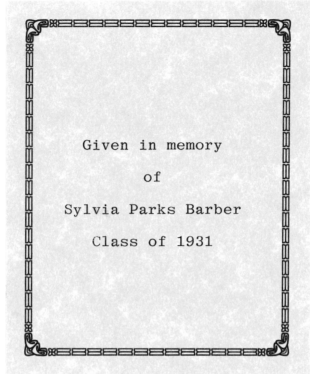

Given in memory

of

Sylvia Parks Barber

Class of 1931

THE POETRY OF VACHEL LINDSAY

volume 3

DENNIS CAMP, editor

The Poetry of

Vachel Lindsay

complete & with Lindsay's drawings

newly edited by

DENNIS CAMP

volume 3
Notes / Appendix / Title Index

SPOON RIVER POETRY PRESS
PEORIA, ILLINOIS

first edition

The Poetry of Vachel Lindsay, edited by Dennis Camp, copyright
© 1986 by Dennis Camp. All rights reserved. No portion of this
book may be reproduced in any manner without written permission
of the copyright holder, except for quotations embodied in reviews
or scholarly articles and books.

Published by Spoon River Poetry Press; P. O. Box 1443; Peoria,
Illinois 61655.

Typesetting by Tom Guttormsson, Minneota (MN) *Mascot*.

Cover design by David R. Pichaske.

Printing by Rodine the Printer, Peoria and M & D Printing, Henry,
Illinois.

ISBN 0-933180-77-2

Acknowledgements are due and gratefully made to the many libraries that assisted in making materials available for this edition. For permission to quote from special collections, we especially wish to recognize the University of Virginia Alderman Library, C. Waller Barrett Library; the State University of New York at Buffalo Library, Poetry/Rare Books Collection of the University Libraries; the Princeton University Library, Vachel Lindsay Collection; the University of Chicago Joseph Regenstein Library, *Poetry* Magazine Papers (1912-1936), Harriet Monroe Personal Papers, and Harriet B. Moody Papers; the New York Public Library, Henry W. and Albert A. Berg Collection, Astor, Lenox and Tilden Foundations; the Harvard University Houghton Library, Vachel Lindsay Manuscripts; the University of Southern California Library, General Manuscripts Collection; the Haverford College Library, Treasure Room Manuscripts Collection; the Newberry Library, Eunice Tietjens Papers; and the Yale University Library, Collection of American Literature, the Beinecke Rare Book and Manuscript Library.

Special thanks to Joanne Sawyer, Curator, the Hiram College Library, for her thoughtful assistance both in person and by letter; to Peter Lennon, my former graduate assistant, for his help in locating many of the materials used in these notes; and to Nicholas Cave Lindsay, Vachel Lindsay's son and literary executor, for his permission and continuing support.

This book is published in part with funds provided by The Illinois Arts Council, a state organization, and by the National Endowment for the Arts. Our many thanks.

TABLE OF CONTENTS

For Trula . . .

of the Palace of Eve

NOTES

Editor's Introduction

The notes for this edition derive from many sources—some published, many unpublished. The greatest number of Lindsay manuscripts is in the Barrett Collection at the University of Virginia. Here I have researched the many Lindsay notebooks, datebooks, scrapbooks, etc., as well as the poetry manuscripts, including the pages that he prepared for the *Collected Poems*. I also have used the hundreds of unpublished letters, not only at Virginia but at libraries around the country.[1] Yale, Dartmouth, Princeton, SUNY at Buffalo, Indiana, Chicago, Texas—not to mention Springfield, Illinois—all have substantial Lindsay materials in various collections. Indeed, Lindsay manuscripts and documents exist in libraries in nearly all forty-eight contiguous states, a situation which reflects the poet's extensive travels and prolific pen. My notes, therefore, are more detailed than perhaps is usual for the standard edition of a poet, but the large amount of relevant material is widely scattered and relatively difficult to consult—without spending a small fortune in travel.

In addition, I have used numerous published sources: books authored by Lindsay's acquaintances,[2] periodicals that published his poetry and articles, the biographies of Masters and Ruggles, and the secondary criticism.[3] I have also researched several newspapers: especially the *Chicago Herald*, where Lindsay had his own poetry column in the fall, 1914, and Springfield's *Illinois State Register* and *State Journal*, both of which printed his poetry and many of his own comments on that poetry. On 28 October 1913, Lindsay writes to thank the editors of *Poetry Magazine* for the $100 prize that he won for "General William Booth Enters into Heaven." He notes that word of the prize will appear in the Springfield papers and adds: "That is always the climax with me—the Springfield papers."[4] Finally, I examined several of the early anthologies that were important in determining the direction of American poetry in the opening decades of this century, including Ferdinand Earle's *The Lyric Year* (1912), which, in the words of Jessie B. Rittenhouse, "broke the ground for contemporaneous anthologies";[5] Rittenhouse's own *The Little Book of Modern Verse* (1913, rev. 1919 and 1927); William Stanley Braithwaite's *Anthology of Magazine Verse . . . and Yearbook of American Poetry* (1913-1929); Harriet Monroe and Alice Corbin Henderson's *The New Poetry* (1917, rev. 1932); Marguerite Wilkinson's *New Voices* (1919, rev. 1930); and four volumes of *A Miscellany of American Poetry* (1920-1927), what was to be a biennial series in which established poets were to edit a section of their own unpublished work. Lindsay is one of eleven poets in volume one. To study Lindsay is, among other things, to learn about the American publishing world from 1900 to 1930, since his work was welcomed in nearly all important circles.

As to variant readings, even a glance at the notes that follow will reveal some of the care and hard work that went into the majority of Lindsay's poems. It is important to realize that what is here is only the tip of the iceberg: he expended far greater effort in preparing a poem for print. His friends all knew how hard he labored, especially at revising his work. People in Springfield still remember his public response when asked if he revised: "Yes, I revise seventeen times seventeen times, and probably will revise seventy times more."[6] To Harriet Monroe, he explains: "a poem is a long time growing with me . . .";[7] to Harriet Moody: "with me the whole pie of writing is revision and revision and revision" (UL-V, 27 October 1917). And John Emerson and his wife-to-be, Anita Loos, are informed: "Almost any poem is three to ten times as long in the first draft as in the final form" (UL-H, 19 March 1920).

Even with this attention, Lindsay seldom relied solely on his own judgment. In *New Voices* Wilkerson notes:

> Vachel Lindsay writes his social or choral poetry very slowly and is grateful for the criticism of his friends. He has rewritten some of his poems as many as forty or fifty times.[8]

The Barrett Collection is physical evidence of the truth of this assertion, as Lindsay's gratitude is evident in many letters to his friends. Ellen Williams certainly understates the case when she suggests that "Lindsay was fairly pliable about revising — if anything, he took too many suggestions from too many people."[9] Louis Untermeyer remembers that, whenever Lindsay came to New York, he brought his manuscripts with him:

> he read them to groups of listeners, to friends and strangers, to poets and business men — and he heeded every comment. If Floyd Dell or James Oppenheim or Sara Teasdale disliked a line, or even a passage, out it went. Sometimes other lines were substituted on the spot; sometimes one of us, prodded on by Vachel, offered lines of our own. My letters from Vachel are full of thanks for what any other poet would have considered effrontery.[10]

Untermeyer's experience is echoed by many others: to his friends and often to his editors Lindsay offered his work carte blanche, not, as Untermeyer explains, because he was excessively modest or servilely fearful, but because he had

> an integral faith in his fellows, a thorough-going belief in the democratic experiment, the collaborative comradeship. We were to make the world over, we brothers in art and industry; we were all to rebuild Springfield into the Golden City, the City of Dream. Again and again this theme occurs in Vachel's life and letters.[11]

Indeed, at times the theme is most intense. In February 1923 Lindsay writes: "I am — not a poet. I am something much darker, deeper and deadlier than that. I am an adventurer. Do not mistake. I want it said when they look at the drawing or the verse — not this was his song — but 'This was his adventure' '' (UDB-V). The following notes should help to demonstrate that he was generally a careful poet and craftsman, as well as an adventurer.

*   *   *   *

Preceding each poem title below is the page number on which the poem begins, then the title, then the places the poem was published during Lindsay's lifetime; the citations to place are generally in chronological order, with the final citation signifying the version chosen for this edition. This copy-text, then, is the latest version that Lindsay himself saw through the press. When a work appeared first in a publication other than Lindsay's own, I have used the citation: *1st* (*v.* "The Queen of Bubbles" below). Thereafter are such notes and comments as may have special significance in understanding a work or its place in the Lindsay canon. Finally, there is a line-by-line presentation of textual variants, including editorial changes made in the copy-text (emendations).

In VARIANTS, after the line number, what precedes the bracket (]) is the way the text reads in this edition (to save space I have abbreviated longer passages with ellipses); what follows the bracket is the variant reading and, *in italics*, the place or places it can be found. Similarly, in EMENDA-TIONS, after the line number, what precedes the bracket is the present text (often followed by a parenthetical explanation for choosing it); what follows the bracket is the reading in the copy-text which has been emended.

As an example, the note for "In Heaven" below indicates that the poem is in volume one of this edition, p. 13.

Besides appearing in *The Tramp's Excuse and Other Poems*, the poem is in the third and fourth editions of *The Village Magazine* and in *Collected Poems*, which provides the copy-text. Moreover, line 19 in the copy-text and in *The Village Magazine* reads: "Over rotted harps and rusted gold"; but in *The Tramp's Excuse* the line is: "O'er the rotted harps and the rusted gold." Similarly, in "Galahad, Knight Who Perished" below, line 15 of *Collected Poems*, the copy-text, reads: "Leave not life's fairest to perish—stranger to thee"; but I have emended the text to: "Leave not life's fairest to perish—strangers to thee"—as the line reads in *Rhymes to Be Traded for Bread*, *The Congo and Other Poems*, and the *Journal of Social Hygiene*.

These notes do not record all variant readings, not even all emendations. I have quietly corrected all obvious errors and have not recorded minor verbal and other changes. Lindsay's poems are filled with variations in punctuation, spelling, stanza and line form, etc. To record everything would easily double these notes. Readers who want this information, none of which seemed very important to Lindsay himself, will at least be able to use these notes to search the appropriate texts.

Footnotes for Editor's Introduction

[1] The Lindsay-Sara Teasdale letters (Y) were restricted at the time I completed my research. I was allowed to read and take notes but was not permitted to quote from them. Many have been published in Carpenter and Drake (see "Bibliography" below). Also see Armstrong, Chénetier, and Reed.

2See especially Dell, Graham, Loos, Melcher, Monroe, Rittenhouse, Trombly, Untermeyer, and Wakefield in the "Bibliography."

3In addition to Masters and Ruggles, see especially Carpenter, Chénetier, Dunbar, Flanagan, Fowler, Kramer, Kuykendall, Massa, Putzel, Sayre, Tanselle, Viereck, Williams, and Yatron in the "Bibliography."

4Chénetier, p. 80.

5"Contemporary Poetry: Notes and Reviews," *The Bookman,* XLVI (January 1918), 578.

6As remembered by the late Miss Elizabeth E. Graham, Secretary of the Vachel Lindsay Association and former colleague of Susan Wilcox.

7Monroe, *A Poet's Life*, p. 383.

8ial*New Voices* (1919), p. 8; (1930), p. 6.

9ia*Harriet Monroe and the Poetry Renaissance*, p. 106.

10*From Another World*, p. 138.

11*From Another World,* p. 139.

See "The Potatoes' Dance" (page 57)

Bibliography

(This is a working bibliography, for use with the "Notes" and the "Editor's Introduction"; no attempt has been made to be exhaustive. Works here have been especially useful in gaining the background for and in the actual preparation of this edition. Further bibliographical information may be found throughout the "Notes" and in the footnotes to the "Editor's Introduction.")

Armstrong, A. Joseph, ed. "Letters of Nicholas Vachel Lindsay to A. Joseph Armstrong," *The Baylor Bulletin*, XLIII (September 1940).

Avery, Emmett L. "Vachel Lindsay in Spokane," *The Pacific Spectator* (Summer, 1949).

_____. "Vachel Lindsay: Spokane Journalist," in *Research Studies*, XXV (Pullman: Washington State University, 1957), 101-110.

_____. "Vachel Lindsay's 'Poem Games' in Spokane," in *Research Studies*, XXX (1962), 109-114.

Blankmeyer, Helen Van Cleave. *The Sangamon Country*. Springfield: Illinois State Register, 1935.

Bonn, George S. *We Need More Lindsay-Hearted Men*. Springfield: The Vachel Lindsay Association, 1961.

Braithwaite, William Stanley, ed. *Anthology of Magazine Verse . . . and Yearbook of American Poetry*. New York: G. Sully & Company, 1913-1929.

Cady, Edwin H. "Vachel Lindsay Across the Chasm," *The Indiana University Bookman*, No. 5 (December 1960), pp. 5-11.

Canby, Henry Seidel. The reference is to a scrapbook Lindsay prepared for Canby while the latter was editor of *The Saturday Review of Literature*. The book was sent on 14 October 1924 and is at the Beinecke Library, Yale University.

Carpenter, Margaret Haley. *Sara Teasdale: A Biography*, 2nd ed. New York: The Schulte Publishing Company, 1960.

Certain, C.C. "Vachel Lindsay at the English Council," *The Elementary English Review*, IX (May 1932), 132-135, 141.

Chénetier, Marc, ed. *Letters of Vachel Lindsay*. New York: Burt Franklin & Co., 1979.

_____. "Vachel Lindsay's American Mythocracy and Some Unpublished Sources," in *The Vision of This Land*, ed. John E. Hallwas and Dennis J. Reader. Macomb: Western Illinois University, 1976.

Chesterton, Gilbert Keith. *All I Survey*. London: Methuen & Company, Ltd., 1933.

Cockrell, Dura Brokaw. "Vachel Lindsay, Artist," *The Shane Quarterly*, V (April-July 1944), 126-130.

Dell, Floyd. *Homecoming: An Autobiography*. New York: Farrar & Rinehart, Inc., 1933.

Drake, William. *Sara Teasdale: Woman & Poet*. San Francisco: Harper & Row Publishers, 1979.

Duffey, Bernard. *The Chicago Renaissance in American Letters: A Critical History*. East Lansing: Michigan State College Press, 1954.

Dunbar, Olivia Howard. *A House in Chicago*. Chicago: The University of Chicago Press, 1947.

Dussert, Pierre, ed. *Springfield Town Is Butterfly Town and Other Poems for Children* (by Vachel Lindsay). Kent, Ohio: The Kent State University Press, 1969.

Felts, David Virgil. *Trading Rhymes for Bread*. Springfield: The Vachel Lindsay Association, 1960.

Flanagan, John T., ed. *Profile of Vachel Lindsay*. Columbus, Ohio: Charles E. Merrill Publishing Company, 1970.

Fowler, Elizabeth Thomas, ed. *Annotated Edition of the Letters of Vachel Lindsay to Nellie Vieira*. Diss. Tennessee, 1968.

Graham, Stephen. *Tramping with a Poet in the Rockies*. New York: D. Appleton and Company, 1922.

Harris, Mark, ed. *Selected Poems of Vachel Lindsay*. New York: The Macmillan Company, 1963.

Jenkins, Alan. *Vachel Lindsay and the Kingdom of God*. Springfield: The Vachel Lindsay Association, 1947.

Kramer, Dale. *Chicago Renaissance: The Literary Life in the Midwest, 1900-1930*. New York: Appleton-Century, 1966.

Kreymborg, Alfred. "Exit Vachel Lindsay—Enter Ernest Hemingway," *Literary Review*, I (Winter, 1957-58), 208-219.

Kuykendall, Radford B. *The Reading and Speaking Vachel Lindsay*. Diss. Northwestern, 1952.

Lindsay, Elizabeth Conner. "A Poet and His Audience," *The Shane Quarterly*, V (April-July 1944), 118-125.

Lindsay, Vachel. "Avanel Boone, and the Young American Poets of Russian Blood," *The Dial*, LXX (May 1921), 540-544.

_____. "The Buggy-Breaking Doctor," in Macmillan's *The News Review*, I (2 March 1931), 4.

_____. "Father Springfield in the Mirror," *Survey*, XXXIII (19 December 1914), 316-318.

_____. *The Golden Book of Springfield*. New York: The Macmillan Company, 1920.

_____. "The Great Douglas Fairbanks," *The Ladies Home Journal*, XLIII (August 1926), 12, 114.

_____. "Home Rule in Poetry," *Reedy's Mirror*, XXV (24 November 1916), 740-741.

_____. "How Mrs. Joy Celebrated Peace," *The New Republic*, XVII (23 November 1918), 102.

_____. "Litany of the Middle West," *Kessinger's Mid-West Review* (April 1930), pp. 27-28.

_____. *The Litany of Washington Street*. New York: The Macmillan Company, 1929.

_____. "The New Localism: An Illustrated Essay for Village Statesmen," *Vision*, No. 4 (Spring, 1912).

_____. "The New Poetry," *The Christian Century*, XLI (10 April 1924), 460-461.

_____. "A Photo-Play," *Reedy's Mirror*, XXV (4 August 1916), 505.

_____. "The Real American Language," *The American Mercury*, XIII (March 1928), 257-265.

_____. "Springfield—A Walled Town," *The Christian Century*, XXXVIII (21 April 1921), 17-18.

_____. "Venus in Armor," *The New Republic*, X (28 April 1917), 380-381.

_____. "Walt Whitman," *The New Republic*, XXXVII (5 December 1923), 3-5.

_____. *War Bulletins I, II, III and V*. Springfield: Jeffersons Printing Company, Fall, 1909.

_____. "What It Means to Be a Poet in America," *The Saturday Evening Post*, CIC (13 November 1926), 12-13, 45-46, 48.

_____. "A Word of Advice about Policy," *The Dial*, LXV (5 September 1918), 176.

Loos, Anita. "Vachel, Mae, and I," *The Saturday Review* (26 August 1961), pp. 5-6.

Lowell, Amy. *A Critical Fable*. Boston: Houghton Mifflin & Company, 1922.

Macfarlane, Peter Clark. The reference is to a scrapbook that Lindsay prepared for Macfarlane sometime early in 1913; the book is now part of the Barrett Collection at the University of Virginia Library. Macfarlane later published a feature article on Lindsay: "A Vagabond Poet," *Collier's: The National Weekly*, LI (6 September 1913), 7-8, 32.

Massa, Ann. *Vachel Lindsay: Fieldworker for the American Dream*. Bloomington: Indiana University Press, 1970.

Masters, Edgar Lee. *Vachel Lindsay: A Poet in America*. New York: Charles Scribner's Sons, 1935.

McInerny, Dennis Q. "Vachel Lindsay: A Reappraisal," in *The Vision of This Land*, ed. John E. Hallwas and Dennis J. Reader. Macomb: Western Illinois University, 1976.

Melcher, Frederic G. "Vachel Lindsay—An Account of a Friendship Recorded from Memory, August, 1957," *The Indiana University Bookman*, No. 5 (December 1960), pp. 12-20.

_____. "Vachel Lindsay in the Schools," *The Elementary English Review*, IX (May 1932), 117-119.

Mencken, Henry Louis. *Vachel Lindsay: The True Voice of Middle America*. Washington, D.C., 1947.

Monroe, Harriet. *A Poet's Life: Seventy Years in a Changing World*. New York: The Macmillan Company, 1938. See also *Poets & Their Art*, 2nd ed. New York: The Macmillan Company, 1932.

Perkins, David. *A History of Modern Poetry: From the 1890's to the High Modernist Mode*. Cambridge: Harvard University Press, 1976.

Phelps, William Lyon. *Autobiography, with Letters*. New York: Oxford University Press, 1939. See also *The Advance of English Poetry in the Twentieth Century*. New York: Dodd, Mead & Company, 1919.

Putzel, Max. *The Man in the Mirror: William Marion Reedy and His Magazine*. Cambridge: Harvard University Press, 1963.

Reed, Doris M., ed. "Letters of Vachel Lindsay in the Lilly Library at Indiana University," *The Indiana University Bookman*, No. 5 (December 1960), pp. 21-63.

Reid, Harriet. *Miss Harriet Reid Tells of Lindsay's Love of Springfield: Teacher of Finest Citizenship*. Pamphlet. Springfield: The Vachel Lindsay Association, n.d.

Ridgely, Frances S. *A City Is Not Builded in a Day: Story of Vachel Lindsay's Background in the City of Springfield, Illinois*. Springfield: The Vachel Lindsay Association, 1968.

Rittenhouse, Jessie B. *My House of Life: An Autobiography*. Boston: Houghton Mifflin Company, 1934.

Roberts, Octavia. "Nicholas Vachel Lindsay," *The American Magazine*, LXXIV (August 1912), 422-424.

Ruggles, Eleanor. *The West-Going Heart: A Life of Vachel Lindsay*. New York: W. W. Norton & Company, 1959.

Sayre, Robert F., ed. *Adventures: Rhymes & Designs* (selections from Vachel Lindsay). New York: The Eakins Press, 1968.

Schenk, William Paul. "Vachel Lindsay," *Inland: The Magazine of the Middle West*, Issue XXIV (Summer, 1959), 9-12. A publication of the Inland Steel Company, Chicago.

Schroeder, Ralph L. *Where a Lad Is: An Account of Vachel Lindsay*. Syracuse: Syracuse University Library, 1962.

Snigg, John P. *I Walked with a Poet*. Springfield: The Vachel Lindsay Association, n.d.

South, Eudora Lindsay. *From the Lindsay Scrapbook: Cousin Vachel*. Lafayette, Indiana, 1978. Private publication.

Spencer, Hazelton, ed. *Selected Poems of Vachel Lindsay*. New York: The Macmillan Company, 1931. See also "The Life and Death of a Bard," *The American Mercury*, XXV (April 1932), 455-462.

Tanselle, G. Thomas. "Vachel Lindsay Writes to Floyd Dell," *Journal of the Illinois State Historical Society*, LVII (1964), 366-379.

Trombly, Albert Edmund. *Vachel Lindsay, Adventurer*. Columbia, Missouri, 1929.

Untermeyer, Louis. *From Another World: The Autobiography of Louis Untermeyer*. New York: Harcourt, Brace and Company, 1939.

Van Doren, Carl. "Salvation with Jazz," in *Many Minds*. New York: Alfred A. Knopf, 1924.

Viereck, Peter. "The Crack-Up of American Optimism: Vachel Lindsay, The Dante of the Fundamentalists," *Modern Age*, IV (Summer, 1960), 269-284.

Waddell, Elizabeth. "Rhymes for Bread," *Reedy's Mirror*, XXII (7 March 1913), 5-6.

Wakefield, Catherine F. "Lindsay as the Poet Uncle," *The Elementary English Review*, IX (May 1932), 126-127.

Wakefield, Olive Lindsay. "Vachel Lindsay, Disciple," *The Shane Quarterly*, V (April-July 1944), 82-107.

Wheeler, Edward J. "An Illinois Art Revivalist," *Current Literature*, L (March 1911), 320-323.

Whitney, Blair. "The Garden of Illinois," in *The Vision of This Land*, ed. John E. Hallwas and Dennis J. Reader. Macomb: Western Illinois University, 1976.

Wilcox, Susan E. "My Tow-Headed Pupil, Vachel Lindsay," *The Elementary English Review*, IX (May 1932), 123-125, 131.

Williams, Ellen. *Harriet Monroe and the Poetry Renaissance: The First Ten Years of Poetry, 1912-1922*. Urbana: University of Illinois Press, 1977.

Winsett, Marvin Davis. *Some Uses of Words*. Springfield: The Vachel Lindsay Association, 1969.

Wolfe, Glenn Joseph. *Vachel Lindsay: The Poet as Film Theorist*. New York: Arno, 1973.

Yatron, Michael. *America's Literary Revolt*. New York: Philosophical Library, Inc., 1959.

Abbreviations

AL   Lindsay, *Where Is Aladdin's Lamp?* (1904—Lindsay's first "book." Two handwritten copies were made; one mutilated copy is extant (V).

AMe   *The American Mercury.*

AMg   *The American Magazine*

AMP   Lindsay, *The Art of the Moving Picture* (rev. ed., 1922).

AWP   Lindsay, *Adventures While Preaching the Gospel of Beauty* (1914).

B   State University of New York, Buffalo, Library.

C   The University of Chicago Library.

CC   Lindsay, *The Candle in the Cabin* (1926).

ChC   *The Christian Century.*

CEP   *Chicago Evening Post.*

CEPF   *Chicago Evening Post Friday Literary Review.*

Cg   Lindsay, *The Congo and Other Poems* (1914).

CH   *Chicago Herald.*

CL   *Current Literature.*

CM   *The Century Magazine.*

CN   Lindsay, *The Chinese Nightingale and Other Poems* (1917).

CO   *Current Opinion.*

CP   Lindsay, *Collected Poems* (1923; rev. ed., 1925).

DJ   Lindsay, *The Daniel Jazz and Other Poems* (1920); see p. 883.

ESC   Lindsay, *Every Soul Is a Circus* (1929).

GSt   Lindsay, *Going-to-the-Stars* (1926).

GSu   Lindsay, *Going-to-the-Sun* (1923).

GWB   Lindsay, *General William Booth Enters into Heaven and Other Poems* (1913).

GWC   Lindsay, *The Golden Whales of California and Other Rhymes in the American Language* (1920).

H   Harvard University Library.

HGB   Lindsay, *A Handy Guide for Beggars* (1916).

Hu   The Huntington Library.

Ind   *The Independent.*

ISJ   *Illinois State Journal.*

ISR   *Illinois State Register.*

JA   Lindsay, *Johnny Appleseed and Other Poems* (1928); see p. 907.

KMR   *Kessinger's Mid-West Review.*

LBMV   *The Little Book of Modern Verse*, ed. Jessie B. Rittenhouse (Boston: Houghton Mifflin Company, 1913). See also SBMV, TMV.

LD   *The Literary Digest.*

LH   Lindsay home (Springfield, Illinois).

LM   *The London Mercury.*

MFP   Lindsay, *A Letter about My Four Programmes for Committees in Correspondence* (1916).

MsAP   *A Miscellany of American Poetry* (1920; 4th ed., 1927). Also entitled *American Poetry: A Miscellany.*

NP   *The New Poetry: An Anthology*, ed. Harriet Monroe and Alice Corbin Henderson (New York: The Macmillan Company, 1917; rev. ed., 1932).

NV   *New Voices: An Introduction to Contemporary Poetry*, ed. Marguerite Wilkinson (New York: The Macmillan Company, 1919; rev. ed., 1930).

P   Princeton University Library.

PA   Lindsay, *The Sangamon County Peace Advocate* (1909).

PM   *Poetry: A Magazine of Verse.*

PP   Lindsay—privately printed material, such as broadsides, rhyme sheets, etc.

RB   Lindsay, *Rhymes to Be Traded for Bread* (1912).

SBMV   *The Second Book of Modern Verse*, ed. Jessie B. Rittenhouse (Boston: Houghton Mifflin Company, 1919). See also LBMV, TMV.

SC   The University of Southern California Library.

SDC   *Spokane Daily Chronicle.*

SP   Lindsay, *Selected Poems*, ed. Hazelton Spencer (New York: The Macmillan Company, 1931); see p. 914.

TE   Lindsay, *The Tramp's Excuse and Other Poems* (1909).

TMV   *The Third Book of Modern Verse*, ed. Jessie B. Rittenhouse (Boston: Houghton Mifflin Company, 1927). See also LBMV, SBMV.

UDB   Unpublished datebook.

UL   Unpublished letter.

UMs   Unpublished manuscript.

UNB   Unpublished notebook.

V   The Clifton Waller Barrett Library of manuscripts at the University
       of Virginia Library.

VM 1   Lindsay, *The Village Magazine* (1910).

VM 2   Second edition of above (1920).

VM 3   Third edition of above (1925).

VM 4   Fourth edition of above (1925).

Y   Yale University Library.

Notes

1 THE TRAMP'S EXCUSE AND OTHER POEMS (Springfield, Fall, 1909)
[This 9¼" by 6" booklet of poems, held together by a hand-tied string,
was privately printed in late summer 1909. Lindsay considered it *War
Bulletin Number Four*. There were five of these *Bulletins* issued between
July 19 and Thanksgiving, 1909, at first costing five cents and, after
Number One failed to sell, thereafter advertised as being "as free as bread
and butter." A facsimile of the first page of *Number One*, including the
important little essay "Why a War Bulletin?," is in Sayre, p. 280.
  Lindsay confessed to Sara Teasdale (UL-Y, 21 March 1914) that TE is
crude autobiography. To Floyd Dell, in a 6 September 1909 letter at the
Newberry Library (reprinted by Tanselle and Chénetier, pp. 35-36),
Lindsay asserts that TE presents his whole system "at one fell swoop."
The high points are "The Little Yellow Bird of Weariness," "The
Sorceress!," "Aladdin's Lamp," and "then the fell swoop at the end of the
book." Dell's account of receiving the booklet is in *Homecoming*, pp.
208-209; his famous review of TE — Lindsay is "indubitably a poet" — is in
the Chicago *Evening Post* for 29 October 1909 (quoted in part by Ruggles,
p. 156).
  As for the drawings, Lindsay wrote to Edward Scribner Ames, the pastor
of the Disciples church he attended while in Chicago: "As for my ideas of
art form in poetry — and pen and ink drawing — they are formed definitely
by four men: Poe, Coleridge (in his two or three *magical* poems) Blake and
Beardsley . . . . These are the *necromancers*, the *Wizards*, the *Magi* in
English — and Beardsley is the solitary magician in pen and ink." ". . . I
will consider I have made myself understood the more my work is
compared with theirs, artistically, and its shortcomings noted from that
standpoint" (21 October 1909, Chénetier, p. 40)].

2 THE TRAMP'S EXCUSE: drawing in VM 2, 3, 4. Note in VM 3, 4: "The
lady is one of twenty fashion plates from fairyland I drew some time ago."
As late as February 1922 Lindsay indicates his love for these "plates"
(several of which are extant in the Barrett Collection at the University of
Virginia): "There is just one standard of drawing for me — The
Fashionplates from Fairyland as I began them about 1906. That was my
highest point of drawing" (UDB-V).

3 STAR OF MY HEART: in AL, GWB, CP. See the "Preface" to TE in
Appendix. In TE Lindsay quotes Matthew 2: 1-2, 9 as an epigraph; the

poem is subtitled "Christmas Eve" in an early manuscript version (UMs-LH).

4 I WANT TO GO WANDERING: in AL, MsAP, CP. Entitled "Wandering" in AL, TE. We have a valuable scrapbook (V) that Lindsay prepared for Peter Clark Macfarlane, who asked to do a feature on the poet (published in *Collier's Weekly*, 6 September 1913); on a copy of this poem in the scrapbook, Lindsay notes: "Written with old W.D. Frazee in mind — my Grandfather's brother. He was the author of Reminiscences and sermons." At the bottom of the page he adds: "About 1903, or 04, sometime before I took to the road." See "Preface" to TE in Appendix. VARIANTS 1] *in TE the poem begins:* Till my footsteps are feeble, an[d] aged my hair, 14 And] I shall *TE* 17 Old] Or old *TE* 25 go] shall go *TE* 27 a feather] feathers *TE* 29 redwood, or] *not in TE* 33 cliff . . . prairie] cliffs and the canons will *TE* 34 sagebrush] moonlight *TE* 35 songs] song *TE* 35 call] fall *TE* 38 The] Yea, the *TE* 39 With . . . river,] With dreams of that rude, haunted river and all *TE* 40 And . . . wandering] Of my wandering, wandering *TE*.

5 CAUGHT IN A NET: in GWB, CP, SP. This poem may be "The Moon Woman," which was sent to Frederick Richardson, Lindsay's art instructor at Chicago, in December 1904 (see Masters, p. 120). EMENDATION 4 night time (as in TE, GWB, CP)] nightime

5 AN AUGUST AFTERNOON: in VM 3, 4. Entitled "The Dreams of God" in a manuscript version (UMs-LH), with note added: "Written for my lady far away" and dated "Sept. 14, 1902."

6 BY THE SPRING AT SUNSET: in Cg, CP.

6 THE FACES THAT PASS: in VM 3, 4.

7 TO THE MAIDEN, HONEST AND FINE: in VM 3, 4. The "maiden" in this and the next two poems was probably Nellie T. Vieira; see Fowler, p. 70.

8 THE BEGGAR'S VALENTINE: in GWB, CP. EMENDATION 38, (as in TE, GWB)].

9 BEYOND THE MOON: in GWB, CP. Entitled "Written to the Most Beautiful Woman in the World" in TE. For a firsthand account of Lindsay's reciting the poem, see Dell, pp. 210-211.

10 HYMN TO THE SUN: in VM 3, 4; CP. In CP as part of the "Invocation for 'The Map of the Universe'" and entitled "Johnny Appleseed's Hymn to the Sun." The seeds of this poem and other like poems (see "The Beggar Monk" below) may be in a notebook for 1907 (see Masters, pp. 184-185).

12 UPON RETURNING TO THE COUNTRY ROAD: in RB; GWB; *Forum*, September 1913; AWP; CP. A 1909 notebook (V) includes this poem in a

list of works dated "1906 or 1908." Entitled "Prologue to 'Rhymes to Be Traded for Bread'" in CP, with headnote: "(A Private Publication Out of Print)." VARIANTS 7 chanting], grimly *TE, RB, GWB, Forum, AWP* 15 slept] had slept *TE, RB, GWB, Forum, AWP* 18 There] Their *GWB, Forum.*

12 A PRAYER TO ALL THE DEAD AMONG MINE OWN PEOPLE: in RB, GWB, CP. In a notebook (V) we learn that the poem was written one week after the death of Lindsay's aunt, Mary Frazee, who died on 2 April 1907. This early version is entitled "A Poem to the Dead Who Are Blood Kin." In TE there is a first stanza:

> Oh, ministers of grace will you be with us
> > When we go forth into the sun and rain?
> Brave aunts beneath the sod, and fair forefathers,
> > Dear cousins, can you thwart the days of pain?

VARIANT 1 clan from Heaven] heavenly kinsmen *TE.*

12 REVELRY: in VM 3, 4; CP. The 1909 notebook (see "Upon Returning to the Country Road" above) includes the title "The Revel in Heaven." This poem and the next, "In Heaven," are included in the section of CP entitled "Invocation for 'The Map of the Universe'"; the poems comprise the two parts of "Johnny Appleseed's Wife of the Mind," with a headnote: "Johnny Appleseed dreamed that because of his monastic self-immolation in the depths of the frontier forest, he would be rewarded in the next life with two very beautiful wives."

13 IN HEAVEN: in VM 3, 4; CP. See "Revelry" above. For Lindsay's view that the poem reflects Swedenborg's "Marriages in Heaven," see Fowler, pp. 201, 203-204. VARIANT 19 Over. . .and] O'er the rotted harps and the *TE.*

14 THE BEGGAR MONK: in VM 3, 4. VARIANT 72 The] 'Tis the *TE.*

16 THE BEGGAR'S VIGIL: in VM 3, 4; CP. In CP as part of the "Invocation for 'The Map of the Universe'" and entitled "Johnny Appleseed's Wife from the Palace of Eve," with headnote: "(See Harper's Monthly Magazine for November, 1871)." VARIANTS 14 in] midst *VM 3, 4* 'mid *TE* 21 out of] out *TE, VM 3, 4* 35 so white] snow-white *VM 3, 4.*

17 THE EARTH-HUNGER: in VM 3, 4. Originally combined with "Couches of Earth and Gardens of Roses" (see below) and with that title. Then written out separately but with the title "Colorado, the Breast of the Earth." These two manuscripts (UMs-LH) date the poem "March 18, 1903." On 4 April 1906 Lindsay transcribed the two poems for Susan Wilcox (UL-LH) with the titles "The Breast of the Earth" and "The Fireflies."

18 WRITTEN FOR A MUSICIAN: in Cg; VM 3, 4; CP; SP. In TE and VM 3, 4, the title is "Faith," with the present title as an afternote. A draft without comment was sent to Nellie T. Vieira on 22 June 1909: see Fowler, pp. 35-37.

18 THE DREAM OF KING DAVID IN HEAVEN: in VM 3, 4. A manuscript version (UMs-P) is dated "August 29, 1903," with a note: "Copied for my fellow traveller in the land of prints and jades and swords, Jessie Kalmback."

19 INDIAN SUMMER: in PP; MFP; VM 2, 3, 4; CP. A manuscript version (UMs-LH) is dated "Sept. 1902" and entitled "Autumn." On 14 October 1924 Lindsay sent a scrapbook with works from VM to Henry Seidel Canby, then editor of *The Saturday Review of Literature.* The book is in the Beinecke Library at Yale University. On a copy of "Indian Summer" Lindsay writes: "First distributed as a Gratuitous and Unwelcome Tract in Springfield."

20 HOW A LITTLE GIRL SANG: in GWB; *Poetry Magazine,* August 1923; *Literary Digest,* 25 August 1923; CP; SP. Braithwaite (1924) lists the poem as one of the best in a magazine for 1923. The little girl was a high school friend, Mary Tiffany. On 26 July 1918 Lindsay apprises Harriet Monroe: "I wrote my first poem to this little girl when she sang at a High School party for us, long ago. The poem was read at her Mother's request at her funeral, which was otherwise the formal Episcopalian service. I was one of the pallbearers. This was all last summer." He identifies the poem as "the first I ever wrote" (UL-C).

20 A SONG FOR GOOD KNIGHTS, STUPID WITH WEARINESS: in VM 3, 4. In two early manuscripts (UMs-LH), one dated "Sept. 1902" and the other "Sept. 22, 1902," and entitled "Sound Sleep" and "Sound Sleep and Sudden Waking," respectively.

21 THE ALCHEMIST'S PETITION: in Cg; VM 3, 4.

21 GOD SEND MY BOSOM A SONG: in VM 3, 4. VARIANT 15, an hour], and hour *TE.*

22 DRINK FOR SALE: poem and drawing in PP; VM 2, 3, 4; CP (hand-lettered poem only). On a copy of the poem in the Canby scrapbook (see "Indian Summer" above), Lindsay writes: "This was once an unwelcome Temperance Tract, hated by both Wets and Drys."

24 TO MATTHEW ARNOLD: in AL; VM 3, 4. Entitled "To One Who Was Almost Forgotten" in AL, TE. Manuscript date (LH): "Christmas night, 1903"; a note on the manuscript reads: "You may apply this poem to Milton or Arnold or Maeterlink as you please!" See the note to "Sons of the Middle West" below. VARIANT 13 prayer . . . young] stern, stern prayer upon his *TE.*

25 THE CUP OF PAINT: in AL; PP; VM 3, 4. One of the poems Lindsay tried to sell on the streets of New York in March 1905. See Masters, pp. 124ff. A manuscript copy (UMs-LH), dated "May 22, 1902," offers the following note: "Dedicated to a decayed tragedian who was leader of

burlesque on my first and last visit to Sam T. Jacks. It was a carnival of sodden paint.'' VARIANTS 3 It] The Cup *PP* 4 will . . . will] do . . . do *PP*.

25 THE DRUNKARDS IN THE STREET: in GWB, CP. A manuscript copy (UMs-LH) is dated "February 18, 1909.''

26 THE SONG OF THE GARDEN-TOAD: in GWB, CP. Several manuscript copies exist (LH, V); one is dated "Hiram '99.'' Another has the subtitle "Concerning rebellious worms''; also, two notes: "this song might be applied to the Ghetto,'' and, "I have gone back to the rose roots for my symbolism in Couches of Earth and Gardens of Roses'' (see "The Earth-Hunger'' above).

27 THE SOUL OF THE SOUBRETTE: in VM 3, 4. VARIANT 22 0] 'Tis the *TE*.

28 SWEET BRIARS OF THE STAIRWAYS: in AL, PP, GWB, CP. The first poem Lindsay tried to sell on the New York City streets in March 1905 (see "The Cup of Paint'' above); entitled then (PP) and in TE: "We Who Are Playing Tonight.'' An afternote in TE identifies the setting: "Souvenir of The Ghetto, Chicago.'' On a copy of the poem in the Macfarlane scrapbook (see "I Want to Go Wandering'' above), Lindsay notes: "Just as I left art school, my grotesques like the above began to win some attention and were much commended by Henri — and I was given much wall space for them in the shows.'' For a firsthand account of the drawing's presentation at the school, see Dura Brokaw Cockrell's essay in *The Shane Quarterly* (April-July 1944). On 1 May 1905, Lindsay writes to Miss Wilcox: "The picture may not be an ideal illustration, but it is the best grotesque I ever did, and illustrates the first verse in a fashion'' (Chénetier, p. 6). The drawing is only in PP.

29 THE BATTLE: in VM 2, 3, 4. See the "Preface'' to TE in the Appendix; an early manuscript title is "The Battle of Love.'' On a manuscript copy (UMs-LH, c. 1904), Lindsay writes: "Read it in a gentle mood — criticise it in a charitable moment — for it is about my first to bloom and certainly the favorite flower in my poor garden. Written all through one night in early '97, at intervals of half an hour or an hour — waking up for it with a line at a time.'' In the "Index'' to VM 2-4 there is an authorial note: "This is indeed a confidential communication. It is my first picture, drawn in 1897, and the verse written the same day. I humbly submit that possibly much of my work is still inscriptional and hieroglyphic, rather than vocal.'' VARIANT 39 hands] hand *TE*.

31 THE SPIDER AND THE GHOST OF THE FLY: in PP; Cg; VM 2, 3, 4; CP. Originally entitled "The Murder of the Butterfly.'' On a copy in the Canby scrapbook (see "Indian Summer'' above), Lindsay writes: "Picture and Verse first distributed as an unwelcome tract, free, on the streets of Springfield Illinois. Verse written to fit the picture. Afterwards inserted in Tramp's Excuse and Village Magazine.'' VARIANT 4 rainbow-dye] pansy dye *VM 2-4*.

32 THE QUEEN OF THE BUTTERFLIES: in VM 3, 4. VARIANT 16 the
wise] the innocent-wise *TE*.

32 THE MYSTERIOUS CAT: in Cg, CP, JA, SP. Entitled "My Lady
Disdain" in TE, with subtitle: "For a picture by George Mather Richards."
Also known as "The Proud Mysterious Cat." After TE, the poem was
considerably expanded; lines 2, 6, 10, 14, 18, 19, 21, and 22 do not appear
in TE.

33 COUCHES OF EARTH AND GARDENS OF ROSES: in VM 3, 4. See
note to "The Earth-Hunger" above. Early titles: "Woe to the Weary
Fireflies" (1903) and "The Fireflies" (1906).

33 BABYLON! MY BABYLON!: in AL; VM 3, 4. An early manuscript copy
(UMs-LH) is entitled "The-Eve-of-Judgement-Day," with a note
preceding: "Rhymes written in Chicago, 1902, but supposed to be written
on." In his diary, 5 December 1901, Lindsay noted that he would like to
write a poem on "The Pleasures of Babylon" (see Masters, p. 110).

34 TO THE SWEET SINGER OF ISRAEL: in AL; PP; VM 3, 4. Printed in
1908 as a broadside to advertise Lindsay's lecture on "The Ghetto Jew,"
which was given at the Springfield YMCA on 18 November 1908. An
afternote reads: "(Founded on the Sixty-eighth psalm, Twenty-third
verse)." On an early manuscript copy (UMs-LH), dated "Jan. 13, 1903,"
Lindsay writes: "As a whole this poem I generally find, quite often
unsatisfactory. But I certainly feel the sentiment most earnestly — and the
vision has haunted me for many a day. It was suggested by finding the last
two lines in a Psalm. — I am proud of the three lines I starred, and of the
rest of the poem to the end." Lindsay "starred" lines 29-31, which then
read:
      Till the Ghastly blood of that Ghastly host
      Has gilded all gutters, has deepened all rivers
      And deepened the Oceans and gilded the tide!

36 THE HUMBLE BUMBLE BEE: poem and drawing in PP; VM 2, 3, 4;
CP. Another tract distributed in Springfield (Canby scrapbook — see
"Indian Summer" above).

37 MARCH IS A YOUNG WITCH: one of Lindsay's first poems, written
while he was still in high school.

37 THE QUEEN OF BUBBLES: *1st* in *The Critic*, March 1904; in AL;
CEPF, 24 September 1909; LBMV; GWB; CP; SP. Lindsay's first published
poem: see "The Map of the Universe," 2nd edition (below); and
"Adventures While Singing These Songs" in CP. The poem is titled "The
Dreamer" in Jessie B. Rittenhouse's *The Little Book of Modern Verse*
(1913). The parenthetical note is not in *1st*, TE; TE has an afternote:
"Printed in the Critic for March, 1904." In a letter to his Father (UL-V, 3
November 1903), Lindsay reports: "I have a drawing in Pen and Ink — the
best I have done of the Queen of Bubbles. It is the figure we had week

before last. I have clothed her in an embroidered cloak and given her a chariot to ride in." Then in a letter to both parents (UL-V, 9 January 1904) he adds: "I have tonight just finished embellishing a printed poem 'The Queen of Bubbles,' for Mr. Torrence [of *The Critic*]. I shall take it up town Monday. He will publish it soon." VARIANTS 1, 6 *not in 1st, TE* 2 Why . . . seek] You will never reach *1st* 14 And] But *1st*.

40 SIX POEMS ON THE MOON, FOR MAN AND BEAST. Lindsay's first published moon poems; he wrote over a hundred of them. Five of these were done for pictures that were used to decorate a little Springfield girl's bedroom in the summer of 1909. There were twelve pictures with poems on the back; nine were lost in a fire, two are apparently lost. The one that remains, "What Grandpa Mouse Said," is in the University of Illinois Library. Lindsay's early love of Keats—he claimed more than once that he had Keats "by heart"—may have influenced this aspect of his work (see "I Stood Tip-Toe," ll. 123-126 especially). See also "The Light O' The Moon" in GWB below and "Adventures While Preaching Hieroglyphic Sermons" in CP.

40 WHAT GRANDPA MOUSE SAID: in GWB; *Forum*, February 1914; AWP; CP; JA; SP. Entitled "The Owl Moon" in TE, with the present title as a subtitle. A dim drawing for this poem, dated 1910, decorates the back covers of VM 2-4. A water color, with the poem hand-lettered, is at the University of Illinois. Lindsay writes: "Picture and poem for Mrs. Haegler"—the mother of Clarissa Jorgensen (née Hagler or Haegler), who, as a little girl, had this and eleven other Lindsay water colors on her bedroom walls. Also on the back of the drawing, in Lindsay's hand, we read: "I feel that this is one of the finest rhymes I have ever written and have kept a copy for publication." The date is 5 August 1909. VARIANTS 13-16 *not in JA* 15 will then] then will then *Forum, AWP*.

40 WHAT THE HYENA SAID: in VM 1, 2, 3, 4; PP (as a broadside c. 1913); GWB; CP. Entitled "The Moon-Worms" in TE, PP, VM 1-4—with the present title as subtitle. Early manuscript (V) title: "The Golden Skull." A note in VM 3, 4 under the drawing reads: "A large colored cut paper replica of this design I made for the Walls of the Pig and the Goose Restaurant. . . ." See "Adventures While Singing These Songs" in CP. The drawing is not in TE, GWB. VARIANT 11 all] our *PP, VM 2-4*.

42 THE CANDLE-MOON: in VM 1, 2, 3, 4; CEPF, 8 October 1909. Drawing not in TE, CEPF. For Lindsay's reaction to publication in CEPF, see Fowler, pp. 140-141.

43 THE ROSE OF MIDNIGHT: in VM 1, 2, 3, 4; AWP; *Forum*, February 1914; CP. All versions except CP subtitled "What the Gardener's Daughter Said." Afternote in VM 3, 4: "Set to music by Albert V. Davies, Gulf Park College, Gulfport, Mississippi." Drawing not in TE, AWP, *Forum*; in VM 3, 4 same note after drawing as "What the Hyena Said" (see above). VARIANTS 7 April] roaring *TE, VM 1* 7 April rain] faint cold light *AWP, Forum* 8 Filling the April] That through the garden *AWP, Forum* 9-12 *not in AWP, Forum* 13 The] All *AWP, Forum* 18 fairy] perfumed *TE, VM 1-4*.

44 THE CENSER-MOON: in VM 1, 2, 3, 4; CP. In VM 3 twice (pp. 44-45, 162); drawing not in TE but is on the back cover of MFP. VARIANT 11 'mid] the *VM 2-4*.

45 THE BEGGAR SPEAKS: in VM 1, 2, 3, 4; GWB; CP; SP. Entitled "What Mr. Moon Said to Me" in VM 2-4; present subtitle serves as title in TE and VM 1. Drawing not in TE, GWB, CP, SP; note added under drawing in VM 3, 4: "Mister Moon with his hand on the bread of idleness, which he has just been cutting." The "bread of idleness" is from Proverbs 31: 27.

47 THE SOUL OF A SPIDER: in ISR, 6 November 1913; MFP; *Current Opinion*, September 1920; VM 2, 3, 4; CP. The drawing, dated 1904, is not in ISR. In VM 2-4 the poem is entitled "Hieroglyphic of the Soul of a Spider"; an afternote in VM 3, 4 reads: "The Soul of the Spider may be seen hovering between The Tomb of Lucifer and the Palace of Eve, in the Map of the Universe. . . ." In a letter to Susan Wilcox (1 May 1905), Lindsay discusses his drawings and concludes: "My figures only excite passing interest. The Soul of the Spider beats them all, so far as staying qualities are concerned" (Chénetier, p. 7). VARIANT 4 And] King *TE, ISR*.

47 THE SOUL OF A BUTTERFLY: the drawing and quatrain are in MFP; VM 2, 3, 4; CP. The earlier version (see p. 50) accompanies the drawing in TE and appears without the drawing in RB and VM 3, 4. The drawing alone is on the back cover of TE and VM 1. In VM 2-4 the quatrain is entitled "Hieroglyphic of the Soul of a Butterfly." An afternote in VM 3, 4 reads: "The Soul of the Butterfly may be seen hovering between the Jungles of Heaven and The Palace of Eve, in the Map of the Universe. . . ." In his notebook (V) — headed "Orange Indiana. June 4, 1906" — Lindsay writes: "As to pictures in the fashion of the Soul of the Butterfly, it is reasonable to draw them and name them. They are the flowers of the designing brain, and it is as fitting to name them, and infuse poetry into them, as into the flowers of the field. The scientist will see that the poetry is merely read into them, but after all, abstract ideas must be visualized, and it is as well to visualize them by beautiful forms, as by the spelled word upon the page. The hieroglyphic has its due excuse." VARIANTS 25 hid] filled *TE* 31 Always it seemed to] It seemed to always *TE, RB*.

51 THE LITTLE YELLOW BIRD OF WEARINESS: in AL; VM 3, 4. Two versions (UMs-LH), both dated "November 1902," are entitled "Comrades. A Fantasy." Two later versions (UMs-LH and V), AL, and TE have the title "The Little Yellow Bird." VARIANTS *after 6 in TE:* And snuggle underneath my gown, 9 cold] wan *TE*.

51 GHOSTS IN LOVE: in AL, GWB, CP. VARIANT 5 that] of *TE, GWB*.

52 PARVENU: in AL; Cg; VM 3, 4; CP. In an early manuscript (UMs-LH) and in AL, the title is "A Parvenu"; in TE the title is "Cinderella." VARIANTS 2 By . . .,] By far-off Daydream River — *TE, Cg, VM 3, 4* 8 We . . . .] We for the Daydream River. *TE, Cg, VM 3, 4.*

52 THE FAIRY BRIDAL HYMN: in GWB, CP.

53 CRICKETS ON A STRIKE: in AL; PP; VM 1, 2, 3, 4; Cg; CP; JA. Early titles (UMs-LH and V): "The Foolish Queen of Fairyland" and "A Strike"; the plate, dated 1904, is not in TE, Cg, JA. In a letter to Harriet Monroe (UL-C, 26 July 1918), Lindsay identifies this as one of his earliest poems, written while he was still in high school. An afternote in VM 3, 4 reads: "This plate, — printed on a separate sheet, and issued to the citizens of Springfield gratis, was received with profound suspicion, about the same days as the War Bulletins — 1908-1909. What war was going on then? The one between me, and my fellow-Babbits." VARIANT 7 Play . . . my] Play broken tunes in the *PP, TE, VM 1-4.*

54 THE SORCERESS!: in GWB; HGB; VM 2, 3, 4; CP; JA; SP. An early (c. 1904) version (UMs-LH) is entitled "The Lamp"; in HGB the title is "Follow the Thistledown." The plate is not in GWB, HGB, CP, JA, SP. An afternote in VM 3, 4 reads: "Another of the set of twenty fashion plates from Fairyland [see "The Tramp's Excuse" above]. Sweetheart Spring, Sweetheart Summer, Sweetheart Autumn and Sweetheart Winter, which appeared in the *Sangamon County Peace Advocate* Christmas 1909, were written for fashion plates that were lost" (see "Sweethearts of the Year," p. 74).

54 TO THE ARCHANGEL MICHAEL: in AL; VM 3, 4. An early version (UMs-LH), dated "January 12, 1904," is entitled "The Archangel Michael"; in AL the title is "To the Archangel Michael."

56 THE WITCH OF LAKE MICHIGAN: in AL; VM 3, 4. An early version (UMs-LH) is entitled "The Water Witch." VARIANT 2 fire-brands] fire-bands *TE.*

57 THE POTATOES' DANCE: in VM 1, GWB, CN, MFP, CP, JA, SP. Entitled "The Potato's Dance" in GWB. In a letter to Lucy Bates (UL-LH, 4 July 1914), Lindsay indicates that the key word is pronounced "*Potatuz.*" See also the "Introduction to 'The Potatoes' Dance'" and "The Poem Games" in the Appendix. After TE, VM 1, and GWB, the poem was considerably expanded to fit Lindsay's concept of the poem games; the following lines are added: 2, 3, 6, 7, 10, 11, 14, 15, 18, 19, 22, 23, 30, 31, 35-38, 40, 41, 44, 45, 56, 57, 59. VARIANTS 27 tiny] airy *CN, MFP, CP, JA* fairy *TE VM 1, GWB* 28 Who] That *TE, VM 1, GWB* 55 dancing] figure *TE, VM 1, GWB* 59 *not in MFP* 65 And *not in TE, VM 1, GWB* 66 glorious] beauteous *TE, VM 1, GWB.*

59 THE ANGEL FROZEN-WINGS: in [AL]; VM 3, 4. An early version (UMs-LH), dated "May, 1902," is titled "The Angel Goldenflesh." A letter to "Papa and Mama" (UL-V, 19 January 1905) reveals that the poem was originally part of AL, but it is not in the mutilated extant copy (V). On a copy of the poem in the Macfarlane scrapbook (see note to "I Want to Go Wandering" above), Lindsay writes: "Another good example of a purely esthetic fantasy in the early manner."

60 ALADDIN'S LAMP: in VM 3, 4. Parenthetical headnote not in TE.
VARIANT 34 spoke] spake *TE*.

62 THE MAP OF THE UNIVERSE: VM 2, 3, 4; CP. For the second edition
of the "Map," see below. See also "Explanation of 'The Map of the
Universe'" in the Appendix — as well as the poems comprising "Invocation
for 'The Map of the Universe,'" "Adventures While Preaching
Hieroglyphic Sermons," and "Adventures While Singing These
Songs" — all in CP. Lindsay advises Edward Scribner Ames (21 October
1909): "Wizards and prophets have always fought for supremacy in my
soul, their work does not always run parallel. Wizardry is the Art of the
Unseen, while by comparison Religion is the Morals of the Unseen. The
Map of the Universe is Wizardry, it has no morals, or logic, to speak of"
(Chénetier, p. 40).

63 TO THE YOUNG MEN OF ILLINOIS: the poem is part of the "Litany of
the Heroes" (*q.v.*). Lindsay published these lines as a complete poem in
TE and GWB (with "Lincoln" as the title in GWB). The plate also appears
on the back cover of "The Heroes of Time," an early edition of the
"Litany" privately published in 1910.

64 WHY I VOTED THE SOCIALIST TICKET: in *Independent*, 19 May
1910; ISR, 20 May 1910; GWB; CP; SP. Early version (UMs-LH) subtitle:
"who am not a Socialist."

64 AT MASS: in GWB, CP. Afternote in TE: "Paulist Father's Church.
New York City." In MFP Lindsay relates: "In reciting The Congo I
unconsciously introduced a new element of chanting, akin to the Gregorian
Chant I had heard in the Paulist Fathers' Church." In a letter to his Mother
(UL-V, 19 February 1904), Lindsay praises the church and adds: "They use
the Gregorian Chant, the oldest and finest Church music in the world. It is
said to be one of the musical treats of New York. It was at least
impressive."

65 HEART OF GOD: in RB; GWB; *Forum*, October 1913; AWP; CP.
Entitled "A Prayer in the Jungles of Heaven" in TE; this is the subtitle in
RB, *Forum*, and AWP. See "Explanation of 'The Map of the Universe'" in
the Appendix. In TE there are two concluding stanzas, dropped from all
other versions:

> The Prophets march to nowhere-land —
> Past treasure-heaps that shine.
> They seek Aladdin's foolish lamp —
> To answer prayers of mine.
>
> And will they find the lamp
> Who search because I pray?
> Oh had I known: oh had I prayed
> For Lamps of God, today!

VARIANTS 15, 16 prophets'] Prophet's *TE*.

65 OUTWARD BOUND: in VM 3, 4; CP. Entitled "Johnny Appleseed's Ship Comes In" in CP—part of the "Invocation for 'The Map of the Universe.'" See "The Boats of The Prophets" in *War Bulletin Number Three*. VARIANT 22 prophet-scrolls] prophets scrolls *TE, VM 3, 4*.

66 I HEARD IMMANUEL SINGING: in *Reedy's Mirror*, 19 December 1913; Cg; DJ; TBM; CP. Headnote and directions not in TE. An early version (UMs-LH), dated "July 13, 1907," is subtitled "(The day after the Millenium)." For Lindsay's account of the circumstances of the poem, see Masters, pp. 179-180 (the date, however, is 1906, not 1905, as Masters has it); see also the "Preface" to TE and the "Explanation to 'The Map of the Universe'" in the Appendix; Putzel, p. 187; and Fowler, pp. 338-339. In a letter to Wilbur L. Cross (4 December 1913), editor of *The Yale Review*, Lindsay writes that the poem reflects "in many ways the most *intense* and *personal* experience of my writing life" (Chénetier, p. 85). After line 56, there is an extra stanza in TE:

> And the fertile, fertile Goldenrod:
> The gay, unbraided head
> Of the sterile Indian Poppy
> Long numbered with the dead:
> The dreaming, proud Chrysanthemum:
> Yellow, bronze and white—
> These perished at the judgment,
> When earth went down in night.

VARIANTS 3 bend] bow *TE* 46 radiant] fading *TE* 51 worshipping,] worship: *TE* 52 shield and] hallowed *TE* 53 thistle or of lotus] Violet and Lotus *TE* 54 Or . . . lily] And curled Acanthus *TE* 61 though the arts] if those flowers *TE* 61 arts] flowers *Mirror* 66 flowers and Arts] all the Songs *TE* 66 Arts] songs *Mirror* 73-76 *not in TE*.

69 THE SANGAMON COUNTY PEACE ADVOCATE. NUMBER ONE (Springfield, Christmas, 1909) [Issued in the aftermath of the *War Bulletins*, the *Peace Advocate* is a broadside of poems. The upper righthand corner reads: "The Peace Advocate is free as bread and butter in a hospitable house. He who helps to establish the Christmas truce for which it stands has done the greatest favor possible to do for the publisher hereof." There is no other number.]

71 SPRINGFIELD MAGICAL: in *Vision*, Spring, 1912; GWB; LD, 21 March 1914; ISR, 12 August 1917; VM 3, 4; CP; SP. Entitled "The City Magical" in *Vision*. On 7 October 1909 Lindsay sent an early draft to Nellie T. Vieira, with the title "In Springfield Town" and a middle stanza that was omitted in all published versions; see Fowler, pp. 131, 95, 184.

71 IN THE DARK CHURCH: in VM 3, 4.

71 THE SHIELD OF LUCIFER: in VM 1, 2, 3, 4. The poem and drawing are in VM 3, 4; the drawing is not in PA but is in VM 1, 2 and CP. A hand-lettered version (UMs-LH) is dated "Friday—September 17, 1909." On a copy in the Canby scrapbook, Lindsay writes: "A Picture of The Spear

and Shield of Lucifer—Hanging on the Walls of a neglected Palace in
Heaven. Where the Roof Has Fallen in.''

73 THE SONG OF THE STURDY SNAILS: in GWC; VM 3, 4; CP.

74 SWEETHEARTS OF THE YEAR: in GWB; VM 3, 4; CP. The overall
title is not in PA; VM 3, 4. See "The Sorceress!" above. On 30 September
1909 Lindsay sent copies of "Sweetheart Summer" and "Sweetheart
Winter" to Nellie T. Vieira, informing her that they were written "today"
for "two old pictures.'' On 21 November 1909 he recopied these and added
"Sweetheart Spring" and "Sweetheart Autumn"; see Fowler, pp. 97-98,
301-304.

75 THE SPRINGFIELD OF THE FAR FUTURE: in GWC; *Survey*, 1 August
1921; VM 3, 4; CP. Entitled "Some Day Our Town Will Grow Old" in PA
and VM 3, 4; a draft with this title was sent to Nellie T. Vieira on 3
November 1909 and again on 21 November 1909: see Fowler, pp. 252, 305.
Lines 1-8 are 17-24 (and vice versa) in PA and VM 3, 4. VARIANTS 8 will]
shall *PA, VM 3, 4* 14 blest] to wean *PA* 16 guest] Queen *PA*.

77 THE SPRING HARBINGER (Spring, 1910) [This small (3½'' by 6½'')
booklet of cartoons, privately printed, is signed: "Nicholas Vachel Lindsay,
Rhymer and Designer: Springfield Illinois." Of the nineteen plates, all but
two are scattered through VM 2, 3, 4. Twelve of the plates are in MFP; two
are in VM 1. In MFP Lindsay avers that the little drawings and verses
comprise an "Irrelevant Section": "They have little reference to anything
in particular, and soberminded citizens should skip to the Village
Improvement Parade" (q.v.).

83 *From* THE VILLAGE MAGAZINE (1st Edition, Springfield, Summer,
1910) [In a letter to Hamlin Garland (UL-SC, 7 March 1911), Lindsay
identifies the essay, "An Editorial for the Art Student Who Has Returned
to the Village," as "the essence of the book"; a reprint of this essay is in
Sayre, pp. 269-271. Sayre also reprints the valuable introductory essay to
the second edition (p. 249). Several drawings in VM 1 appear without the
poems later written for them, including the plates for "The Village
Improvement Parade." These drawings are published below, with their
respective poems.]

87 THE GAMBLERS: in GWB, CP. Subtitled "Supposed to Be Spoken by
a Dreaming Idler of the Slum" in VM 1. VARIANTS 30 Turn the bolt—]
—Fit the lock, *VM* 1 32 sunrise] God's own *VM* 1 35-36 *God . . . wine.*]
Land of light! Our flesh will be reborn!/—God will give us fields of flowers
and corn. *VM* 1.

88 ON READING OMAR KHAYYAM: in *Current Literature*, March 1911;
GWB; VM 2, 3, 4; CP. In the Summer of 1910, Lindsay lectured on "The
Saloon. America's Menace. The Situation in Illinois"—throughout
Sangamon and nearby counties. In a notebook (V), Lindsay includes a copy
of the poem and writes: "A Loud Blast on the tin horn, the worst and last.

Henceforth the tin horn becomes a little more like a flute or cornet [*sic*]."
The headnote in parentheses is part of the title in VM 1-4; "in Central
Illinois" is not in CL. See AMP, pp. 235-244.

89 THE EMPTY BOATS: in *Current Literature*, March 1911; GWB; MFP;
VM 2, 3, 4; CP. The drawing is not in GWB; note in VM 3, 4: "See Map of
the Universe. Written remembering my Art Student Days in the Attic of a
New York Boarding House." Also see "Explanation of 'The Map of the
Universe' " in the Appendix. VARIANT 3 near] to *MFP*.

90 THE CORNFIELDS: in GWB; VM 2, 3, 4; CP.

90 THE ANGEL AND THE CLOWN: in GWB; CP; VM 2, 3, 4. Drawing
not in GWB, CP.

92 GENESIS: in GWB, CP.

93 THE WIZARD IN THE STREET: in ISR, 23 October 1910; CEPF, 19
May 1911; GWB; CP; SP. Lindsay's attitude toward Poe can be judged
from notebook entries cited by Masters, pp. 62ff., and Ruggles, p. 101; see
also AMP, pp. 153-160, 303. In a letter to George Sterling (1 June 1913),
Lindsay writes: "From my 13th to my 17th year Poe was the passion of my
life. No other poet-enthusiasm has quite equalled it since" (Chénetier, p.
69). Lindsay's letter to Dell (21 May 1911), thanking him for publishing the
poem in CEPF, has been published by Tanselle. The poem was published
in ISR to commemorate Poe's election to the Hall of Fame. VARIANT 16
reverenced] reverend *VM 1, ISR, CEPF*.

94 THE STORM-FLOWER: in VM 2; CP; VM 3, 4.

96 AN APOLOGY FOR THE BOTTLE VOLCANIC: in RB; Cg; VM 2; CP;
VM 3, 4. The "Self portrait of the author" from *The Spring Harbinger*
(Vol. I, p. 78) also goes with this poem, although the drawing is not in RB,
Cg, CP. The poem is not in VM 1 and is not titled in VM 2, 3; the title is
simply "The Bottle Volcanic" in VM 4.

97 CONTENTS OF AN INK BOTTLE: in *Current Literature*, March 1911;
VM 2, 3, 4; CP. This drawing is a companion to the "Self portrait of the
author" (see p. 78) and "An Apology for the Bottle Volcanic" above. Note
in VM 3, 4: "My drawings always come first. The above Cat is probably the
very lecherous Slant-Eyed Mountain Cat who appeared twelve years later
shouting 'So Much the Worse for Boston' in 'Going to the Sun' " (*q.v.*).

99 QUIZ, OR THE BEETLE'S DREAM: in VM 2, 3, 4.

99 THE WIZARD WIND: in RB; MFP; VM 2; CP; VM 3, 4. Drawing not in
RB. VARIANTS 1 wizard . . . most] Wizard Wind is my fine friend, so *MFP*
7 of] or *CP* 12 did . . . giant] knew not 'twas a giant *VM 1-2, RB, CP* knew
not the transcendent *MFP* 14 silky] silken *VM 1-2, RB, MFP, CP* 20
perfume, fire] perfume fire *VM 1-2, CP* 19-20 *not in RB, MFP*.

101 WHAT THE GREAT CITY SAID.

101 THE AIRSHIP OF THE MIND.

102 THE MILKWEED, THE SUNFLOWER AND THE ROBIN: in VM 2, 3, 4.

102 CONCERNING THE ACORNS ON THE COVER, AND THROUGH THE BOOK: in VM 2, 3, 4. Drawings of acorns decorate many pages of the four *Village Magazines*.

105 RHYMES TO BE TRADED FOR BREAD (Springfield, May 1912) [A facsimile edition is in Sayre, pp. 231-246; Sayre also reprints "The Gospel of Beauty," the small broadside that Lindsay distributed with RB—see inside the back cover of *Adventures: Rhymes and Designs*.]

108 THE KING OF YELLOW BUTTERFLIES: in CN; *Independent*, 29 September 1917; CP; JA; SP. See "The Poem Games" in the Appendix. Lines 2-3, 9-12, 14-15, 21-24, 31-32, 34-36 are not in RB; lines 7-8 and 30 are repeated one extra time in *Ind*. VARIANTS 17 A frail] 'Tis a *RB* 17 frail] light *Ind* 25 Gentlemen . . . whit!] They're gentlemen—adventurers, they're gipsies every whit, *RB*.

109 A DIRGE FOR A RIGHTEOUS KITTEN: in Cg, CP, JA, SP. Lines 1 and 14 are not in RB; the headnote is not in RB. Entitled "The Grave of the Righteous Kitten" in RB.

109 AN INDIAN SUMMER DAY ON THE PRAIRIE: in *Reedy's Mirror*, 7 March 1913; Cg; CP; JA; SP.

110 WHY I FLED FROM DUTY: in VM 3, 4. Lindsay wrote the poem for Nellie T. Vieira when she ended their relationship; see his letter to her on 10 August 1910 in Fowler, p. 360.

110 MACHINERY: in VM 3, 4. A large water color in the Lindsay home—with the poem hand-lettered down each side—is signed and dated "May 1904."

111 LOVE AND LAW: in Cg; *Christian Century*, 16 May 1918; CP; VM 3, 4. VARIANTS 4 'mid], in *ChC* 7 It is] 'Tis *RB, Cg, ChC, CP*.

111 THE FLIGHT OF MONA LISA: in VM 3, 4. One Vicenzo Perugia stole the Mona Lisa from the Louvre in August 1911; it was not recovered until December 1913. On a copy of the poem in a scrapbook (V, c. 1916), Lindsay adds an epigraph: "and the return thereof, which was never quite explained till now."

113 THE PATIENT WITCH: in *Poetry Journal*, March 1914; VM 3, 4.

114 EDEN IN WINTER: in GWB; *Current Opinion*, April 1914; CP. VARIANT 40 eyes] eye *RB, GWB*.

116 THE TOWER BUILDER: in VM 3, 4.

116 QUEEN MAB IN THE VILLAGE: in GWB, CP. VARIANT 1 Once] Oh, once *RB*.

119 THE MASTER OF THE DANCE: in Cg, CP. The headnote is not in RB. VARIANTS 34 to] into *RB* 115 upward] up *RB* 116 The thrill] The vast thrill *RB* 138 glory untold.] white-bannered days, *RB* 140 unfold] upraise *RB* 146 starlit] starlighted *RB*.

122 THE DANDELION: in GWB, CP, JA.

123 THE LAMP IN THE WINDOW: *1st* in *Vision*, Spring, 1912; in VM 3, 4. This poem, considerably revised, is the basis of what is often thought to be one of Lindsay's last poems—"Mentor Graham" (*q.v.*). VARIANTS 9 homes] home *1st* 23-25 *italicized in 1st*.

123 THE HEARTH ETERNAL: *1st* in *Vision*, Spring, 1912; in Cg, CP. VARIANTS 7 and] yet *1st* 14 old] green *1st*.

124 THE BUSH OF BURNING SPICE: in VM 3, 4.

125 THE WOMAN CALLED "BEAUTY" AND HER SEVEN DRAGONS: in VM 3, 4. In a scrapbook (V, c. 1916), Lindsay entitles the poem "Avanel Boone." VARIANTS 17 over-field] o'er the field *RB* 38 with] with the *RB*.

127 HERE'S TO THE SPIRIT OF FIRE: in AWP; *Forum*, January 1914; CP. VARIANTS 18 sea-rose] sea-roses *RB* sea-rose's *AWP* sea-roses' *Forum* 19 men] can but *RB, AWP, Forum*.

128 LOOK YOU, I'LL GO PRAY: in GWB; VM 3, 4; CP. A copy of the poem was pasted beside a picture of Tolstoi in a scrapbook Lindsay brought with him on the 1912 tramp (see Ruggles, pp. 177-178).

128 THE MISSIONARY MISGIVING: in VM 3, 4.

129 FOREIGN MISSIONS IN BATTLE ARRAY: in GWB; VM 3, 4; CP. In a review of GWB in the *Illinois State Register* (28 November 1913), obviously based on an interview with Lindsay, we read: "The poem 'Foreign Missions in Battle Array' commemorates the work of Dr. and Mrs. Wakefield in the foreign missionary field in China." Paul Wakefield married Lindsay's older sister Olive in June 1904; both served as missionaries in China, with occasional furloughs, from fall, 1905 to 1927, when Christians were forced out of China.

130 GALAHAD, KNIGHT WHO PERISHED: in Cg; *Journal of Social Hygiene*, January 1921; CP. VARIANTS 6 the bound] white slaves *RB* 8 intricate, desperate] desperate, desperate *RB* EMENDATION 15 strangers (as in RB, Cg, JSH)] stranger.

130 THE PERILOUS ROAD: in VM 3, 4. Headnote in RB: "A Poem for Spiritualists." On one copy of the poem (V), Lindsay writes in a subtitle: "and a warning to the followers of men like William Blake." In a letter to Harriet Monroe (UL-C, 14 March 1914), Lindsay encloses a copy of the poem and comments: "A poetic transcript of my first evening with Yeats at Mrs. Letts—before we became acquainted. Written long ago—but prophetic." VARIANTS 1 boy] youth *RB* 4 the bright] bright *RB* 7 while] the while *RB* 12 the night] eve *RB* 15 No] Nay *RB* 17 And] Nay *RB* 17 my son] good youth *RB* 19 my] mine *RB* 31 crying] weeping *RB* 33 He . . . alone] When he wakes once more, *RB* 38 Yes] Yea *RB*.

131 IN MEMORY OF A CHILD: in Cg, CP. There is a fifth stanza in RB:

> Yet, he is lost to us,
> Far is his path of gold,
> Far does the city seem,
> Lonely our hearts and old.

132 IN PRAISE OF SONGS THAT DIE: in Cg; *Literary Digest*, 21 November 1914; CP.

132 FORMULA FOR A UTOPIA: in VM 3, 4. For Lindsay on utopias, see AMP, pp. 272-279; *The Golden Book of Springfield*; and *The Litany of Washington Street*.

133 THE PERFECT MARRIAGE: in Cg, CP, SP. In RB there are four extra lines at the end:

> We will do well. We'll save through life
>   love's spark, love's gem,
> We'll guard no man-made heap of coins or
>   diadem—
> But clasp worn hands, and vow great vows
>   to God above,
> Keeping unquenched through storm and fear,
>   one spark of love!

134 THE LEADEN-EYED: in Cg; *Christian Century*, 19 July 1917; NP; NV; *Survey*, 16 October 1920; *Playground*, May 1924; CP; SP. The title is from Keats's "Ode to a Nightingale," 1. 28.

135 TO THE UNITED STATES SENATE: *1st* in ISR, 2 March 1911; in GWB. No headnote in ISR; the afternote is not in ISR, RB. To date, the best study of Lorimer is Joel Arthur Tarr's *A Study in Boss Politics: William Lorimer of Chicago* (Urbana, 1971). On a copy of the poem in a scrapbook (V, c. 1916), Lindsay writes: "Sent twice to every member of the Senate and House. Then Lorimer was expelled! Probably in spite of the poem!" VARIANTS 1, 5, 13 the] a *1st*.

136 DREAMS IN THE SLUM: in VM 3, 4.

136 THE EAGLE THAT IS FORGOTTEN: *1st* in ISR, 15 April 1911; in *Public*, 24 May 1912; *Reedy's Mirror*, 7 March 1913; *Current Opinion*, May

1913; ISR, 3 May 1913; LBMV; GWB; *Literary Digest*, 21 March 1914; NP; CP; KMR, April 1925, July 1927, February 1930; SP. After its first appearance in ISR, newspapers around the country printed the poem. There are no significant variants, although the details in the headnote do change from copy to copy. The title in *Current Opinion* is "John P. Altgeld." To Sara Teasdale in March 1914 (UL-Y), Lindsay reveals that the poem is part paraphrase of Tennyson's "A Dirge." Altgeld, of course, was one of Lindsay's heroes; he wrote several unpublished essays on Altgeld—one while at Hiram College—and kept a scrapbook on the Governor's career. All of this is extant as part of the Barrett Collection (V). For a study of Altgeld, see Harry Barnard, *Eagle Forgotten: The Life of John Peter Altgeld* (Indianapolis, 1938). See also Rittenhouse, p. 298.

137 TO THOSE THAT WOULD MEND THESE TIMES: in VM 3, 4.

138 TO THOSE THAT WOULD HELP THE FALLEN: in VM 3, 4. VARIANT 3 at] at the *RB*.

138 THE TRAP: *1st* in ISR, 2 June 1911; *Current Opinion*, August 1913; ISR, 31 July 1913; GWB; CP. Headnote in *1st*: "(A Discussion of the White Slave Traffic.)" VARIANTS 2 angels'] Angel's *1st*, ISR *(1913)* 24 in] of *CO* 39-40 *not in RB* 44 daughters] daughter *RB* 49-50 *follow 54 in 1st* 60 brides] bride *CO* EMENDATION 11 ?" (as in RB, GWB)] "?

140 TO REFORMERS IN DESPAIR: in GWB, CP.

140 THE LEGISLATURE: in VM 3, 4.

140 THE PILGRIMS FROM ASIA: in VM 3, 4.

141 WE CANNOT CONQUER TIME: in VM 3, 4. A revised version of this poem was published posthumously in the *English Review* (March 1932) with the title "Epitaph for Henry Ford" (*q.v.*). In the Fall, 1915, Ford had asked Lindsay to join him on his Peace Ship. Lindsay refused and Ford himself abandoned the effort in December of that year. As early as 1916, Lindsay's notebooks reveal that he is thinking of Henry Ford in the light of this poem.

141 LAZARUS AND DIVES: in VM 3, 4. VARIANT 10 It is] 'Tis *RB*.

142 ON THE ROAD TO NOWHERE: in GWB; *Forum*, November 1913; AWP; CP.

145 GENERAL WILLIAM BOOTH ENTERS INTO HEAVEN AND OTHER POEMS (New York: Mitchell Kennerley, 1913) [After this volume appeared in late November, a fair number of newspapers and periodicals offered reviews. None, however, could have meant as much to Lindsay as the long review in Springfield's *Illinois State Register*, 28 November 1913. The reviewer comments on several poems in the book, noting that some had been published in the *Register*. He asserts that Lindsay chose his sixty

poems from out of three hundred possible ones and adds: "Without doubt the book is a modicum of Mr. Lindsay's best work."]

148 GENERAL WILLIAM BOOTH ENTERS INTO HEAVEN: *1st* in *Poetry Magazine*, January 1913; *Current Opinion*, March 1913; ISR, 7 March 1913; *Literary Digest*, 8 March 1913; *Independent*, 13 March 1913; *Christian Century*, 10 April 1913 and 5 February 1914; NP; SBMV; CP; KMR, April 1925; *Bibliothea Sacra*, January 1931; SP. For background on the poem, see "Adventures While Singing These Songs" in CP; Carpenter, p. 300; Schroeder, pp. 14-15; Monroe, pp. 279-282; and G. Thomas Tanselle, "Lindsay's *General William Booth*: A Bibliographical and Textual Note," in *Papers of the Bibliographical Society of America*, Vol. 55 (1961), pp. 371-380. In 1931 Lindsay informs Sara Teasdale (see Carpenter, pp. 298-300) that the poem goes back to a 1902 Chicago drawing of Jacob's ladder, adding that his poetry is always preceded by his art studies. The editor of *The Independent* notes parallels with Erasmus' account of scholar Johann Reuchlin's entering into heaven and also with Bunyan's *Pilgrim's Progress*. The greatest number of variants is in the directional sidenotes; I have not recorded these because Lindsay himself did not take them seriously. In MFP he asserts: "The devices of marginal directions, the naming of the tune, printing with dots, dashes and capitals, etc., are not an integral part of the original theory. They are a concession to the tired business man, just as books printed by embossed points are a concession to the blind." In the same context Lindsay reveals that, during his 1912 tramp, he "evolved the theory that the natural meter for writing a projected poem might be found by seeking a hymn or ballad of long standing somewhat parallel in thought." He reminds us that Burns wrote "in this fashion" and adds: "The first set of verses where I applied the notion was The Flute of the Lonely [*q.v.*]. . . . When I wrote General Booth, in Los Angeles, a month or two later, the method was an old story with me." VARIANTS 21 trumpets blowed a] bazoos blowing *PM, CO, ISR, LD, Ind, ChC* 34 Then,] Yet *PM, CO, ISR, LD, Ind, ChC, GWB*.

149 GOD LOVES A GAMBLER LADY: *1st* in ISR, 23 October 1912; *Reedy's Mirror*, 27 June 1913; *Forum*, July 1913; ISR, 3 July 1913; CP; SP. All versions of the poem except *1st* and SP are titled "The City That Will Not Repent"; Lindsay also referred to the poem as "San Francisco" (ISR, 19 September 1913). Following the title in *1st* is a note: "(Written expressly for the newspapers of Springfield, Illinois.) . . . A poem on San Francisco, showing how she is planning to build a magnificent fair on perilous earthquake ground." After the poem in *1st* we read: "Nicholas Vachel Lindsay. Visiting Prof. E. Olan James . . . Berkeley, Cal., Oct. 18, 1912" — in other words, directly after leaving Los Angeles and the writing of "Booth." The "magnificent fair," of course, will be the 1915 Panama-Pacific Exposition, at which thousands of copies of Lindsay's "The Wedding of the Rose and the Lotus" (*q.v.*) will be given away. VARIANTS 3 new San Francisco] the new-built 'Frisco *1st* 12 store and] 'Frisco *1st* 12 store] spire *ISR, Mirror, Forum* 39 should] would *ISR* 41 Nay, she] 'Frisco *1st* 49 a gambler lady] this rebel city *ISR, Mirror, Forum, GWB, CP* 49 a] this *1st* 50 foemen] foeman *1st*.

151 IN WHICH ROOSEVELT IS COMPARED TO SAUL: *1st* in *Forum*, March 1913; ISR, 4 March 1913; *Literary Digest*, 21 March 1914; GWC; CP. Entitled "Where Is David, the Next King of Israel" in *Forum*, ISR, GWB, LD; headnote in ISR: "Appropriate for Inauguration Day." Nearly six years later (7 January 1919), the *Register* reprints the poem under the headline: "In Memoriam: Theodore Roosevelt"—whose death was on the day before. For Lindsay on Roosevelt, see Graham, pp. 165-170, 174, 217. VARIANTS 22 born] made *ISR* 28 tunes] words *ISR*.

152 HONOR AMONG SCAMPS: *1st* in *American Magazine*, January 1912; CP.

152 INCENSE: *1st* in *Outlook*, 23 September 1911; ISR, 24 September 1911; CP; SP. On 21 May 1922 Lindsay wrote the poem into the autograph book of Mrs. Arthur T. Aldis (Y).

153 THE WEDDING OF THE ROSE AND THE LOTUS: in PP (1913); *Sunset Magazine*, June 1914; MFP; VM 2, 3, 4; CP. Drawings not in GWB, *Sunset* (a San Francisco periodical). An early copy (UMs-V), dated "May 1, 1912," is titled "The Marriage of the Rose and the Lotus"; in MFP and *Sunset* the title is "The Rose and the Lotus." A large water color, with the poem hand-lettered down the sides, is in the Lindsay home (dated "March 1913"). See "The History of the Rose and the Lotus Rhyme" in the Appendix and "Adventures While Preaching Hieroglyphic Sermons" in CP; see also "Lady Iron-Heels" in HGB and Graham, p. 118. The poem was recited before Woodrow Wilson's Cabinet (Massa, p. 10), and Franklin K. Lane, then Secretary of the Interior, ordered ten thousand copies—with the drawings. These were given to members of both Houses of Congress on the opening day of the Panama-Pacific Exposition (20 February 1915) and given away at the Exposition itself. In a letter to Hamlin Garland (31 March 1913), Lindsay explains his symbolism and then adds: "Now when we approach the first hour in history when East and West meet, never again to be parted it is fitting and proper we should weave these two flowers together as our sign of spiritual courtesy to the East; as our expression of the hope of ultimate Peace and Justice and highmindedness between Asia and the World, as well as a sign of their sure inter-dependence. . . . I think the *idea* is better than the design or poem which I send—I think it has a fundamental historical vitality. I have not copy-righted it, and I want a great many people persuaded to steal it, or persuaded it is their own. . . . I do not see why the internationalism of this design cannot be made a substitute for or supplement to the violent internationalism of the Socialist flag" (Chénetier, pp. 67-68). VARIANTS 1 Flags of the Pacific] The wide Pacific waters *PP, GWB, Sunset* 3-4 Captain . . . fleet] With cries of joy they mingle, / In tides of love they greet *PP, GWB, Sunset*.

156 KING ARTHUR'S MEN HAVE COME AGAIN: *1st* in *Outlook*, 28 May 1910; CP. A hand-lettered version (UMs-LH) is dated "May 3, 1910." On a copy of the poem in the Macfarlane scrapbook (see note to "I Want to Go Wandering" above), Lindsay writes: "Quoted in many religious and anti-saloon papers. The Epworth Herald has just reprinted it."

157 WITH A BOUQUET OF TWELVE ROSES: in GWB, CP, SP. Published with "The Firemen's Ball" (*q.v.*) in SP, under the title "Poems Speaking of Buddha." In CP we have the same title, but "To Buddha" (*q.v.*) is added to the two poems.

157 THE KNIGHT IN DISGUISE: *1st* in *American Magazine*, June 1912; *Reedy's Mirror*, 13 June 1912; *Current Literature*, July 1912; CP; SP. Chosen by Ferdinand Earle for *The Lyric Year* (1912) — with the title "O. Henry"; listed in the *Boston Evening Transcript* as one of the forty best poems of the year by William Stanley Braithwaite (1912). Also see Putzel, pp. 177-179. VARIANT 18 banter . . . and] revel and absurdity's *AMg, Mirror, CL.*

159 THE TREE OF LAUGHING BELLS: in AL, PP (1905), CP; SP. On 31 January 1904 Lindsay writes to his Mother (UL-V) that he is about to send his sister Joy a copy of one of his "latest poems—the 'Wings of the Morning.'" His notebooks reveal that he continued to work on the poem for over a year; then, under the date "July 5, 1905," he writes (UNB-V): "Up to this date—500 copies of the Tree of Laughing Bells have been printed. Grandma has paid the bill of the printer, $43.63 and incidentals—string for tying, envelopes, etc., bringing the total of fifty dollars. This payment she made a gift but I consider a loan." This little booklet, of course, is what Lindsay carried on his 1906 tramp from Florida to Kentucky (see HGB). During this tramp, he writes in his notebook (UNB-V, 23 April 1906): "After much reading and explaining of the Bells, to many people, I have arrived at the definition of a symbol. It should reflect the experience of the man reading, as a pool reflects a passing cloud. It should be like a flower, the basis of many metaphors, yet always a flower in the end. It should be intricately significant for the mind desiring meaning, it should be simple, for the mind desiring a story. It should have more thought, rather than less, in its make-up, than it appears to have. It should have not only a vigorous decorative organization, but a philosophic anatomy." Lindsay's letter to Henri, requesting the chance to read the poem, is extant (UL-Y, 21 March 1905); see Masters, p. 121; Ruggles, pp. 93-94; Rittenhouse, pp. 299-300. A watercolor-collage for the poem, dated "June 15, 1908," is at LH and is reproduced as the frontispiece for volume one of this edition. For "the wings of the morning," see Psalm 139:9 and Bryant's "Thanatopsis," 11. 50-51. VARIANTS 29 from *not in PP, GWB, CP* 88 0 . . . wounded] The Chaos wind was *PP* 108 straining] trailing *PP, GWB* training *CP.*

163 THE OLD HORSE IN THE CITY: CP, JA, SP. An early version is written into Lindsay's 1912 hiking diary (V).

164 WHAT THE SNOW MAN SAID: CP, JA. Also written into the 1912 hiking diary (V).

164 WHAT THE SCARECROW SAID: CP; JA. Read in Springfield as "The Proud Scarecrow" (ISR, 19 September 1913).

165 WHAT THE FORESTER SAID: in CP, JA.

165 A NET TO SNARE THE MOONLIGHT: *1st* in *American Magazine*,
April 1913; *Reedy's Mirror*, 11 April 1913; *Public*, 25 April 1913; CP; JA;
SP. Letters and newspaper items reveal that Lindsay also referred to the
poem as "The Dew, the Rain and Moonlight." VARIANT 4 Descend] Come
down *1st*, *Mirror*, *Public*.

166 THE PROUD FARMER: *1st* in *American Magazine*, September 1912;
Literary Digest, 7 September 1912; *Christian Century*, 5 February 1914; PP
(1915); CP; KMR, July 1926; SP. Beginning with GWB, this and the
following two poems comprise Lindsay's "A Gospel of Beauty." In AMg
and LD the title is "The Grave of the Proud Farmer"; in PP, which is a
booklet with the title *Community Poems for Illinois* and includes "The
Illinois Village" and "On the Building of Springfield" (see below), the title
is "The Illinois Farmer." VARIANT 31 build] built *1st, LD, GWB*.

167 THE ILLINOIS VILLAGE: in VM 1, 2, 3, 4; *Current Literature*, March
1911; PP (1915); CP; KMR, July 1926; SP. See "The Proud Farmer"
above. VARIANTS 19 inspired, aflame] creative men *VM 1-4, CL* 31 touch]
gush *VM 1-4, CL* 52 Artist's] artists' *VM 1-4, CL*.

168 ON THE BUILDING OF SPRINGFIELD: in TE; VM 1; *American
Magazine*, May 1913; ISR, 22 April 1913; LBMV; PP (1915); CP; KMR,
July 1926; SP. See "The Proud Farmer" above; in PP the title is "The
Illinois City." In ISR we read: "The poem was originally written and
recited by Mr. Lindsay as the climax and summary of a lecture course on
composite citizenship delivered in the YMCA five years ago. The title of
the lecture was, 'How to Make Springfield Unique.' " The lecture was on
16 December 1908: see the note to "The Dance of Unskilled Labor" below.
Lindsay informs Sara Teasdale (UL-Y, December 1913) that the poem is
based on the same experience that led to "I Heard Immanuel Singing"
(*q.v.*); much later, 21 March 1931, he relates to Sara that the poem is the
very soul of his soul (UL-Y). See also Carpenter, p. 298; Rittenhouse, pp.
307-308; Fowler, p. 184. In TE and VM 1, there is an extra stanza after line
16:

> Like Nuremburg against the robber knights
>   Let her keep out the wealth bereft of sense —
> Putting her ban upon the stupid toys
>   Of private greed and greasy arrogance.

171 THE CONGO AND OTHER POEMS (New York: The Macmillan
Company, 1914) [The "Introduction" is by Harriet Monroe, though she
does offer a long quotation from Lindsay himself. Taking a page from
Wordsworth, Lindsay submits his poems "as experiments," but these
experiments are an endeavor to carry the "vaudeville form back towards
the old Greek precedent of the half-chanted lyric." One-third of the music,
Lindsay avers, "must be added by the instinct of the reader." In a letter to
Miss Monroe (UL-C, 18 May 1914), Lindsay names the first three poems in
this volume as his "principal exhibits" of chant poetry. Later, after he had

recited them in New York, he writes Miss Monroe: "Last evening had a big roaring session at the Poetry Society, and spread myself like a battercake on a griddle" (UL-C, 27 October 1914). Lindsay's later disillusionment—not so much with the chants themselves as with the incessant demands of audiences that he perform them—is a well-known story.

Sara Teasdale's role in this volume, both as principal character and as a help in preparing the edition, is also a well-known story—see Carpenter, pp. 192-193. Before deciding on Gloriana for her name, Lindsay's letters reveal that he tried "little girl" and "Polly Ann." His pet name for the real Sara was suggested by his young sister Joy: "Saraphim" (Carpenter, p. 177).

Finally, the war poems at the end are eleventh-hour additions; in late summer and during the fall, 1914, Lindsay worked feverishly to complete them for the book—see Ruggles, pp. 230-232.]

174 THE CONGO: in NP; DJ; CP; JA; *Golden Book*, September 1929; SP. Published many times during Lindsay's lifetime, including as one of the *Linweave Limited Editions* (Mt. Vernon, 1931), with illustrations by Alexander King. For firsthand accounts of the poem and of Lindsay's performance of it, see Monroe, pp. 329-339; Untermeyer, p. 152; Ruggles, pp. 209-218; Rittenhouse, pp. 301-305; Carpenter, p. 300; and "The Poetry of Vachel Lindsay," *The Dial*, LVII (16 October 1914), 281-283. A.L. Bader has reprinted Lindsay's own explanation from the *Illinois State Register* (13 February 1914), in the *Philological Quarterly*, XXVII (April 1948), 191-192; see also "How 'The Congo' Came to Be Written," *Christian Century*, XXXII (4 February 1915), 104-105. The *Illinois State Journal* (13 February 1914) reveals that Lindsay received more than "a word of introduction" (Ruggles, pp. 214-215) when he recited the work for his Springfield, Lincoln Banquet audience. The *Journal* reports the synopsis of the poem and the poet's intent given by Judge Humphrey when he introduced Lindsay. If the audience was abashed, as Ruggles suggests, a Lindsay letter to Harriet Monroe discloses that the poet himself remained undaunted: "I have just recited it ['The Congo''] for the big fat-sides Lincoln banquet here—audience of 1000 in the Arsenal and boomed it to the very back of the building" (16 February 1914, Chénetier, p. 88). One aspect of the work that has gone relatively unnoticed is the influence of Springfield black attorney Charles Gibbs, who was, in many ways, as audacious as his friend Lindsay. Another Lindsay friend, John P. Snigg, remembers the poet saying that "he had conceived the idea for one of his best known poems, 'The Congo,' from conversations with a colored lawyer in Springfield, shortly after the race riots here. He informed me that many times he had climbed the stairs to the office of Charley Gibbs, on the second floor of a building in the middle of the 1908 riot area, and had talked with him about the riot and the problems of the Negro" (*I Walked with a Poet*, pamphlet published by the Vachel Lindsay Association, Springfield, 1947); see also Graham, p. 277. For the importance of the Gregorian chant, see "At Mass" above; for the influence of G.K. Chesterton's "Lepanto," see Dell, pp. 210-211. *The Metropolitan* paid Lindsay for the work (Monroe reports $75, Ruggles $50), and the poet expected it in the August 1914 issue. Instead the editors published "Sunshine" (*q.v.*); Monroe suggests the "eastern magazine . . . never dared print so eccentric a manifestation

of poetic genius!''—in *Poets & Their Art* (New York, 1932), p. 269. The parenthetical headnote and the final note are not in Cg, DJ.

179 THE SANTA-FÉ TRAIL (A HUMORESQUE): *1st* in *Poetry Magazine*, July 1914; NV; DJ; CP; JA; SP. Lindsay's letters to Sara Teasdale (Y) reveal that most of the work on the poem was done in March 1914. For background on the work, see AWP, especially pp. 20, 43-44; Carpenter, pp. 190, 260; Rittenhouse, p. 305; and Graham, p. 69. For Lindsay on revising, see Williams, pp. 106-108; for the rhythms of the poem, see NV, pp. 64-65. On 13 May 1914 Lindsay writes to Harriet Monroe: ''. . . I have entitled this a humoresque—to disarm the reader, and prepare him for *anything*. When I first conceived it, the piece started with three long pages of rat-horn, bat-horn, fat-horn, cat-horn, hog-horn, dog-horn, grog-horn, and so forth. A sort of three times ugly kallyope yell to express my wrath and lifelong aversion to the automobile. It stands as a sign, as a symbol of *America*, from the standpoint of those who despise her most and get her superficial aspects in a triple dose. I have considered the voice of the auto at its worst—the most obscene and unclean sound on the face of the earth. (Also very mechanical. Hence the forced rhymes.). . . . Gradually I added the twilight zone—and the sweetness of the horns—in the distance—and the Rachel Jane was the very last afterthought, put in as a sort of final concession to the ladies who shrunk from the rude blasts of my satire, and the mechanical rhyme-repetitions. . . . I have tried—like the lion in Pyramus and Thisbe—to roar so as not to frighten the ladies—still I must roar,'' Chénetier, p. 98. VARIANTS 26, 107 *not in 1st, Cg, DJ* 49, 102 And *not in 1st, Cg, DJ.*

183 THE FIREMEN'S BALL: *1st* in *Poetry Magazine*, July 1914; CP; SP. Published by Braithwaite (1914) as one of the best poems of the year; included in ''Poems Speaking of Buddha'' in CP, SP (see ''With a Bouquet of Twelve Roses'' above). Lindsay's letters to Sara Teasdale (Y) reveal that most of the work on the poem was done during December 1913 and January 1914, although Masters (p. 108) mentions ''The Ding Dong Doom Bells'' as an early (April 1901) part of the poem. Headnote in PM: ''In which the music of the Ball imitates the burning of a great building.'' See also Dunbar, p. 110; Rittenhouse, pp. 304-305. VARIANT 73 *not in Cg.*

189 YANKEE DOODLE: *1st* in *Metropolitan*, February 1914; ISR, 4 February 1914; CP. Published by Braithwaite (1914) as one of the year's best poems; the poem was read in Springfield as early as 19 September 1913 (ISR article). ISR not only publishes the poem but also a long interview with the poet: ''The piece . . . supports the Wilson-Bryan peace policy, as well as the anti-militarist propaganda of international socialism. It has in mind the liberators of the present day, who, above all things, abhor old-fashioned war and jingoism. The battles of the world that are henceforth worth while, are those fought in times of ostensible peace. The American flag and the old-fashioned tune of Yankee Doodle ought to be symbols of this kind of war and this kind of liberation.'' Lindsay intends the poem as a ''national hymn'' and hopes grade school children everywhere will learn to sing it. A late version (UMs-V, 1931), with the title ''Our

Banner Splendid,'' is evidence that he was working on the poem at the end of his life, obviously trying to get it ready for Washington's bicentennial birthday (February 1932). For more on Washington, see Lindsay's *The Litany of Washington Street* (1929). Edwin Howland Blashfield (1848-1936), American genre and mural painter, published *Mural Painting in America* in 1913; this may have been the stimulus for the poem. VARIANTS 6 rode] charged *1st, ISR* 20 demons' rumbling] demon's tyrant-*1st, ISR* 21-24 *not in 1st, ISR* 43 Valiant citizens] Spirits living yet *1st, ISR* 44 Of] In *1st, ISR* 51 today] the flag *1st, ISR* 52 flag the] marching *1st, ISR.*

190 THE BLACK HAWK WAR OF THE ARTISTS: *1st* in *Poetry Magazine,* July 1914; Cg. The instructional headnote is not in *1st*; lines 7-12 are repeated at the end of *1st*. Lindsay's letters to Lorado Taft are at the Chicago Historical Society. On 5 June 1913, Lindsay sends a copy—with the title ''Hawk of the Rocks''—to Taft and to Hamlin Garland (UL-SC). He advises Taft that his statue ''is the one thing of its kind in America. It is just as necessary a symbol—this statue of Black Hawk, as the Statue of Liberty in New York Harbor.'' A year later Lindsay sends a revised version to Garland, with the present title, and comments that the work ''is a sort of Battle-Cry for Western Art'' (UL-SC, 26 June 1914). On 11 July 1922, Lindsay writes into his datebook: ''There is one thing a man can be in this mixed world—without pretense:—He can be a Hawk and he can waken the flying Hawk in other men'' (UDB-V).

192 THE JINGO AND THE MINSTREL: *1st* in *Independent,* 6 November 1913; ISR, 13 November 1913; CP. Read in Springfield (ISR, 19 September 1913) as ''Japan''; the last sentence of the headnote is not in *1st*, ISR, Cg. See ''The History of the Rose and the Lotus Rhyme'' in the Appendix; AMP, pp. 64-65, 79-81; and the note to ''Young Daughter of the Ancient Sun'' below. VARIANTS 3 as rare a] the rarest *1st, ISR* 4 As] That *1st, ISR* 61 this day] venom *1st, ISR, Cg* 78 The] Though *1st, ISR.*

194 AN ARGUMENT: *1st* in *Little Review,* June 1914; CP. In the fall, 1913 Lindsay sends ''Incense and Splendor'' to Harriet Monroe; later he advises her that the work will not ''attract the languid reader . . . but I think it has staying powers, for the meditative'' (UL-C, 21 January 1914). VARIANTS 17 Never] And never *1st* 36 wreath] wreaths *1st, CG.* A slightly revised version of ''The Rhymer's Reply'' appears in the section of CP entitled ''Invocation for 'The Map of the Universe.''' Here the title is ''Johnny Appleseed Speaks of Great Cities in the Future,'' and there are four additional lines at the end:

> And scattering dreams, and glory,
> Prophets' boats sailed in from far away,
> And angels' boats sailed in
> From chaos-seas and many a stormy bay.

VARIANTS 23 naught] nothing 28 o'er the] over

195 A RHYME ABOUT AN ELECTRICAL ADVERTISING SIGN: in CP.

197 THE SOUL OF THE CITY RECEIVES THE GIFT OF THE HOLY
SPIRIT: in PP (1913); MFP; VM 2, 3, 4; CP. The drawings are not in Cg.
See the essay in the Appendix with the same title; see also Lindsay's *The
Art of the Moving Picture*, Chapter XI (1915, rev. 1922). The drawings
were completed in the spring, 1913; sometime after, the poem was written
and the whole published in the fall, 1913. On 1 June 1913 Lindsay writes
tongue-in-cheek to George Sterling: "Pity Springfield. Do not pity me. The
poor little town is in for it. People have tried every kind of purgation from
assaults upon Lorimer [see note to "To the United States Senate" above] to
the establishment of Commission Government. Now I will see what the
angels can do—each one with a censer in its hand. Springfield shall be
whipped by these angels and sent to Sunday School like a naughty child.
That is—I hope so" (Chénetier, p. 70). Lindsay's interest in censers may
reflect his love for Keats: see especially "Ode to Psyche."

213 I WENT DOWN INTO THE DESERT: *1st* in *Little Review*, June 1914;
Chicago Herald, 2 September 1914; CP. Headnote in the *Herald:* "A
souvenir of my walk into New Mexico two years ago." See Ruggles, p. 196.
VARIANT 3 Arisen] Or some one like, arisen *1st*.

213 DARLING DAUGHTER OF BABYLON: *1st* in *Little Review*, June
1914; CP. The "darling daughter" is Octavia Roberts; see Lindsay's
description of her in a letter to Harriet Moody (Dunbar, p. 117). Lindsay's
letters to Sara Teasdale (Y) reveal that he took up the poem in the spring,
1914, having first written it in late 1912. An early version sent to Sara
(UMs-Y) has the unlikely title: "From a Sweat-shop Hand to a Certain
Ex-worker in Settlements."

214 THE AMARANTH: *1st* in *Little Review*, June 1914; CP; SP. For a later
version, with many variants, see "Explanation of 'The Map of the
Universe'" in the Appendix. This version is also in the section of CP
entitled "Invocation for 'The Map of the Universe'"; here the title is
"Johnny Appleseed Speaks of the Apple-Blossom Amaranth That Will
Come to This City." VARIANT 12 our . . . or] now our youths are strident,
or are *1st*.

215 TWO EASTER STANZAS: *1st* in *Reedy's Mirror*, 10 April 1914; CP.
Lindsay's letters to Sara Teasdale (Y) reveal that the "you" is Octavia
Roberts (see "Darling Daughter of Babylon" above). The poems were not
written at Easter but during the late fall, 1912, after Lindsay had returned
from the West.

216 THE TRAVELLER-HEART: *1st* in *Chicago Herald*, 3 September 1914;
CP; SP. Read in Springfield on 19 September 1913 (ISR). VARIANT 17 all
not in 1st.

217 THE NORTH STAR WHISPERS TO THE BLACKSMITH'S SON: *1st*
in *Chicago Herald*, 31 August 1914; DJ; CP. VARIANT 3 but are] but you
are *1st*.

218 THIS SECTION IS A CHRISTMAS TREE: in CP. Lindsay uses this poem to introduce the next four in CP. Originally these four were published under the title "Rhymes for Gloriana."

218 THE DOLL UPON THE TOPMOST BOUGH: *1st* in *Chicago Herald*, 1 September 1914; CP. See "This Section Is a Christmas Tree" above.

218 ON SUDDENLY RECEIVING A CURL LONG REFUSED: *1st* in *Chicago Herald*, 1 September 1914; CP. On 8 February 1914 Lindsay sends Sara Teasdale an early draft of the poem (UMs-Y), with the title "To My Present from Sara."

219 ON RECEIVING ONE OF GLORIANA'S LETTERS: *1st* in *Chicago Herald*, 1 September 1914; CP. A Lindsay letter to Sara Teasdale (UL-Y, 13 April 1914) reveals that an early title was: "On Receiving a Good Letter from Polly Ann."

219 IN PRAISE OF GLORIANA'S REMARKABLE GOLDEN HAIR: *1st* in *Chicago Herald*, 1 September 1914; CP. Early titles from the Teasdale letters (Y): "In Praise of a Little Girl's Golden Hair" (27 January 1914), and "In Praise of Polly Ann's Remarkable Golden Hair" (13 April 1914). For "the treasure-pits of Heaven," see "Explanation of 'The Map of the Universe'" in the Appendix.

220 THE SUN SAYS HIS PRAYERS: in CP.

220 THE LION: *1st* in *Tuck's Magazine*, Winter, 1914; CP; JA; SP. A small article in ISR (9 April 1913) reports the origin of *Tuck's*, a tiny Springfield periodical. Two high school girls, Alice Catherine Warren and Elizabeth Stebbens Brown, wrote much of it and printed it themselves; they named it after the Warren dog. Lindsay published several of his poems here, and, quite characteristically, put *Tuck's* on an equal footing with *Poetry: A Magazine of Verse, The Bookman, The Independent*, and others on the credits page of *The Chinese Nightingale and Other Poems* and CP.

221 AN EXPLANATION OF THE GRASSHOPPER: *1st* in *Tuck's Magazine*, Winter, 1914; CP; JA; SP. A letter to Sara Teasdale (UL-Y, 28 January 1914) gives the poem the title "Natural History Note."

221 THE DANGEROUS LITTLE BOY FAIRIES: in CP.

221 THE MOUSE THAT GNAWED THE OAK-TREE DOWN: *1st* in *Little Review*, June 1914; CP; SP. The title in *1st* is "The Stubborn Mouse." A letter to Sara Teasdale (UL-Y, 12 March 1914) notes that the poem was written on 2 March 1914.

222 HOW A LITTLE GIRL DANCED: *1st* in *Little Review*, March 1914; *Current Opinion*, May 1914; ISR, 4 May 1914; CP; SP. Headnote in *1st*, Cg, CP: "Dedicated to Lucy Bates." ISR also publishes a report obviously

based on a personal interview with Lindsay: "While the poet does not
openly condemn the modern dances the verses reveal his partiality for all
that is aesthetic and refined. He sees in the dancing that he writes about an
unselfish and inspired spirit."Lindsay sent a letter of praise to Lucy the
very night he first saw her dance (26 May 1910). She is perfection: "I feel
that I understand for the first time what a free spirit is, delivered from
mortal mind." He concludes: "I have seen thousands of dancers, but have
never seen dancing before" (Chénetier, p. 43).

223 FACTORY WINDOWS ARE ALWAYS BROKEN: *1st* in *Chicago
Herald*, 4 September 1914; DJ; CP; SP. Headnote in *1st*: "Written when I
was last in Chicago." The poem is also known as "The Factory Window
Song."

223 TO MARY PICKFORD: *1st* in *American Magazine*,   April 1914;
Current Opinion, November 1914; *Playboy*, January 1919; Cg. Read in
Springfield 19 September 1913 (ISR); Lindsay also published a note on the
"Pickford Popularity" in ISR (10 June 1917): "Why do the people love
Mary? Because of a certain aspect of her face in her highest mood.
Botticelli painted her portrait many centuries ago, when by some
necromancy she appeared to him in this phase of herself. The people are
hungry for this little fine and spiritual thing that Botticelli painted in the
faces of the muses and heavenly creatures." See AMP, pp. 3-4, 54-56.
Lindsay's laudatory review of Pickford and her film, "A Romance of the
Redwoods," is in *The New Republic*, 7 July 1917, under the title "Queen of
My People." VARIANT 29 swains] films *1st*.

224 BLANCHE SWEET: *1st* in *Little Review*, June 1914; Cg. On 3 January
1914 Lindsay indicates to Sara Teasdale that he wants to write a poem on
Blanche (UL-Y). See AMP, pp. 4, 72. VARIANT 5 Rank] Dour *1st*.

225 SUNSHINE: *1st* in *Metropolitan*, August 1914; *Current Opinion*,
August 1914 and August 1923; CP; JA. Only Catharine's initials are in *1st*;
her name does not appear in CO. She is Olive Lindsay Wakefield's
daughter, and thus the poet's niece.

227 WHEN GASSY THOMPSON STRUCK IT RICH: *1st* in *Chicago
Herald*, 29 August 1914; Cg. Headnote in *1st*: "A souvenir of my walk
through Colorado two years ago. Gassy Thompson, I am told, walked into
the Telegraph office on the same occasion here described, slammed down
$25 and said: 'Telegraph all four corners of the earth, "Gassy Thompson
has struck it rich!"'" VARIANT 7, 13, 19 *stress not in 1st*.

228 TO GLORIANA: *1st* in *Reedy's Mirror*, 12 June 1914; CP. The title in
1st is "For Gloriana, Poet of St. Louis"; in Cg the title is "Once More—For
Gloriana." In *1st*, Cg, and CP the work is used to introduce other "moon
poems." When Lindsay returned from the West in late 1912, he sent
Harriet Monroe twelve poems on the moon. On 22 January 1913 he sent
fourteen more, with a letter (UL-C), explaining that these are the last he
plans to write. He would like them published in a series—"as a set of

waves, each separate piece a new wave of Fancy dashing upon the reader, and not quite like the one before.'' He adds: ''I want enough waves to make a reasonable bath.'' See also ''Six Poems on the Moon, for Man and Beast'' in TE, and ''The Light o' the Moon'' in GWB. VARIANT 5 snowy] mists and *1st*.

228 EUCLID: *1st* in *Poetry Magazine*, July 1913; CP; *Current Opinion*, August 1923; *Golden Book*, April 1931; SP.

228 THE HAUGHTY SNAIL-KING: *1st* in *Reedy's Mirror*, 12 June 1914; CP; JA.

229 WHAT THE RATTLESNAKE SAID: in CP; JA; SP. An early version, written in Lindsay's 1912 hiking notebook, has the title ''The Rattlesnake'' (UNB-V).

229 THE MOON'S THE NORTH WIND'S COOKY: *1st* in *Reedy's Mirror*, 12 June 1914; CP; *National Education Association Journal*, January 1926 and March 1928; JA; *Golden Book*, September 1931; SP. Early manuscript title: ''What the Little Girl Said'' (UNB-V, 1912). VARIANT 7 greedy] hungry *1st*.

230 DRYING THEIR WINGS: *1st* in *Poetry Magazine*, July 1913; CP; JA; SP. VARIANT 2 folks] folk *1st*.

230 WHAT THE GRAY-WINGED FAIRY SAID: *1st* in *Reedy's Mirror*, 12 June 1914; CP; JA.

230 YET GENTLE WILL THE GRIFFIN BE: *1st* in *Poetry Magazine*, July 1913; CP; JA; SP. Read in Springfield as ''The Moon's a Griffin's Egg'' (ISR, 19 September 1913). Also referred to as ''The Griffin's Egg'' (MFP).

231 A SENSE OF HUMOR: *1st* in *Poetry Magazine*, July 1913; CP; SP. Entitled ''Prologue. A Sense of Humor'' in Cg; it is the first of ten moon poems in *Poetry* and has the following headnote: ''Spoken by the Author in his own person.'' VARIANTS 5 us] him *1st* 15 or suchlike] and merry *1st*.

231 ON THE GARDEN-WALL: *1st* in *Reedy's Mirror*, 12 June 1914; CP; JA.

232 THE MOON IS A PAINTER: *1st* in *Reedy's Mirror*, 12 June 1914; CP. Manuscript titles: ''The Painter,'' changed to ''Indirect Moonlight,'' and finally to ''A Moonlight Transformation'' (UNB-V, 1912).

233 THE ENCYCLOPAEDIA: *1st* in *Reedy's Mirror*, 12 June 1914; CP; SP.

233 WHAT THE MINER IN THE DESERT SAID: *1st* in *Poetry Magazine*, July 1913; KMR, December 1927; CP. VARIANTS 1 brass-hooped] brazen *1st* 3 ridge] sands *1st*.

233 WHAT THE COAL-HEAVER SAID: in KMR, December 1927; CP. Manuscript title (UNB-V, 1912): "The Coal-Heaver Says."

234 WHAT THE MOON SAW: *1st* in *Poetry Magazine*, July 1913; CP; SP.

234 WHAT SEMIRAMIS SAID: *1st* in *Reedy's Mirror*, 12 June 1914; CP. Manuscript title: "What the Young Jezebel Said" (UNB-V, 1912).

235 WHAT THE GHOST OF THE GAMBLER SAID: *1st* in *Poetry Magazine*, July 1913; CP. Title in *1st*: "The Soul of the Gambler"; manuscript title: "The Ghost of the Gambler" (UNB-V, 1912).

235 THE SPICE-TREE: *1st* in *Chicago Herald*, 8 September 1914; CP; SP. A letter to Sara Teasdale (UL-Y) dates the poem exactly: Sunday morning, 28 June 1914. The poem is for Sara: see Dunbar, p. 117 and Carpenter, pp. 206, 216.

236 THE SCISSORS-GRINDER: *1st* in *Poetry Magazine*, July 1913; CP. The first parenthetical headnote is not in *1st*, Cg. VARIANTS 19, 31 that] the *1st* 39-40 *not stressed in 1st.*

237 MY LADY IN HER WHITE SILK SHAWL: *1st* in *Reedy's Mirror*, 12 June 1914; CP. Among ideas for poems in Lindsay's 1912 hiking notebook (UNB-V), we find: "Tribute to my lady in the white silk shawl, as the appreciator of all types of Beauty and Culture. The problem to make her fit for America or America fit for her. Say she lies over the sea and comes back fewer and fewer times." An early version of the poem soon follows. Lindsay may have associated the poem with Sara Teasdale, but it could not have been written for her (see Carpenter, p. 265). VARIANTS 7 moods,] thoughts *1st* 8 With thoughts that] That seem to *1st* 8 place.] place *Cg* 9 harsh] raw *1st.*

238 ALADDIN AND THE JINN: *1st* in *Poetry Magazine*, April 1914; NP; NV; TBM; CP. When Lindsay first sent the poem to Harriet Monroe, line 11 read: "Forgetting the drum of the Muezzin." On 30 May 1913 he writes (UL-C): "I find that I have mispronounced and misdescribed Muezzin in the first stanza of Aladdin. Please rewrite the line for me at once. Make it: — 'Forgetting the shouting Muezzin.'"

239 THE STRENGTH OF THE LONELY: *1st* in *Reedy's Mirror*, 12 June 1914; CP.

239 ABRAHAM LINCOLN WALKS AT MIDNIGHT: *1st* in *Independent*, 21 September 1914; *Survey*, 6 March 1915; NP; *Literary Digest*, 18 January 1919; *Independent*, 15 February 1919; *Public*, 15 March 1919; DJ; KMR, April 1925; SBMV; JA; CP; SP. Published many other times during Lindsay's lifetime: the copy in LD, for example, is from The Advocate of Peace (December 1918). On 1 August 1914 Lindsay informs Sara Teasdale that he is working on a poem about Lincoln (UL-Y); see also Ruggles, p. 231. VARIANTS 5 in] the *1st* 13-16, 21-24 *not in Public.*

240 A CURSE FOR KINGS: *1st* in *Chicago Herald*, 10 September 1914; CP; SP.

242 WHO KNOWS?: *1st* in *Chicago Herald*, 12 September 1914; CP.

242 TO BUDDHA: *1st* in *Chicago Herald*, 15 September 1914; CP. One of the "Poems Speaking of Buddha" in CP (see note to "With a Bouquet of Twelve Roses" above); for Lindsay on Buddha, also see "Litany of the Heroes" and "Adventures While Preaching Hieroglyphic Sermons" in CP.

243 THE UNPARDONABLE SIN: *1st* in *Chicago Herald*, 16 September 1914; *Methodist Review*, May 1930; CP.

243 ABOVE THE BATTLE'S FRONT: *1st* in *Chicago Herald*, 17 September 1914; CP.

244 UNDER THE BLESSING OF YOUR PSYCHE WINGS: *1st* in *Chicago Herald*, 26 August 1914; DJ; SP. Strangely, the poem is not in CP. The title in *1st* is "When All the World Is at War"; on 5 August 1914 Lindsay sent a copy to Sara Teasdale entitled "With All the World at War." VARIANTS 8 And . . . now] The fratricidal cries made dim, *1st* 13 I thought myself] The one who was *1st* 14 And yet I come] Has come to you *1st* 15 Hiding] To hide *1st* 16 Against . . . your] To flutter near your pallid, *1st*.

245 FROM ADVENTURES WHILE PREACHING THE GOSPEL OF BEAUTY (New York: The Macmillan Company, 1914) [published at about the same time as *The Congo and Other Poems*, the prose and poetry of this work are from and about Lindsay's 1912 tramp from Springfield to Wagon Mound, New Mexico.]

247 THE KALLYOPE YELL: *1st* in *Forum*, November 1913; *Reedy's Mirror*, 14 November 1913; *Current Opinion*, December 1913; CP; JA; SP. Published by Braithwaite (1913) as one of the year's best poems in a magazine; only sections II and III in CO. A headnote in AWP reads: "Loudly and rapidly with a leader, College yell fashion"; in CP this is changed to: "To be given in the peculiar whispered manner of the University of Kansas 'Jay-Hawk Yell.'" There is no headnote in SP. From the pages Lindsay used to prepare CP (V), it is clear that he originally planned a more elaborate headnote than above. He wrote and then crossed out: "It is to be noted that this song is marked 'College Yell fashion.' But, judged by the best 'Yells,' that does not mean strain, speed or racket. The best yells prophecy great music. The University of Kansas 'Jay Hawk' yell is slowly and beautifully whispered by four thousand students, and is quite close to UNITED STATES grand opera and epic poetry. So epic poetry began." In MFP Lindsay discusses his symbol: "The 'kallyope' is selected as a symbol of many things — among them are street-car advertisements, bill boards, automobile horns, electric signs, megaphones, phonographs, motion pictures, uplift magazines, girl-and-music shows, brass bands, yellow journals, and the like. By these the powers of attention of the tired business man, highly concentrated in office

hours, are frayed into a thousand pieces once the roller-top desk is closed. The 'kallyope' stands for many deeper, finer things as well. But I had for years been facing the kallyope question, helpless, furious and defiant, an avowed follower of Ruskin. Then I wrote a few of a new kind of verses, part irony, part admiration, listing in metaphor the things that perplex and distract, thereby trying to conquer and assimilate them, instead of running away.'' He complains that now ''the tired business man'' listens to him but misses the irony, ''the thread of silver music under the toot.'' He warns that ''the Higher Vaudeville'' brings with it ''higher irony as well.'' See also ''Adventures While Singing These Songs'' in CP; Carpenter, p. 178; and Putzel, pp. 185-187. VARIANT 87 a] the *1st, Mirror, AWP.*

250 KANSAS: *1st* in *Forum*, December 1913; CP; SP. VARIANT 47 sunrise] sunlight *1st.*

252 THE FLUTE OF THE LONELY: *1st* in *Forum*, February 1914; *Reedy's Mirror*, 27 February 1914; CP; SP. No headnote in *1st*; see note to ''General William Booth Enters into Heaven'' above.

252 THE SHIELD OF FAITH: *1st* in *Forum*, February 1914; CP; SP. There are two extra stanzas at the beginning in *1st*, AWP:

> The full moon is the Shield of Faith,
>   And when it hangs on high
> Another shield seems on my arm
>   The hard world to defy.
>
> Yea, when the moon has knighted me,
>   Then every poisoned dart
> Of daytime memory turns away
>   From my dream-armored heart.

253 THE PATH IN THE SKY: *1st* in *Forum*, February 1914; CP; JA.

254 EPILOGUE TO THE ADVENTURES WHILE PREACHING THE GOSPEL OF BEAUTY: *1st* in *Forum*, February 1914; CP. VARIANT 20 soul's] lost *1st.*

255 A LETTER ABOUT MY FOUR PROGRAMMES (Springfield, Summer, 1916) [This sixty-eight page booklet was ready for distribution early in July. It was an attempt to introduce recital organizers to the poet's work, enabling them to select from the four programs he was prepared to give.]

257 THE VISIT TO MAB: in GWC; VM 1, 2, 3, 4; CP. Only the drawing is in VM 1; it is not in GWC. A headnote in MFP and VM 2-4 reads: ''A parable in which those people are reproved who refuse to read verses.'' VM 3-4 adds: ''But the parable, now in circulation five years, has yet to produce any noticeable effect.'' VARIANTS 2 A] The *MFP, VM 2-4* 30 well could say] could express *MFP* 31 ''pride and stay,''] emperess, *MFP.*

258 THE VILLAGE IMPROVEMENT PARADE: in VM 1, 2, 3, 4; *Current Literature*, March 1911; *Vision*, Spring, 1912; GWC; PP (October 1930);

CP. The poem is not in VM 1, CL, *Vision*; the drawings are not in GWC. Lindsay carried the drawings on his 1912 tramp: a note in PP relates that the verses "were written several years later." The title in GWC is "A Hot Time in the Old Town"; a note to sing the poem to this tune is in MFP and VM 2-4. MFP continues: ". . . to be sung with a certain high seriousness and oratorical dignity sometimes lacking in the delivery of that famous refrain. If this seriousness is maintained along with a proper sense of humor the reader may grasp one aspect of the Higher Vaudeville." On the drawings, Lindsay comments to Macfarlane (V) in 1913: "The Village Improvement Parade—poor as it is—is the climax of this 13 years of endeavor, and most of what I can do artistically has gone into it." A headnote in MFP reads: "A parade held for the purpose of making over the village from the standpoint of beauty and art. The parade is celebrated in hieroglyphics and rhyme." Lindsay experimented with various forms for the refrain, often repeating words and phrases. In VM 3-4, the first line of each stanza concludes with "(drum, drum, drum.)"; lines 2, 8, 14, 20, 38 end with "(march, march, march.)"; and lines 26, 32, 44, 50 end with "(dance, dance, dance.)." VARIANTS 21 Tom turkeys] Our blacksmiths *MFP* 39 A scroll] Scrolls *VM 3-4, PP* EMENDATION 1 crows] crowds.

265 DANCING FOR A PRIZE: in VM 1, 2, 3, 4; GWC; CP; JA. The poem is not in VM 1; the drawing is not in GWC, JA. Headnote in VM 3, 4: "Inscribed to the Poet, Sara Teasdale."

267 *From* A HANDY GUIDE FOR BEGGARS (New York: The Macmillan Company, 1916) [The prose covers Lindsay's 1906 tramp from Florida to Kentucky and his 1908 tramp through New Jersey and Pennsylvania to Hiram, Ohio. Most of the poetry, however, was written later.]

269 THE WOULD-BE MERMAN: *1st* in *Chicago Herald*, 28 August 1914; CP. The title in *1st* is "Why I Want to Be a Tramp, Scamp and Harvest Hand Again"; a headnote in *1st* reads: "(Addressed to a respectable friend who desired me to quit the disgraceful business.)." VARIANTS 4 folk] snobs *1st* 22 wide] dire *1st*.

270 THE TRAMP'S REFUSAL: *1st* in *Yale Review*, October 1914; CP; SP. VARIANTS 9 Sometimes, while] And oft when *1st* 15 wrought] writ *1st* 16 stranger] human *1st* 19 heart] heart's *1st* 20 Has changed and] Deep change has *1st* 27-28 *stressed in 1st*.

270 WITH A ROSE, TO BRUNHILDE: in CP. Written for Octavia Roberts (see Ruggles, pp. 173-174).

271 THE TOWN OF AMERICAN VISIONS: *1st* in *Little Review*, June 1914; KMR, July 1928; CP. In *1st* the title is "Encountered on the Streets of the City"; a headnote reads: "The Church of Vision and Dream." On 3 May 1914 Lindsay informs Sara Teasdale (UL-Y) that he is working on "The Chinese Nightingale" (*q.v.*) and walking in downtown Springfield. He would like to write a poem on the mystic heart of the little town.

272 WHAT THE SEXTON SAID: *1st* in *Forum*, July 1916; CP. The poem was sent to Harriet Monroe on 23 April 1915; on 21 October 1915 Lindsay writes Miss Monroe (UL-C): ". . . use the Sexton to point out that I can write the ancient Wordsworthean Gray's Elegy thing as well as *most anybody!*"

273 LIFE TRANSCENDENT: in CP.

273 IN THE IMMACULATE CONCEPTION CHURCH: in CP, SP. Lindsay informs Sara Teasdale (UL-Y, 1 August 1914) that the poem was written sometime during 1913; he originally entitled the poem "A Prayer in the Immaculate Conception Church." For Lindsay's drawing of the Church, see "The Soul of the City Receives the Gift of the Holy Spirit" above.

275 THE CHINESE NIGHTINGALE AND OTHER POEMS (New York: The Macmillan Company, 1917) [On 15 September 1917 — about a month before this volume was out — Lindsay writes Louis Untermeyer (UL-B) that the book is "a regularly graded series showing the development or change from a Jane Addams and Bryan follower to a Kerensky follower. That is a pro-ally follower of the Russian Revolutionary mood." At the same time he echoes these thoughts to Sara Teasdale (UL-Y), adding, though, that he has not lost his sympathy for Jane Addams and others in the peace movement. In the letter to Untermeyer, Lindsay explains his position in the following: "It seems to me Wilson's course has been absolutely clear, and one which would lead any open liberal mind," but he adds that he "quit arguing two months ago." The Kerensky poem (see "This, My Song, Is Made for Kerensky" below) is his "final position."]

277 THE CHINESE NIGHTINGALE: *1st* in *Poetry Magazine*, February 1915; NP; *Journal of the American Asiatic Society*, January 1918; SBMV; CP; JA; SP. Headnote in all but SP: "A Song in Chinese Tapestries"; no dedication in *Asia*, CN, CP, JA. Early subtitle: "A San Francisco Fantasy."On 15 December 1914 the *Illinois State Register* reports that Lindsay will read his new poem, "The Chinese Princess," and then gives the poet's own synopsis: "The story opens in a laundry shop in San Francisco, a little after midnight. The Chinaman is asked why he works on the lonely night shift, instead of the day shift. He answers that when all is still his Nightingale from Shanghai sings to him. Chang works the proper magic. The bird appears on the wrist of the idol in the corner. The bird calls for the princess who was Chang's mate in China many times, through many incarnations, while he was again, and again king. The princess appears and with the help of the Joss, tells two stories, and hints at others. She tells how on a certain day there was a great children's festival to honor the king and queen, and what a sight it was, and how the nightingale sang all day, and again in the evening. Then there is a story of how the king and queen, in another incarnation flew away on a dragon's back to the dragon-mountain, there to have their loves in secret, while dragons flew about the mountain's base. And how, while thus away from their capital, fierce pirates descended upon the town, and it was only through the wizard power of the Joss, who was a sage in ancient times, that the pirates were

drowned and the city saved. Then the lovers returned from the mountain on the dragon's back, and found the city decked out in magical splendor by the Joss, awaiting their coming back. They flew in the path of the guiding nightingale and reached the city, and made the Joss a Knight. But the nightingale remembers none of these things. He only remembers that from the beginning of time, lovers met under the trees in spring and spring came always after winter.'' Almost a year later—1 November 1915—the *Register* reports that the poem has won Harriet Monroe's Levinson Prize for 1915. Lindsay is said to be ''partial'' to the poem, ''because, as he says, it is one of his best literary efforts and has in it none of the 'Sarsaparilla' or 'Peruna' of some of his other verses.'' The paper then quotes the major part of the poem. Lindsay's letters reveal that he began work on the poem in late April 1914 and was essentially finished in early October of the same year. For Sara Teasdale's influence, see Carpenter, pp. 193-194, 223, 260; see also Untermeyer, pp. 139, 156; Ruggles, pp. 223-224; and ''Adventures While Singing These Songs'' in CP. VARIANTS 57 blue] white *1st* 72 Flourished] Opened *1st* 72 her shimmering] closed her *1st* 106 For] And *1st*, *Asia*, *CN* 109 the] a *1st*, *Asia*, *CN* 200 final] answering *1st*.

282 WHERE IS THE REAL NON-RESISTANT?: in *Literary Digest*, 15 December 1917; *Christian Century*, 21 August 1919; CP. See Ruggles, pp. 248-249.

283 HERE'S TO THE MICE!: *1st* in *Tuck's Magazine*, Spring, 1915; *Masses*, October-November 1915; SP. The title in *1st*, *Masses* is ''Mice''; the headnote is not in *1st*, *Masses*. For *Tuck's*, see the note to ''The Lion'' above. Throughout 1914 Lindsay reports to Sara Teasdale (UL-Y) that he is working on a socialist poem called ''A Song for Strikers.''

284 WHEN BRYAN SPEAKS: *1st* in ISR, 15 February 1915; CN. The *Register* reports: ''Nicholas Vachel Lindsay, 'the bard of the Sangamon,' arrived in Washington the other day—in more senses than one. He descended like a meteor into the fold of official Washington and in a night proved conclusively that the Minnesingers are not all dead yet. At a brilliant reception following a dinner given to the Secretary of State and Mrs. Bryan by the Assistant Secretary of Agriculture and Mrs. Carl Vrooman, he intoned, in his inimitable fashion, several of his better known poems, adding a new one written for the occasion—'When Bryan Speaks.''' The poem was reprinted in June 1915, at the time of Bryan's resignation, and in August 1917, when Bryan came to speak in Springfield. Because Bryan could move the masses, Lindsay thought him ''the one living American poet'' (MFP, p. 6). The poem was reworked considerably; the line, ''When Bryan speaks,'' follows lines 4, 8, 12, 16, and 20 in *1st*. Other significant VARIANTS: 8 springtime fancy] hot excitement *1st* 13 sky] land *1st* 19 many] ninety *1st* An extra stanza follows line 16 in *1st*:

''When Bryan speaks the sky is wide,
The people are a tossing tide,
And all good men the world around
With our heart-strings seem allied—
When Bryan speaks.

Finally, there are three extra stanzas at the end in *1st*:
"The world breaks up—
For little things:
For hats of women—crowns of kings—
For rumors over cups of tea—
For tweedledum and tweedledee—
For this taboo and that desire
We war like water mixed with fire.

"Hail to the fundamental man
Who brings a unifying plan
Not easily misunderstood,
Chanting men toward brotherhood.

"So be you glad, American,
When, after planning many weeks,
The folks by thousands come to town
And Bryan
                SPEAKS!''

285 TO JANE ADDAMS AT THE HAGUE: *1st* in *Chicago Herald*, 11 May 1915; *Christian Century*, 13 May 1915; CP. On 3 May 1915 Lindsay writes Harriet Moody (UL-V): "I want Jane Addams to do wonders at the Hague. I cannot help but feel that she will. She has given me my first happy though[t] about the war—since it has begun. I think she is the most wonderful woman of her kind in the world—and may even pull the thorn from the lion's foot, like Androcles." Another letter to Mrs. Moody—this one 7 June 1917 (UL-C)—reveals that Lindsay is not yet pro-Wilson: "I have sat all evening listening to a room full of ex-pacifists, pro-Wilson radicals, trying to argue the last Tolstoyan non-resistant into line for the war. It was a heroic and high minded battle . . . but our Tolstoyan is still so." For Lindsay on Tolstoi, see Graham, pp. 240, 246. VARIANTS 9 promise] vision *1st* 13 taller] higher *1st*.

285 THE TALE OF THE TIGER TREE: in CP. On 15 September 1916, at the end of a ten-day stay at the Moody farm in Massachusetts, Lindsay writes Harriet Moody (UL-C): "I feel now that all the kinks are out of my brain, and I can go home and start new—with hope of writing The Tiger Tree, having wrestled with trees living and dead." His letters reveal, however, that the poem did not come easily: he struggled for nearly a year, making innumerable copies and versions. Most of his friends complained that the work was vague and obscure. At one point Lindsay writes to Harriet Monroe with some exasperation: "There is absolutely no complicated parable. It is a battle—that is all—set against the picture of a pleader for peace. It isn't Pilgrim's Progress—and it isn't Aesop's fables. It is just war in the Jungle—in contrast with the eternal peace principle. If you get that—you get it all—plus the color" (2 April 1917, Chénetier, p. 146). In the end, the only close friend who seems to have liked the poem was Jessie Rittenhouse. An early version (UMs-Y) has two headnotes: "A story showing the death of the Mound-Builder Nation, in spite of the

forging of the first sabre,'' and, ''While walking by the capitol building, I
go back to the stone age.'' See also Monroe, p. 383; Rittenhouse,
''Contemporary Poetry: Notes and Reviews, ''*The Bookman*, XLVI
(January 1918), 576-577.

292 THE MERCIFUL HAND: *1st* in *Red Cross Magazine*, September
1917) *Christian Century*, 30 August 1917; CP. The poem is first mentioned
in Lindsay's 1916 Datebook (V), with the title ''To a Muse Going to the
Front.'' An early copy, with the title ''To Miss Fitzgerald—Going to the
Front'' and dated ''Feb. 15, 1916,'' is at the Maryland Historical Society.
In both *1st* and ChC, Lindsay signs himself ''of the Vigilantes.''

293 OUR MOTHER POCAHONTAS: *1st* in *Poetry Magazine*, July 1917;
Literary Digest, 4 August 1917; DJ; CP. Published with ''Niagara'' and
''Mark Twain and Joan of Arc'' (see below) in PM as war poems. On 5
April 1917, when Lindsay submits a revision to Harriet Monroe, he writes:
''I had many sad thoughts about the war last night. I love Jane Addams
dearly—and her brave fight for peace pulls at my heart. But Wilson also
has my heart, and I cannot see any other course for him'' (UL-C).
VARIANTS 21 And bird-like *in 1st, LD* 22 grape-vine] ivy *1st, LD* 35 *not in
1st, LD, DJ, CN.*

295 CONCERNING EMPERORS: ''God Send the Regicide'' is a part of
''Litany of the Heroes'' (*q.v.*).

296 NIAGARA: *1st* in *Poetry Magazine*, July 1917; *Literary Digest*, 4
August 1917; DJ; CP; SP. Lindsay advises Sara Teasdale (UL-Y, 13 June
1917) that he has just added a war stanza to the poem; the rest, he claims,
he has thought about for two years. This stanza is in all versions except SP:

II
What marching men of Buffalo
Flood the streets in rash crusade?
Fools-to-free-the-world, they go,
Primeval hearts from Buffalo.
Red cataracts of France today
Awake, three thousand miles away
An echo of Niagara,
The cataract Niagara.

There is also an extra stanza in *1st*, after 1. 35:

By the quaint market proudly loom
Church walls. Kind altars gleam within,
Confession boxes crowd the gloom,
Baptismal fonts, in Buffalo.
St. Michael fights the dragon drear;
The stations of the cross are here.
But my church is Niagara.

VARIANT 30 are lost in] burnt out with *1st, LD.*

297 MARK TWAIN AND JOAN OF ARC: *1st* in *Poetry Magazine*, July 1917; CP. Included with "The Raft" and "When the Mississippi Flowed in Indiana" (both below) under the title "Three Poems about Mark Twain" in CP. The stimulus for this poem is clearly Jesse L. Lasky's film, *Joan the Woman*, starring Geraldine Farrar. See Lindsay's review of the film: "Venus in Armor," in *The New Republic*, X (28 April 1917), 380-381—a review that reflects Lindsay's ambivalence toward the warring Saint and Mark Twain's praise for her. See also *The Litany of Washington Street*, pp. 48, 61-63; and AMP, pp. 172-174.

297 THE BANKRUPT PEACE MAKER: in CN. Lindsay's own appraisal of the poem is written in his datebook on 16 January 1922: "My best attack was my worst failure" (UDB-V).

299 "THIS, MY SONG, IS MADE FOR KERENSKY": *1st* in *Poetry Magazine*, October 1917; ISR, 7 October 1917; *Literary Digest*, 15 December 1917; CN. The title in *1st* and ISR is "The Soap-Box," with the present title as subtitle in *1st*. The *Register* reports that the poet wants the work given in "college yell fashion, but more musically." Lindsay began a poem on the soap box in the summer of 1915 (UL-V, 10 June 1915—to Harriet Moody); he rewrites this poem in the summer of 1917 with Kerensky in mind (UL-Y, 11 September 1917—to Sara Teasdale). Lindsay's interests in the soap box go back at least to the spring of 1912, when he concludes his illustrated essay—"The New Localism" in the periodical *Vision*—with a little prose piece entitled "On the Soap Box." His conclusion here is that all artists belong on soap boxes, preaching "that all men are born unique in power to create beauty, that now we are engaged in a great civil war, an epic struggle for the abolition of the slavery of ugliness, and the giving of eyes to a nation of ninety million blind, and the putting of creative power into ninety million hands." In 1917, the *Register* reports, the soap box is a symbol of free speech, "of all that civilization holds dear, a symbol of the dreams that France is dying for." VARIANTS 32 *not in LD* 49 *not in 1st, ISR* 64 peoples . . . mad] people of the world, little folk *1st, ISR* 65 rolling] tramping *1st, ISR* 76 and *not in 1st, ISR* 79 the *not in 1st, ISR*.

301 OUR GUARDIAN ANGELS AND THEIR CHILDREN: *1st* in *Bookman*, June 1917; CP. VARIANTS 44 touch] wrap *1st* 50 make of worth] justify *1st* 51 All . . . youth] The time we cried and parted, *1st* 52 all . . . earth] every dream and sigh *1st*.

303 EDWIN BOOTH IN CALIFORNIA: *1st* in *The Trimmed Lamp*, October 1915; *Current Opinion*, December 1915; CP; SP. In *1st* and CO the title is "Prince Hamlet in California"; in CN and CP the poem is included with "Epitaph for John Bunny" (see below) in "Epitaphs for Two Players." The title in CN and CP is "Edwin Booth." The last two stanzas are not in *1st*, CO; the third stanza in both reads:

Who would have thought, in this rough room
The prince could move such bravos grim?
Miners and pioneers no more.

VACHEL LINDSAY

The wind-blown lamp-wick spluttered dim.
And Hamlet knelt in fear and pride.
"Swear by my sword" three times he cried.
They bent like Danish knights to him.

The editor of CO comments that the poet "is a little 'off' in his geography," obviously leading to Lindsay's revision of 1. 7. VARIANTS 7 high and solemn] dark Sierra *1st, CO* 22 haunted . . . harsh] magic place, tho bleak and raw *1st, CO* 27 court-] proud *1st, CO* 30 prince] man *1st, CO* 35 A brave lad] The brave prince *1st, CO*.

304 EPITAPH FOR JOHN BUNNY: *1st* in *Chicago Herald*, 30 April 1915; *Reedy's Mirror*, 7 May 1915; CP. There are six additional lines at the end in *1st* and *Mirror*:

> Not so, but here in Springfield's crowded street
> The grocer's children miss their heart's delight.
> The proud young newsboy bears a heart of lead;
> The children of the wise and soundly bred,
> And children of the ragman, mourn their dead.
> John Bunny acts upon the films of night.

See AMP, pp. 50-51. VARIANT 3 oddities] quiddities *1st, Mirror*.

305 MAE MARSH, MOTION PICTURE ACTRESS: in CP. Lindsay's review of "The Wild Girl of the Sierras" is in ISR, 7 July 1916; it was one of his favorite pictures. See also "A Doll's 'Arabian Nights'" below and AMP, pp. 4, 12, 32, 35.

306 TWO OLD CROWS: *1st* in *Tuck's Magazine* (June 1915); CP: JA.

307 THE DRUNKARD'S FUNERAL: *1st* in CEPF, 25 June 1915; *Current Opinion*, August 1915; DJ; CP. In a letter to Sara Teasdale (UL-Y, 1 August 1914), Lindsay indicates that he is working on a new poem—"The Saloon Must Go." A manuscript copy (V) and CEPF both indicate that the poem is a Cruikshank drawing or grotesque in verse. The editor of CO reports that Lindsay has penned in the margin of his copy: " 'The Drunkard's Funeral' is more effective if you pound on the table when you read it." VARIANTS 9 The] That *1st, CO, CN* 24-29, 32 *not in 1st, CO* 30 Force] Till we force *1st, CO* 42 little] stubborn *1st, CO*.

308 THE RAFT: *1st* in *Chicago Herald*, 3 November 1915; *Reedy's Mirror*, 3 December 1915; *Current Opinion*, January 1918; CP; KMR, May 1928; SP. See "Mark Twain and Joan of Arc" above; headnote in *1st, Mirror*: "An Inscription for Your Volume of *Huckleberry Finn*." Lindsay's titanic struggle with his "Mark Twain" poem is evident from the following letter to Harriet Monroe (UL-C, 21 October 1915): "I send you Mark Twain. It was first blocked in this time last year—and I have been polishing it at odd times while correcting proof. . . . I suppose I have revised it three times every day since. I never polished anything more elaborately. . . . It is a sort of Literary Declaration of Independence—and Western Manifesto—and written with the Poetry Magazine particularly in mind." The poem was

rejected as being too "journalistic." Lindsay continued to revise the work even after it was published: the *Herald* version is forty-five lines longer than what we now have, the *Mirror* version is nearly forty. In cutting inferior lines, Lindsay helps to tighten his focus on the theme stated in lines 43-45. The following variants are most selective: after 1917 the work does not change in any essential way. After what is here the opening stanza, there is an extra stanza of more than usual interest in *1st:*

> *Why do I sing these whelps in vulgar bond,*
> *When I might sing of perfumed Samarkand?*
> *Once I wooed a muse in filmy silks,*
> *Kissed her hands, beneath a white-rose bower;*
> *And she was crowned with pearls, herself a pearl.*
> *But that was long ago, a dressed-up hour.*
> *Farewell, my flute! Farewell, O silver lyre!*
> *I dare the mist, the sunstroke and the mire.*
> *I am eating yellow petals of the sunflower,*
> *And all my blood, that once was fainting music,*
> *Is turned to glory, and mid-western fire.*
> *This unke[m]pt river is my rank desire.*

In the *Mirror*, this stanza follows line 79:

> Beside glad Omar, who of wine could sing
> As our wild river to a shadowed spring.
> Beside Dean Swift, that black-browed scourge of men,
> As is the Mississippi to a fen.
> Beside Cervantes, deathless Spanish knight,
> As our wild river to some fountain white.
> Beside Moliere, with plume and sword and cane,
> As is the Mississippi to the Seine.
> By Jonson with his masques and classic gems
> And Marlowe with his antique diadems,
> As our sweet ragged river to the Thames.

VARIANTS 26 Christian] lonely *1st* 80-86 *these serve as an introductory stanza in 1st, Mirror.*

310 THE GHOSTS OF THE BUFFALOES: *1st* in *Chicago Herald*, 17 November 1914; DJ; CP; JA; SP. In CN and DJ, lines 177-184 of the "Litany of the Heroes" (*q.v.*) serve as an introductory stanza; headnote in *1st*: "The Indian and buffalo sections of the piece are for the most part to be read with a heavily accented imitation of the galloping of cavalry. The Indian section shrill and rapid, the buffalo section as heavy as possible and slower. The interludes to be nearly whispered." Lindsay's letters reveal that he worked hard on the poem—sometimes using the title "The Red Gods"—in late summer and fall, 1914, although the seeds of the work can be found in his 1905 datebook (see Ruggles, pp. 101, 230; Monroe, pp. 281-282; Carpenter, p. 212). Legend has it that the Lindsay backyard was once part of a buffalo run. In December 1921 the poet writes in his datebook (UDB-V): "The only dragon that haunts me is the fire-breathing

bison of Central Illinois.'' VARIANTS 13 aged and sere] swift-winged, flying low *1st* 16 ghost- . . . below,] their torches, and how they did go: *1st* 17-21, 24 *not in 1st* 39, 72 thinking] half-thinking *1st* 42-43 *in 1st*: And mourned a long-forgotten slaughter, / The wind cried and cried . . . 72 *repeated in 1st* EMENDATIONS In the title: GHOSTS (as in *1st, CN, DJ*)] GHOST 36 are] were 86 storm's] storms'

313 THE BRONCHO THAT WOULD NOT BE BROKEN: *1st* in *Seven Arts*, August 1917; NV; *Chapbook*, May 1920; CP; JA; TBM; SP. Published by Braithwaite (1917) as one of the year's best works in a periodical. In *1st*, ''of Dancing'' is added to the title. Lindsay worked on the poem in late summer and fall, 1914; but the circumstances, of course, date back to his 1912 tramp. In AWP, after recounting the story of the colt (pp. 129-137), the poet concludes: ''I think I want on my coat of arms a broncho, rampant.''

314 THE PRAIRIE BATTLEMENTS: *1st* in *Forum*, August 1916; *Literary Digest*, 15 December 1917; CP. No dedicatory note in *1st*. VARIANTS 2, 16, 22 our] my *1st* 7, 9, 11, 19 Silver] Many *1st* 9 gray] old *1st*.

315 THE FLOWER OF MENDING: *1st* in *Forum*, August 1916; *Current Opinion*, October 1916; SBMV; CP; JA. Eudora Lindsay South (see ''Bibliography''), to whom the poem is dedicated, dates the poem in the summer, 1906, when Lindsay completed his Florida-to-Kentucky tramp with a short stay at her mother's farm.

316 ALONE IN THE WIND, ON THE PRAIRIE: in CP. Lindsay sends two versions of this work to Sara Teasdale in May 1914 (UL-Y).

316 TO LADY JANE: *1st* in *Chicago Herald*, 25 September 1914; CP. The title in *1st* is ''Romance Was Always Young''; headnote in *1st*: ''Written to little Miss Jane, whom I met at the end of a day in which I had been reading Longfellow's translation of Dante. The discourse before us ends by asking that when she is to be married she will wear one rose for the author.'' In the Lindsay home there is a hand-lettered copy of the poem decorated with several small, water-color drawings. The title is ''Her Name Is Romance''; the date is ''June 30, 1907.''

317 HOW I WALKED ALONE IN THE JUNGLES OF HEAVEN: *New Republic*, 10 November 1917; CP. In CP twice, the second time as part of ''Invocation for 'The Map of the Universe,' '' with the title ''How Johnny Appleseed Walked Alone in the Jungles of Heaven.'' Published by Braithwaite (1918) as one of the year's best. For more on heaven's ''jungles'' see ''Explanation of 'The Map of the Universe' '' in the Appendix, and the final chapter of *The Golden Book of Springfield*.

318 THE BOOKER WASHINGTON TRILOGY [This work, the individual poems of which are below, was begun immediately after the death of Booker Washington, 14 November 1915. The trilogy was first read in Springfield on 19 January 1916 (ISR, 20 January 1916), as a memorial to

the black educator. In an essay on the trilogy (UMs-H), Lindsay notes that "several years ago a band of able people from his school" came to Springfield and gave a performance for Tuskegee. "The leader explained in plain white man's English, that while there were trained musicians in the company who could do the average concert thing after the manner of white people, the music department of Tuskegee was bending such skill as it had to the development of the old plantation songs and camp-meeting spirituals, as a real basis for the future music of the race. So we had the original melodies, plus brains.

"I have tried to assimilate their idea, in this Booker Washington memorial.

"Simon Legree is an Afro-American Grotesque, John Brown an Afro-American hero tale, King Solomon an Afro-American Jubilee Song. Legree is a serious attempt to record the devil-fear that haunts the race, though it is written with a humorous close. John Brown records the race-patriotism, with a flare of rebellion. King Solomon the race Utopianism, with an overgrowth of the tropical. . . . . Their year of jubilee is indeed distant. The King Solomon poem looks as far into the future as the Chinese Nightingale into the past, and may be considered the direct antithesis of the Nightingale in many ways. . . .

"The stanza that directly applies to [Booker Washington] is the one on King Solomon's shepherds, for Booker Washington was certainly a shepherd of the sheep. A mere incident of his shepherding was the correct art theory of his Tuskegee singers." See also Dunbar, p. 140; Armstrong, pp. 5-6; "The Poem Games" in the Appendix; and Chénetier, pp. 128-129, 134-135.]

318 SIMON LEGREE—A NEGRO SERMON: *1st* in *Poetry Magazine*, June 1916; CP; SP. VARIANTS 3 had] kept *1st* 3 opulent cattle,] fine swine. *1st* 4 And . . . rattle] He had cool jugs of cider and wine *1st* 22 that] who *1st* 24 poor] kind *1st* 25 last] parting *1st* 49 red] raw *1st*.

320 JOHN BROWN: *1st* in *Poetry Magazine*, June 1916; NP; DJ; CP; SP. Also known as "A Visit to Palestine" (MFP). For Lindsay's early interest in John Brown, see Fowler, pp. 76-77. VARIANT 10 the] a *1st*.

322 KING SOLOMON AND THE QUEEN OF SHEBA: *1st* in *Poetry Magazine*, June 1916; CP; SP. After *1st*, the poem was expanded to fit the poem games concept; lines added are 3-4, 6-7, 21, 23, 26-27, 31, 33, 36-37. There are no marginal directions in *1st*. VARIANTS 2, 5 am] was *1st* 8 We will] You shall *1st* 50 These] That *1st* 76 These keep] That makes *1st* 101 King . . . chieftains] The teeth of all his chiefs were set with diamonds *1st* 110 by] at *1st*.

329 HOW SAMSON BORE AWAY THE GATES OF GAZA: *1st* in *Poetry Magazine*, October 1917; NP; DJ; CP; SP. Published by Braithwaite (1918) as one of the year's best works. On 8 September 1917 Lindsay writes Harriet Monroe (UL-C): "Perhaps you could make Samson the basis of an editorial on folk poetry, and use it in the editorial section. Every town has its negro churches worth attending seriously, but few people who go have

little idea of the richness of race genius that is laid before them. They think it is all a laughing matter, and so they are likely to take any serious rendering of the event as a laughing matter also.''

331 THE GOLDEN WHALES OF CALIFORNIA AND OTHER RHYMES IN THE AMERICAN LANGUAGE: (New York: The Macmillan Company, 1920) [A letter to Mary Humphrey (UL-LH, 8 April 1919) reveals that many of these poems were written in 1919, when Lindsay was hard at work on *The Golden Book of Springfield*. This latter book he believed to be his masterpiece; he already had more than three years' labor into it. On 28 October 1919 Lindsay writes to Christopher Morley: ''I am not much interested in 'The Whales,' but I cannot drive the 'Golden Book' all the time. It seems to be a kind of vampire, and use me up, but I may beat her up yet! The 'Whales' is a sort of interlude, between drives at the G.B.'' (UL-Haverford College Library, Treasure Room Manuscripts Collection. Published with permission.) See AMP, pp. 245-252, and ''A Word on California, Photoplays, and Saint Francis'' in the Appendix.]

335 THE GOLDEN WHALES OF CALIFORNIA: *1st* in *Chicago Daily News*, 21 May 1919; ISR, 25 May 1919; DJ; CP; SP. ISR is a reprint of *1st*. In all versions except SP, Section I, ''The Voice of the Earthquake,'' is the final section; the other sections of SP then follow the order of the other versions. There is a headnote in CP: ''(Inscribed to Isadora Bennett Reed).'' Lindsay made numerous changes between *1st* and GWC and several after, including the omission of several lines. In all versions except SP, two lines precede what is here line 1:

But what is the earthquake's cry at last
Making St. Francis yet aghast: —

Two more lines then follow in *1st*:

Shaking each whale feeder's flag bright mast,
Drowning the voices of the swans going past? —

All versions except SP have four extra lines after line 20:

What is the hue of the big whales' hide?
Gold, gold, gold.
What is the color of their guts' inside?
Gold, gold, gold.

After line 34, *1st* reads:

And the cattle on the hills of California
Eat cactus for butter-grass,
And their sides sag down in California
And their milk is like wine at the mass,
To the priestly sons of California.

After line 105, *1st* reads:

For the freeborn flesh of California,
The royal iron and bones,
Is a breed of such devil-humans
As never before were known.

The following are very selective: VARIANTS 43 Goshawfuls] Jabberwocks *1st* 69 sunstruck] beach combers *1st* 70 quinces, cherries] prickly pears *1st* 147 them made holy,] in far valleys *1st* 148 White-souled] Girls and boys *1st* EMENDATION 45 wriggle (as *1st*, GWC)] wiggle

339 KALAMAZOO: *1st* in *Poetry Magazine*, August 1919; CP. When Lindsay sends the poem to Harriet Monroe, 3 November 1918, he writes: "When I was at the University of Wisconsin last spring I maintained that Kalamazoo could be made the most romantic word in America if only one could write the right poem about it. That there was nothing essentially absurd or unmusical in the name. The reason people smiled at Oshkosh and Kalamazoo was that the cities were not consistent with the names, and had, to ordinary American eyes, nothing to satisfy the curiosity provoked by the challenging names. Yet there is as much queer and dear romance in those two cities as any cities ever held, no doubt, and it is for us to unfold it. The point is to bring out the Kalamazooishness of Kalamazoo, and avoid emphasizing too strongly the Kalamazoo-fool-ishness of Kalamazoo. The very words Oshkosh and Kalamazoo imply a special idiom, which I hope I have approximated" (Chénetier, p. 174). See Peter Viereck, "The Crack-Up of American Optimism: Vachel Lindsay, the Dante of the Fundamentalists," *Modern Age*, IV (Summer, 1960), 269-284. VARIANTS 15 that] the *1st* 31 shame,] heat — *1st* 46 Lorna . . . O'Grady] Cinderella, Becky Thatcher *1st* 53 valiant] dead, the *1st*.

340 JOHN L. SULLIVAN, THE STRONG BOY OF BOSTON: *1st* in *New Republic*, 16 July 1919; CP; KMR, September 1927; SP. Headnote in *1st*, GWC, CP: "Inscribed ["Dedicated" in *1st*] to Louis Untermeyer and Robert Frost." For the story of the poem's origin, see Untermeyer, pp. 139-144. VARIANTS 41 called . . . hound] named along with Cain *1st* 42 And . . . Judas,] Voltaire, Appolyon, and *1st* 44 fried] tried *1st* 47 pet and] and our *1st* 50 raw saloon] crimson dive *1st* 77-81 *not in 1st* 77 the . . . allied,] and the world one posy. *1st* 77 lands] world *CP* 78 *not in GWC*.

343 BRYAN, BRYAN, BRYAN, BRYAN: in *London Mercury*, February 1920; DJ; CP; KMR, July 1927; SP. Lindsay's 1919 datebook (UDB-V) reveals that he began thinking about the poem in January. On 1 January he writes: "In mood of Whales of California write a memorial of Bryan and Campaign of '96 of which he is the one survivor and has not long to live. Show how each figure has gone, make war cries Bryan, Bryan etc. All election cries full lunged." On 8 January he adds: "In Bryan poem use best phrases from his lifetime speeches: The people have a right to make their own mistakes." See also Ruggles, pp. 50-55, 264; Graham, pp. 35, 69, 248-249. Headnote in LM: "A Rhyme in the American Language." VARIANTS 38 The rakaboor *not in LM* 103 rag and flag] flag in town *LM* 104 dusty *not in LM* 105 Jammed our streets] Reached the town *LM After 180 in LM:* Swivel chairs, bulls and bears, 230 glorious] wonderful *LM* 239 mighty] pious *LM*.

350 A RHYME FOR ALL ZIONISTS: *1st* in *Contemporary Verse*, April
1918; *Current Opinion*, July 1918; DJ; CP; SP. In *1st* and CO the title is
"The Eyes of Queen Esther, and How They Conquered King Ahasuerus";
published by Braithwaite (1918) as one of the year's best works in a
magazine. On 24 August 1917 Lindsay writes Harriet Monroe that he is
working on a new poem: "Ahasuerus in His Prime" (UL-C); see also
Untermeyer, pp. 144-146. VARIANTS 46-48 He . . . secret] The fern
before the grazing fawn / Bends down with dew, a thing of naught, / Only
the *1st, CO* 49 his . . . her] her Shushan from the walls (*with a footnote*:
"Shushan—the royal city") *1st, CO, GWC, DJ* 50 hated them] saw it not
1st, CO, GWC, DJ.

352 A MEDITATION ON THE SUN

354 THE COMET OF PROPHECY: in CP. VARIANT 31 will *not in GWC*.

355 SHANTUNG, OR THE EMPIRE OF CHINA IS CRUMBLING DOWN:
1st in *Poetry Magazine*, September 1918; CP. The title in *1st* is "The
Empire of China Is Crumbling Down"; published by Braithwaite (1919)
with this title. The headnote is not in *1st*; the third paragraph is not in
GWC. Several Lindsay letters in May 1918 advise people to read the poem
in a Daniel-Webster-oratorical fashion. Interestingly, after performing the
poem a number of times, Lindsay changes his mind. On 21 June 1918 he
writes Katharine Lee Bates (who was at Wellesley College): "I was
mistaken about reading the poem in an orotund way. 'The Empire of
China' is to be read with a touch of *humor* till the last seven lines, which are
supposed to be solemn" (UL—published by permission, New York Public
Library, Henry W. and Albert A. Berg Collection, Astor, Lenox and Tilden
Foundations). When the poem was sent to Harriet Monroe—on 23 May
1918 (UL-C)—Lindsay suggested the last two lines of Benét's (William
Rose) "Merchants from Cathay" as an epigraph:

. . . Holy Blessed Mary, preserve us as you may
Lest once more those mad merchants come chanting
from Cathay.

After *1st*, Lindsay added several lines: 3, 10, 20, 68, 89-90, 126-128, 198,
200-201, 215. The following are selective: VARIANTS 11 walls.] walls the
bookworms come; *1st* 35 sage of Shantung] sunrise of Lu *1st* 38 tempting]
swarming *1st* 91 His . . . wide,] Her witch-ways all *1st* 153 Impudent . . .
rioting,] Learned paupers riot yet *1st* 206 O . . . Sphinx] O drownéd cat *1st*
213 patient] civil *1st*.

361 THE LAST SONG OF LUCIFER: in [AL], PP (1908), CP. In a letter to
Eunice Tietjens (21 May 1923), Lindsay dates the poem 1898 and adds:
". . . technically and musically it is as well as I have done"(UL-published by
permission, Eunice Tietjens Papers, The Newberry Library). However, in
preparing the pages for CP, he penned the following, finally deleting it (a
revised version is in "Adventures While Singing These Songs" in CP): "I
wrote this chant of Lucifer at Hiram College in 1899, obviously when I was
rereading John Milton. I presume I read Lucifer to fifty fellow-students,

one at a time, correcting by their suggestions every time, and, of course, correcting by ear. All this in a college which undertook to make every student a trained orator, capable of holding the entire assembly, a place of the old New England type, full of the most fastidious and non-rhetorical oratorical standards. So from the first, the oratorical test had something to do with this style of poetry with me. I submit the poem as one containing most of the tunes which are assumed to have appeared in much later work. People insist that I talk technique. If I do so, in the matter of oratory, let it be from this Hiram College Chant'' (UMs-V). Two early manuscript versions (LH), with the titles ''The Prince of Art'' and ''Silence Borne from Afar'' (dated ''August 31, 1901''), indicate that the Hiram poem was only about one-quarter of what we now have. Comparatively, the focus is blurred and the hero is ''Israfel,'' not Lucifer. The mutilated extant copy of AL (V: 1904) does not have the poem, but PP is an obvious adaptation of this. Typically, the song is intertwined with a story: a young violinist—through the machinations of an old wizard—hears the song recited by the Demons themselves. In preparing the text for GWC, Lindsay makes only a few changes, obviously dropping the story and also dropping several direct references to Satan and the pains of hell. Also the archaic *thou* is changed to the familiar *you*. Masters (pp. 107-108) gives two other early titles: ''The Dream of Lucifer'' and ''First Dream of Lucifer.'' See also ''Explanation of 'The Map of the Universe' '' in the Appendix. VARIANT 150 forest] forests *GWC.*

369 A DOLL'S ''ARABIAN NIGHTS'': in CP, SP. Manuscript title (V): ''Bagdad, Bagdad.'' VARIANT 79-82 *not in GWC, CP.*

372 THE LAME BOY AND THE FAIRY: in CP, JA, SP. Headnote in CP: ''(To the rhythm of Chopin's Berceuse)''; said to be a ''poem game'' in GWC, with headnote: ''To be Chanted with a Suggestion of Chopin's Berceuse.'' See ''The Poem Games'' in the Appendix. The late Elizabeth E. Graham, Secretary of the Vachel Lindsay Association, remembered that on the night of 30 November 1931, directly after his most successful Springfield recital, Lindsay took Susan Wilcox aside, read the poem, and announced: ''You were the fairy to me; you understood.'' He then implored, rather darkly: ''Be kind to Elizabeth [his wife], no matter what happens.'' One week later—the night of 5 December—he was dead. Miss Wilcox, of course, was his beloved high school English teacher (see ''Adventures While Preaching Hieroglyphic Sermons'' in CP). The version of the poem in SP has been drastically cut; all other versions begin with the following 72 lines:

A lame boy
Met a fairy
In a meadow
Where the bells grow.

And the fairy   5
Kissed him gaily.

And the fairy
Gave him friendship,
Gave him healing,
Gave him wings.   10

"All the fashions
I will give you.
You will fly, dear,
All the long year.

"Wings of springtime,   15
Wings of summer,
Wings of autumn,
Wings of winter!

"Here is
A dress for springtime."   20
And she gave him
A dress of grasses,
Orchard blossoms,
Wild-flowers found in
Mountain passes,   25
Shoes of song and
Wings of rhyme.

"Here is
A dress for summer."
And she gave him   30
A hat of sunflowers,
A suit of poppies,
Clover, daisies,
All from wheat-sheaves
In harvest time;   35
Shoes of song and
Wings of rhyme.

"Here is
A dress for autumn."
And she gave him   40
A suit of red haw,
Hickory, apple,
Elder, pawpaw,
Maple, hazel,
Elm and grape leaves,   45
And blue
And white
Cloaks of smoke,
And veils of sunlight,
From the Indian summer prime!   50
Shoes of song and
Wings of rhyme.

"Here is
A dress for winter."
And she gave him   55
A polar bear suit,
And he heard the
Christmas horns toot,

```
And she gave him
Green festoons and                                    60
Red balloons and
All the sweet cakes
And the snowflakes
Of Christmas time,
Shoes of song and                                     65
Wings of rhyme.

And the fairy
Kept him laughing,
Led him dancing,
Kept him climbing                                     70
On the hilltops
Toward the moon.
```

Finally, in lieu of 37-44, GWC and CP read:

```
And the lame child
And the fairy
Journeyed far, far
To the North Star.
```

373 THE BLACKSMITH'S SERENADE: in CP, SP. Lindsay sent the poem
to Harriet Monroe on 24 May 1913, advising her that it is "Apocalyptic" —
his "last word" (UL-C). He has had the notes for the poem for two years
and keeps going back to the idea. On 27 April 1914, however, he indicates
to Sara Teasdale (UL-Y) that the poem has been damned; two days later he
tears it up. On 21 February 1925, the poem was performed at Spokane;
Lindsay's manuscript (V) for the occasion has this note at the end: "The
basic sound of this poem is the letter N, repeated in all sorts of ways, and
the Iron Guitar is really the letter N, *one string*, one iron string of the voice,
not the guitar." VARIANT 59-62 *not in GWC, CP*.

376 THE APPLE BLOSSOM SNOW BLUES: *1st* in *Forum*, August 1916;
GWC. The title in *1st* is simply "The Apple-Blossom Snow"; headnote in
1st: "(A poem to be danced by a chosen couple while the audience chants it
with a delicate syncopation, along with the dancers.)." Manuscript note
(V): "A 'Blues' is a piece in the mood of Milton's Il Penseroso, or a
paragraph from Burton's Anatomy of Melancholy. This present production
is the chronicle of the secret soul of a vaudeville performer, as he dances in
the limelight with his haughty lady." When Lindsay reworked the poem for
GWC, he made more than forty minor verbal changes, tending to stress
blues and jazz and deemphasize ragtime.

378 DANIEL: *1st* in *Others*, January 1919; *New Statesman*, 14 June 1919;
Current Opinion, March 1920; DJ; CP; SP. The title in *1st*, *Statesman*,
GWC, CO, DJ is "The Daniel Jazz"; headnote in GWC, DJ: "Let the
leader train the audience to roar like lions, and to join in the refrain 'Go
chain the lions down,' before he begins to lead them in this jazz." In *1st*
and CP the poem is inscribed to Isadora Bennett Reed. On 8 March 1918
Lindsay writes to Harold Mills Salisbury (UL-V): "I have just blocked in a

song about Daniel this *morning*." The poem was finally sent to Harriet
Monroe on 29 August 1918 (UL-C). After 1920 and the publication of *The
Daniel Jazz and Other Poems* in England, Lindsay discovered—to his
horror— that he was being labeled a "jazz poet." His reaction was fierce,
and continued to the end of his life. On 9 March 1921 he writes Frances
Charles Macdonald (UL-P): ". . . since it has been used to slander me, I
hate the Daniel Jazz like poison, and do not want to recite it under any
circumstances." The following reflect his feeling: VARIANTS 6 music] jazz
1st, Statesman, GWC, CO, DJ 9-10 *not in 1st* 14 scamps] sinners *1st* 32
Daniel] boy *1st* 38 tender *not in 1st*. After 52 there are two long lines of
"Grrrr . . ." in *1st, Statesman, GWC, CO, DJ.*

380 WHEN PETER JACKSON PREACHED IN THE OLD CHURCH: in
CP.

380 THE CONSCIENTIOUS DEACON: *1st* in *Poetry Magazine*, August
1919; DJ.

381 DAVY JONES' DOOR-BELL: *1st* in *Poetry Magazine*, August 1919;
GWC. VARIANTS 3 calls] rings *1st* 21-22 *not in 1st*.

382 THE SEA SERPENT CHANTEY: *1st* in *Others*, March 1919; *Current
Opinion*, May 1919; *Christian Century*, 24 July 1919; DJ; CP; JA; SP.
Headnote in *1st*, CO, ChC: "Dedicated to Isadora Bennett"; manuscript
note (V): "Sometimes called by my friends The Submarine Chantey."
There are minor variations in the use of the chorus from version to
version.

383 THE LITTLE TURTLE: in *Current Opinion*, August 1923; CP;
Kindergarten and First Grade, April 1925; JA; SP.

384 ANOTHER WORD ON THE SCIENTIFIC ASPIRATION: *1st* in *Poetry
Magazine*, August 1919; GWC. The title in *1st* is "The Horrid Voice of
Science." See also the final two chapters of AMP. VARIANTS 7 *not in 1st* 8
And] With *1st*.

384 COLD SUNBEAMS: in AL, CP. Early titles: "Fairy Queens" (AL),
"Fairy Bridal Veils" (UMs-V), and "Bridal Veils" (Masters, p. 120).

384 FOR ALL WHO EVER SENT LACE VALENTINES: in DJ, CP, SP.
Early title (UMs-V): "The Little Boy Lover, and Little Girl Lover."
VARIANTS 33-34 *not in GWC* 35 *not in CP*.

386 MY LADY IS COMPARED TO A YOUNG TREE: *1st* in *Poetry
Magazine*, August 1919; CP. Written for Isadora Bennett (see Ruggles, p.
264).

386 TO EVE, MAN'S DREAM OF WIFEHOOD AS DESCRIBED BY
MILTON: in DJ, CP, SP. In CP twice: first as part of the "Invocation for
'The Map of the Universe.'" On 7 July 1924 Lindsay writes Elizabeth

Mann Wills: ". . . my dream of Eve and of my bride was fixed for ever at nine years old by reading the most holy, yet voluptuous lines of Milton's Paradise Lost, and I have walked in flame and splendor yet kept from women all these years looking for that White Eve, that mate before the fall, who was destined for me from the beginning, and who is as far from a prude, or a 'suppressed desire,' as far from what they call a Puritan as could well be imagined. Yet Eve till the Fall was praying a little harder than she loved, no matter how desperately she loved" (Chénetier, p. 157). See also Ruggles, p. 109.

387 A KIND OF SCORN: in CP. This and the next two poems were begun in early January 1919, after Lindsay had had several long talks with Octavia Roberts. Octavia, now married and with the name Corneau, was living in New England and had visited Springfield for Christmas. An early manuscript (V) reveals that the poems began as one—with the title "The Celestial Circus."

388 HARPS IN HEAVEN: in CP. See "A Kind of Scorn" above.

389 THE CELESTIAL CIRCUS: in CP. See "A Kind of Scorn" above. EMENDATION 18 heaps (as in GWC)] leaps

390 THE FIRE-LADDIE, LOVE: early manuscript title (V): "The Factory of Fate." The Springfield newspapers reveal that "fire-laddie" was as common in Lindsay's day as "fireman" is today.

391 IN MEMORY OF MY FRIEND, JOYCE KILMER, POET AND SOLDIER: 1st in New York Sun, 16 February 1919; CP. Published by Braithwaite (1919) as one of the year's best in a periodical. The poem may have been written as part of Lindsay's preparation for an address on the life and work of Kilmer—given to Springfield's Women's Club on 11 January 1919 (ISR).

392 THE TIGER ON PARADE: in CP.

393 THE FEVER CALLED WAR: sent to Harriet Monroe on 5 June 1917, with the title "The Scarlet Fever."

393 THE MODEST JAZZ-BIRD: 1st in Poetry Magazine, August 1919; GWC. Lindsay's letters reveal his drastic change in attitude toward jazz; on 5 August 1918 he writes Katharine Lee Bates: "I insist that Jazz does not discredit America. I think the Jazz element in America is a sure sign of health. I have the utmost respect for [the] Jazz in the young people, and I feel that without it there would be no American armies in Europe today. I do not claim that the Jazz Bird is a poem. It is a humoresque, of course. But it is the Jazz in these youngsters that will win this war. It is the same thing that Yankee Doodle was in the days of Washington" (Chénetier, p. 169). Manuscript title (V): "The Jazz Bird."

394 THE STATUE OF OLD ANDREW JACKSON: *1st* in *Independent*, 25 January 1919; CP. No headnote in *1st*; the title in *1st* is "Old Andrew Jackson." In preparing the poem for CP, Lindsay added to the headnote (and then crossed out): "I hope some day to write a much more serious rhyme about Jackson than the following. But even as it stands it is my most popular political rhyme south of Mason and Dixon's line" (UMs-V). The more serious rhyme is "Old, Old, Old, Old Andrew Jackson" (*q.v.*). VARIANTS 1 Andrew] Old Andrew *1st* 2 His arm was] With an arm like *1st* 13 And *not in 1st*.

396 SEW THE FLAGS TOGETHER: *1st* in *Boston Evening Transcript*, 23 November 1918; *Literary Digest*, 14 December 1918; ISR, 18 December 1918; *Christian Century*, 2 January 1919; CP. The poem was written for William Stanley Braithwaite's anthology, *Victory! Celebrated by thirty-eight American Poets*, with an introduction by Theodore Roosevelt (Boston, 1919). ISR reports that Lindsay wants poets to design a flag for "the forthcoming League of Nations." His suggestions are: "Make the tentative design by using all the flags on the Standard Dictionary flag page. Cut them out and shuffle them, using one representative of every nation there included. This will produce a set of forty-nine flags, seven each way, in even rows. The advantage of this form is that it disturbs no old loyalty, while establishing a new one. No element is introduced except the idea of union." For Lindsay's own "flag," which was on display in a local bookstore window, see the "Golden Book Section" in VM 2-4. VARIANTS 5 overwhelm] overwhelms *LD, ChC* 26 fine and dear] bright and clear *1st, LD, ISR, ChC*.

397 THE VOICE OF ST. FRANCIS OF ASSISI: *1st* in *Chicago Herald*, 11 September 1914; CP. The title in *1st* is "St. Francis"; manuscript title (V): "When Will the War End?" At the end of Lindsay's 1919 datebook (V) we read: "St. Francis receives my heart again after these many days I have gone with Buddha."

398 HAIL TO THE SONS OF ROOSEVELT: *1st* in *New York Sun*, 9 February 1919; CP. On 21 January 1919 Lindsay writes William Lyon Phelps (UL-Y) and advises that the poem is "a companion piece" to "In Which Roosevelt Is Compared to Saul" (*q.v.*).

398 WHEN THE MISSISSIPPI FLOWED IN INDIANA: *1st* in *Red Cross Magazine*, December 1919; CP. In CP with "The Raft" and "Mark Twain and Joan of Arc" (see above) under the title "Three Poems about Mark Twain." Title in *1st*: "The Cave of Becky Thatcher." On 21 December 1917 Lindsay writes Louis Untermeyer: "I went to Jack Pickford's Tom Sawyer last night, and could hardly keep from crying like a matinee girl. It was a fair performance, but that was not the point. The point was that it reminded me of the book, which I read at my Grandfather's in Indiana (the proud farmer) every year, with all my cousins, from the time I was eight till I was fifteen. We all took turns reading it and re-reading it. I hope to write a poem to Becky Thatcher yet. It was an innocent America we lived in then, and what little lambs Tom Sawyer and Becky Thatcher seem in memory"

(Chénetier, p. 157). VARIANTS 6 wonders] marbles *1st* 8 young] sweet *1st* ground,] towers: *1st* 12 Where . . . found,] All these, are ours—*1st* 19 Indiana] rag carpet *1st* 24 Trips] Walks *1st* 28 little] playing *1st* 36 Nothing] No fiend *1st*.

399 THE FAIRY FROM THE APPLE-SEED: in VM 1, 2, 3, 4; CP; JA. The poem is not in VM 1; it is untitled in VM 2. In VM 3, 4 the title is "A Little Dryad." On a copy of the poem in the Canby scrapbook (see note to "Indian Summer" above), Lindsay notes that it was written for VM 2. The drawing is not in GWC, JA. Unfortunately, an error was made in preparing the text for JA: we have only the first sixteen lines. The final ten are from the end of "The Village Improvement Parade" (*q.v.*). An early manuscript (V) title is "The Fairy from the Amaranth Apple."

401 THE DREAM OF ALL THE SPRINGFIELD WRITERS: *1st* in *Little Review*, June 1914; CP. The title in *1st* is "The Sword-Pen of the Rhymer." VARIANTS 13 beneath the] 'mid orchard- *1st* 14 bound for] struggling *1st* 17 the winter] December *1st* 21 winter's . . . floor] snow my hopes of your, *1st* 24 Amid] 'Mid those *1st*.

402 AFTER READING THE SAD STORY OF THE FALL OF BABYLON: in CP.

402 ALEXANDER CAMPBELL: *1st* in *New York Sun*, 26 October 1919; *Current Opinion*, January 1920; *Christian Century*, 5 February 1920; *New York Evening Post*, 16 June 1923; CP. Only "My Fathers Came from Kentucky" in CO, *Post*; variant manuscript titles (V) for the second part: "My Dead" and "In Robes of Sunrise." On 24 March 1916 Lindsay writes to his former Chicago pastor, Edward Scribner Ames, thanking him for being elected as an honorary member of the Campbell Institute. Lindsay adds: "I am sorry to ask you not to rush me about the poem about Alexander Campbell. I generally take two to four years to write a poem—and then—it doesn't always turn out right" (UL-C). See Lindsay's letter to Marguerite Wilkinson (4 July 1927) in *The Shane Quarterly*, V (April-July, 1944), 115-117; see also "Adventures While Singing These Songs" and "Adventures While Preaching Hieroglyphic Sermons" in CP.

409 *From* THE VILLAGE MAGAZINE: (2nd Edition, Springfield, June 1920) [The second edition of the *Magazine* is nearly double the size of VM 1. A few poems are added to go with drawings that were done for VM 1, but the bulk of the new material is in two new sections: "Interregnum of about Ten Years" and the "Golden Book Section." The latter is Lindsay's summary of the ideas in *The Golden Book of Springfield* (New York: The Macmillan Company, November 1920). For additional information, see Massa, pp. 29-32 and Armstrong, pp. 23-28.]

411 THE TRAVELLER: in MsAP; VM 3, 4; GSu. A new poem and drawing added to the moon poems in VM 1. For an explanation of the hieroglyphics in this and other plates from GSu, see the introductory note to GSu below. The hieroglyphic signature is not in VM 2-4. VARIANTS 5 he *not in VM 2-4* 6 in] is in *VM 2-4*.

412 A SONG IN JULY: in CP; VM 3, 4. Note in VM 3, 4: "Between this picture and the next section occurs an interregnum of about ten years." "A Page of Owls" follows (see below).

413 A PAGE OF OWLS: in MsAP; *Current Opinion*, November 1920; VM 3, 4; GSu. Only the first poem is in CO, GSu; the title in CO and MsAP is "Writing Wills, and So Forth"; the title in GSu is "Old Judge Hoot Owl." In MsAP the second poem is entitled "One of the First Families of Carmi." In the commentary-index that Lindsay prepared for VM 2-4 we read: "All the pictures that follow have been made this year; — all of them through ['A Frank Contribution to Current Discussion'], on Pullman Cars with a fountain pen, and afterwards retraced in black. They may be considered among other things, a protest against being classed by hasty newspaper editors who have not read a line of my books, as being exclusively an exponent of jazz. These same editors also miss the point that there is a touch of irony in the few jazzes I have written, and in the kallyope yell also." Lindsay then refers said editors to the second poem on "A Page of Owls."

414 THE LAND HORSE AND THE SEA HORSE: in MsAP; VM 3, 4; GSu.

415 A PAGE OF DANGEROUS BEASTS: in VM 3, 4. The drawings of the "Bat" and "The Big Eared Rat" are in GSu — as part of the illustrations for "So Much the Worse for Boston" (*q.v.*). The third poem is also in Lindsay's *Springfield Town Is Butterfly Town*, ed. Pierre Dussert (Cleveland: The Kent State University Press, 1969).

416 GIRLS WE ALL KNOW: in VM 3, 4; GSu. Only the second poem is in GSu — with the title "A Political Campaign."

417 A NATURE STUDY PAGE: in VM 3, 4.

418 A FRANK CONTRIBUTION TO CURRENT DISCUSSION: in VM 3, 4. In his commentary-index Lindsay writes: "A Roast on the Imagists. I hope this will not be taken too seriously by the Imagists. But I am remembering newspaper editors who send young reporters to me asking me if I am an imagist, and then asking me what an imagist is, anyway, and then asking me if I was not born in Scandinavia, and then asking me if I have written any books, and then asking me my laundry mark, and what my sorrow is and the romance of my life. Incidentally I would like to congratulate Upton Sinclair most heartily on his book, The Brass Check. But as to the Imagists . . . . " The reference to *The Brass Check* (1919), Sinclair's scathing indictment of modern journalism, is dropped from VM 3, 4. For more on Lindsay and imagism, see AMP, pp. 267-269; Williams, pp. 41-42; and Massa, pp. 228-230.

419 FANTASY ON THE GOLDEN BOOK AND ITS ESCORT: in VM 3, 4. The poem is untitled in VM 2; the commentary-index reads: "Verse concerning The Angels of the Angels, with the flags of the Angels." The poem, then, which concludes the "Golden Book Section" (see above),

clearly relates to Chapter XVIII of *The Golden Book of Springfield*. This final work of VM 2, with some adapting, becomes the prologue poem of GSu, where the title is "We Start West for the Waterfalls" (*q.v.*).

THE DANIEL JAZZ AND OTHER POEMS: (London: George Bell & Sons, September 1920) [Although every poem in this volume had already been published, it is worthy of mention since it, more than any other book, led to Lindsay's reputation as a jazz poet. On 28 August 1920 Lindsay writes Harriet Moody (UL-V): "George Bell and Son bring out 'The Daniel Jazz' and other poems—September 20th. The 'other poems' are well chosen, and the Jazz is the only doubtful one. The rest are the usual list of verses generally first named by my best friends. I suppose the Jazz is the point of the arrow—to help make way for the others, an 'ad' *inside* the book!" Lindsay was more than proven right in this observation, and, as is well known, he ever after declared his contempt for jazz. A letter to Katharine Lee Bates (28 October 1924), for example, manifests his repugnance: "You see I was caught between two millstones. I was born with a voice so they thought me a weaker Bryan. I was born with dancing feet so they thought me Jazz. I used the word once or twice when it meant spice. But *just after that* the world, the whole world went jazz-mad—a thing none of us could have prophesied and I have been worn to my soul, welcomed to a thousand towns where I have had to explain to thousands I was *not* a Jazz artist—and the Saxophone, which I hate—was read into everything I ever did" (Chénetier, p. 331). For a time Lindsay went so far as to accuse his English publishers of treachery. In a reflective moment (25 February 1923), however, he writes in his datebook (V): "George Bell & Son had a perfect *Legal* and *moral* right to do as they did, but exhibited remarkable *feebleness*. As I examine the actual contents of *The Daniel Jazz* volume I feel my wrath was in some ways unjustified. My wrath was really baffled egotism and baffled priestcraft. It was the baffled ambition of the scheming ecclesiastic. I know it." Later that same day, though, he pencils in his most intense desire—that which he feels the jazz epithet has distorted or destroyed—"I want to write books, that, by their incantations will make beautiful cities, as the Koran by its incantations made bloody armies." *The Daniel Jazz* was not Lindsay's first English volume: Chatto and Windus had brought out the *General William Booth* volume in the fall of 1919.]

421 *From* COLLECTED POEMS (1st Edition, New York: The Macmillan Company, Spring, 1923) [For the second edition of CP (1925), which added forty drawings and ten new poems to this first edition, see below. When CP was published, there were countless reviews across the country, but the one that meant most to Lindsay—and the one of greatest historical significance—is that of Susan Wilcox, in Frank Waller Allen's column, "Books and Bookmen," *Illinois State Journal* (Springfield), 24 June 1923. Allen reports that he received a letter from Lindsay when the poet learned that Miss Wilcox was to review the volume: "I am mighty glad Susan Wilcox is to review the collected works. No person in the world could understand it better and no one could read so deeply between the lines." After a long, thoughtful review, Miss Wilcox concludes:

The man who brought poetry from the corner cupboards of magazines and the treasure-chests of poetic coteries to delight audiences of common people wrought the miracle by the spell of rhythm. He himself felt the pulse of life beating and he translated it into his poems. The most popular chants are in the pounding rhythms that appeal to the child-mind, but this is only one variety. His rhythms vary from the blatant blare of the Calliope through the sharp staccato of rag time, sometimes merely rumbling and repeating, to sweeping and surging choruses and delicate echo-like cadences.

No poet of today is more impetuous than Lindsay and his work contains a number of unpoetic and flat passages. Too frequently the "Chautauquan Jay" takes the perch; too often the evangelistic note is too strident and the millennial vision, according to one critic, "shows a world of moral Dutch Cleanser and spiritual Sapolio [brand-name for a white cake soap] — a sort of perpetual World's fair, Christmas card and Sunday school picnic rolled into one." The strangeness sometimes degenerates into the bizarre.

The recent revolt against the new localism led by Mencken and others, because they maintain that the village has nothing to contribute, does not invalidate the appeal of Lindsay's poems on this theme. It is too early to estimate the contribution of the Middle West to art. Lindsay does not merely write history, he transfigures it till sometimes it is myth instead. Persons neglected by other poets become through the fire of his imagination saints and heroes.

All must grant him a poet of whimsical laughter, of fascinating pictures, of homely fancies, of joyous exaggeration, of appealing rhythms. Some may not thrill to his apocalyptic visions. To be fully attuned to these last the reader must come from the same spiritual environment from which the poet sprang. Yet granting his shortcomings enough remains of powerful and original work to give Mr. Lindsay a place among the best exponents of American life today. He has done for the spirit of the Middle West what Robert Frost has done for rural New England. His poems are a delight to the natural person uncontaminated by literary prejudices.

He is truly a democratic poet, believing that our present life is very much worth while and having a faith in the common man that is akin to Lincoln's. "Where else," asks Francis Hackett, "in this country of emergence is there in combination nationalism so free and swinging, religion so vigorous, human contact so unprejudiced, beauty so adored?"

For the structure of the book, see "Adventures While Singing These Songs" in CP; also see Armstrong, pp. 87-88.

423 I KNOW ALL THIS WHEN GIPSY FIDDLES CRY: *1st* in *New Republic*, 18 May 1921; *London Mercury*, September 1921; MsAP (1922); SP. An early version of the poem appears in *The Enchanted Years: A Book of Contemporary Verse Dedicated by Poets of Great Britain and America to the University of Virginia on the Occasion of Its One-Hundredth Anniversary*, ed. John Calvin Metcalf and James Southall Wilson. New York: Harcourt, 1921. In his datebook (19 March 1922), Lindsay writes: "Johnny Appleseed [see below] represents an intellectual mood. But the Gipsies is a little more honest — representing a mood more fundamental

than the intellectual—a minimum rather than a maximum of the soul—the clean cut indestructible cat in a man" (UDB-V). See AMP, pp. 16-17.

426 HAMLET: *1st* in *London Mercury*, December 1920; SP. The words "in Springfield so often" are added to the headnote in *1st*. On 20 December 1922 Lindsay writes Armstrong (pp. 90-91): "I am far more of a Hamlet than you know, far more given to enjoying walking the battlements alone than ever my crowds need to believe or would believe if told. My whole literary world has met me, necessarily in my social mood, and thinks foolishly enough that is where I have always lived and always choose to live."

428 IN PRAISE OF JOHNNY APPLESEED: *1st* in London *Spectator*, 21 May 1921; *Century Magazine*, August 1921; MsAP (1922); JA; SP. The title in *1st* is "A Song for American Children in Praise of Johnny Appleseed"; *The Bookman* (November 1921) published a selection from sections II and III; also published by Braithwaite (1922). On 28 March 1921 Lindsay writes Frances Charles Macdonald (UL-P) that the poem is "the effort of my life, poor as it may be"; see the note to "I Know All This When Gipsy Fiddles Cry" above. On 11 December 1921 Lindsay writes Mrs. Dorothy Bohnhorst (née Runyan), who had asked for advice on publishing creative work, warning her against göing "into literature for an income. Every boot-black in America makes as much as the nearest author." He adds, as an example, "It took me two years to write the poem Johnny Appleseed and I received a month's salary for it" (UL—quoted with permission of Mrs. Bohnhorst). For Lindsay on John Chapman, see the "Golden Book Section" of VM 2-4; Graham, pp. 177-182; AMP, pp. 22-23; and *The Litany of Washington Street*, pp. 75-76. From 1921 to 1931 Lindsay made numerous changes in the text; the following are selective: VARIANTS 30 foggy *not in 1st*, CM 106 forest . . .,] , fairy-enchanted forest, *1st, CM, MsAP, CP* 121 river reed] river and reed *1st, CM, MsAP, CP* 150 all . . . weathers] the whole young earth, *1st, CM* 166-167 *not in 1st, CM* 167 *not in MsAP* 170 *not in 1st, CM, MsAP* 195 brooding] dreaming *1st, CM* 228, 229 his] their *1st, CM, CP* 228 broken *not in 1st, CM* 229 juicy *not in 1st, CM* 232 An angel] A presence *1st, CM* 241 And . . . expectations] All color and all glory *1st, CM* 241 written] tangled *1st, CM* 243 the merciful] thousand *1st, CM* 254 *not in 1st, CM* 255 ten] a *1st, CM* 256-258 *not in 1st, CM, MsAP, CP* 267 stone . . . white] bump on a log, like a stone washed white *1st, CM, MsAP.*

435 LITANY OF THE HEROES: in PP (1908); PP (1910); *New York Evening Post*, 24 February 1923; SP. On 5 February 1923 Lindsay writes Christopher Morley, suggesting the *Litany* appear in Morley's column in the *Post*. Lindsay describes the work as "THE new poem of the Collected Works," and adds that it is "made up of many old stanzas—but in an order which makes them a new poem." Each of the twenty-four characters is "set in abrupt and challenging contrast to his predecessor," closing "with Socrates and Woodrow Wilson as the heroes of the series, and the two men who point to the future, and repeating the note of Amenophis IV (Akenaton) with which the song began. Socrates is the only man out of

chronological order. Wilson and The League of Nations are the final thoughts in the Reader's mind, both of them thoughts of the future—and in a way the solution of the 24 porcupine contradictions of these 24 porcupine historic characters who seemed otherwise to have no unity at all. It is my outline of history . . . ," Chénetier, p. 276. Morley includes an edited version of the letter as a headnote in the *Post*, as Lindsay suggests. Lindsay also stresses the topical appropriateness of his poem: the splendid grave of Tutankhamen has just been discovered (November 1922) and the body is presently being unwrapped. Lindsay believed "King Tut" was the son of Amenophis IV, with whom this poem begins. For information on the background of the poem, see Fowler, pp. 130, 220-222.

From 1906 to 1931 Lindsay worked with his poem, sometimes publishing parts as complete poems, sometimes changing the whole entirely. The following demonstrate how flexible the poem was:

PP (1908): entitled "God Help Us All to Be Brave"; the headnote reads: "A poem concerning the twenty-six representative citizens of the world from Rameses II to Roosevelt." The first stanza is not here, the poem beginning with what is now line 9; this stanza, then, is entitled "Rameses II." Socrates is placed in chronological order following Phidias, and the Cromwell-Milton and Titian-Michelangelo stanzas are interchanged. The Wilson stanza, of course, is not yet written.

PP (1908): entitled "A Memorial of Lincoln, Called The Heroes of Time"; the headnote reads: "A poem illustrating the position of Abraham Lincoln among the dominating personalities of history." This shortened version follows the order of PP (1908) above, but omits the stanzas on Alexander, Justinian, Darwin, Emerson, and Roosevelt. The following serves as "Prologue":

Sons of Lincoln! Sons of Freedom!
They lived through Freedom's second dawn;
Or, smitten with untimely arrows,
By cabins rude as the nests of sparrows,
Or wagons wandering to the sunset
On strange old plains in days long gone;
Or swept with prairie fires or floods,
They died, with their toiling all undone,
By the gray Ohio, or black Missouri,
Or wan and haunted Sangamon.

Say not, "That wild land is no more
Whose voice was in the soul of Lincoln"—
Yea, Lincoln! How he haunteth us!
Yea, unseen fires from buried breasts
Rise into the living hearts of us.
Rise into these mongrel days for us—
No other soil is haunted thus.
Can the East have such a glory—
The storied East, with its lotus wonders—
Today, when the voice of Lincoln thunders?

The Lincoln plate from TE—"To the Young Men of Illinois"—is on the back cover. See "Sons of the Middle West," p. 794.

GWB: includes "St. Francis of Assisi," "Buddha," "Shakespeare," "Michelangelo," "Titian," and "Lincoln."

HGB: includes "Columbus," "Phidias," "Confucius," "In Lost Jerusalem" (Christ), "That Which Men Hail as King" (Caesar), and "That Men Might See Again the Angel-Throng" (Milton).

CN: the opening poem of "Concerning Emperors"—"God Send the Regicide"—is the Cromwell stanza.

Christian Century, 19 December 1918: "Columbus."

GWC: includes "Rameses II," "Moses," "Dante," "The Scientific Aspiration" (Darwin), "Stanzas in Just the Right Tone for the Spirited Gentlemen Who Would Conquer Mexico" (Alexander, Mohammed, Napoleon), "Justinian" (with headnote: "The Tory Reply"), and "The Spacious Days of Roosevelt" (the two Roosevelt and the two final stanzas).

Post, CP: both omit Cromwell; both are inscribed to George Mather Richards. Headnote in CP: "Being a chant about many men, good and bad, who have led and misled mankind, from the earliest times until now."

JA: includes Columbus, St. Francis, Michelangelo, Shakespeare, Lincoln, and the concluding stanza ("Grand and Still Forgotten").

PP (1910), "The Heroes of Time," was prepared for the annual banquet of the Lincoln Centennial Association (12 February) and was printed on the menu cards (ISR, 13 February 1910). For more on the work, see "Adventures While Singing These Songs" in CP; and Masters, pp. 22, 134; Ruggles, pp. 102, 128-129, 316. VARIANTS (all from *PP* 1908 unless indicated otherwise) 9 Still . . .-loving] Would that the brave Rameses, *PP* (*1908*), (*1910*), *GWC* 10 Be] Were *PP* (*1908*), (*1910*), *GWC* 10 deep hearts] souls *PP* (*1908*), (*1910*), *GWC* 11 The . . . well] Vast immemorial dreams dark Egypt *PP* (*1908*), (*1910*), *GWC* 14 triumphant] all-consuming *PP* (1908), (1910), *GWC* 17 Then] Yet *PP* (*1908*), (*1910*), *GWC* 23-24 *PP* (*1908*) *repeats 15-16* 24 help us to be] make us meek and *PP* (*1910*), *GWC* 28 makes] made *PP* (*1908*), (*1910*) 50 the] the old 62 fearful] red-black 65 Behold the] Would we were 66 themselves] ourselves 68 Then] All *PP* (*1908*), (*1910*) 70 looked] did *PP* (*1908*), (*1910*) 70 beneath] look in *PP* (*1908*), (*1910*) 76 dreadful] cruel *PP* (*1908*), (*1910*) 76 light] smite *PP* (*1908*), (*1910*) 92 Fanatics] Religions 95 all crazy] fanatic 100 New. . . . ancient] Europe, China, India, *PP* (*1908*), (*1910*) 101 Allah is] God one God, *PP* (*1908*), (*1910*) 170 hope] hopes *PP* (*1908*), (*1910*) 173 shining flowers,] Amaranth *PP* (*1908*), (*1910*) 183 Abraham's] Abram's 193 Then . . . shining] God give us yet the poise of 194 Teacher . . . better] Armored in sunrays, strange wise 195 The . . . granite] Strong, self-reliant king- 196 sent] born 196 strike] smite 197 wools and hair-shirts] calm assurance 198-200 *in PP* (*1908*): Make us as brothers of the blessed Sun— / Speaking fair runes that drive away the night. / God give us robes of light. 201 were] are 233 forgotten] forgot 236 Egyptian] far Coptic *PP* (*1908*), *GWC*.

441 WHAT THE CLOWN SAID: *1st* in *Chicago Herald*, 7 May 1915; MsAP; JA. An early version appears in Lindsay's 1912 tramping notebook (V). In *1st* the title is "The Circus Clown" and there are three extra stanzas at the beginning:

> "Black horses gallop through my sleep,"
> Said the spangled clown to me.

"Spreading fins of gray or green
   They rise from a black sea.

"And I do crack great jests when they,
   Surmounting that deep tide,
Go foaming up the airy steep
   A-taunting me to ride.

"I crack my whip at them and shout
   Until the far stars hear.
The seraphs dare me on to ride,
   And the little cherubs cheer.

VARIANTS 4 of] in *1st* 7 aggravating hoop] tempting hoop tonight *1st* 8
make my finest] through the paper *1st*.

442 BEING THE DEDICATION OF THE MORNING.

443 TO A GOLDEN-HAIRED GIRL IN A LOUISIANA TOWN: in MsAP,
CP. On 19 March 1920 Lindsay writes John Emerson and Anita Loos that
he has written a poem for a "red-gold head (of hair)" that he saw in New
Orleans (UL-H).

445 GOING-TO-THE-SUN (New York: D. Appleton and Company, Fall,
1923) [GSu is perhaps the least known of Lindsay's books. None of the
poems appears in CP, JA, or SP; only "So Much the Worse for Boston"
was published in a periodical. Six of the poems are in VM 2 (see above), but
VM 2 was a limited, private publication. Most of the poems, of course, are
based on the tramping trip with Stephen Graham in Glacier National Park
at the end of the summer, 1921. Graham's book on the same
experience — *Tramping with a Poet in the Rockies* — was published by
Appleton in 1922. For the coordination of the two books, see Lindsay's
prefatory essay — "The Elements of Good Tea" — in the Appendix; see also
Armstrong, pp. 78, 88.
   GSu is the first result of Lindsay's determination to illustrate all of his
books, a decision he made while he was preparing the first edition of CP.
That he saw his drawings as a way of correcting his false public image is
clear from his datebook (UDB-V, January 1921): "My drawings enable me
to touch the irony, realism and ritual which my chants have led me from.
They go back to High School." His letters reveal that most of the drawings
for GSu were finished during the summer of 1922, when he was staying at
the Cleveland home of his sister, Joy Blair. In fact, as Lindsay informs
Armstrong (p. 88), he saw GSu as "a *book of drawings*," with Glacier Park
as "merely a cloudy background for a book of fantasies." However, his
prediction that the volume "will be welcome as a *light* but amusing book,
much gossiped about" proved wrong.
   Many of the verses, of course, are light, but much of the fun in GSu is in
the hieroglyphic signatures. These often serve as amusing, meaningful
'last words' — in exactly the way political cartoonist Pat Oliphant uses his
tiny figure (usually at the bottom) to give humorous, anticlimactic
comments on his subjects. Lindsay explains how to read the

hieroglyphics—several of which are greatly enlarged in GSt (see below)—in "The Elements of Good Tea" (see the Appendix). The formula, generally, is: 'the living truth about (the subject of the poem and drawing) as told in words and pen and ink by the writer (the scribe of Thoth), who admires or, often ironically, "marvels at" (the subject).' So that in "The Land Horse and the Sea Horse" (see above), the hieroglyphics for the former read; 'the living truth about the land horse as described by the writer who "marvels at" such beasts of burden.' For the sea horse, on the other hand, the signature reads: 'the living truth about the sea as described by the writer, who admires the mountains (where he is) and the sea,' both of which suggest the freedom of the sea horse. Lindsay's interest in hieroglyphics and Egyptology dates back to his art student days in New York (c. 1906) or even before (see Ruggles, p. 42). He renewed his interest in 1914-1915, while working on AMP (see Chapters XIII and XIX), stressing at one point that "the Egyptian scholar was the man who could not only compose a poem, but write it down with a brush. Talent for poetry, deftness in inscribing, and skill in mural painting were probably gifts of the same person. The photoplay goes back to this primitive union in styles" (AMP, p. 210). Finally, in the summer of 1922, he became an even more serious student of the subject; see Ruggles, pp. 302-303. Also see "Adventures While Preaching Hieroglyphic Sermons" in CP and preface for GSt—"Going-to-the-Stars"—in the Appendix; "'Now Comes a Cartoon Letter'" in "Unpublished Poems and Juvenilia" in this edition; and Masters, pp. 174-177; Untermeyer, pp. 131-137; Massa, pp. 255-265; Phelps, pp. 631-632.

447 WE START WEST FOR THE WATERFALLS. See "Fantasy of The Golden Book and Its Escort" in VM 2 above and "Going to the Sun. Waterfalls, Remembered Long After" in "Unpublished Poems and Juvenilia" in this edition.

448 GOING-TO-THE-SUN. In Glacier Park Lindsay discovered a pamphlet entitled *Picture Writing by the Blackfeet Indians of Glacier National Park, Montana*, published by the Great Northern Railway. In late summer, 1922, he sends a copy to Harriet Moody and writes on the cover: "When I am West of the Rockies, I am not afraid the Study of Egypt will ruin my American soul!" (UL-V).

449 THE MYSTIC ROOSTER OF THE MONTANA SUNRISE. For Lindsay on turkeys, see Untermeyer, pp. 148-149.

450 THE BIRD CALLED "CURIOSITY." The hieroglyphic signature indicates that the sunrise or the idea of youthfulness is as much the subject of the poem and drawing as the bird.

452 THE THISTLEVINE. Manuscript title (V): "The Butterflies and the Thistlevine."

452 AND THEY LAUGHED.

454 THE FAIRY CIRCUS. The hieroglyphic signature reads: 'The living truth about the man who looked at the clouds as told by the writer, who admires the man who embraces or adores clouds.'

455 THE BATTLE-AX OF THE SUN.

456 THE CHRISTMAS TREES. The signature reads: 'The living truth about Christmas trees as told by the writer, who admires or wants lots of candles' (the three vertical lines at the end indicate the plural).

456 THE PHEASANT SPEAKS OF HIS BIRTHDAYS. The hieroglyphics indicate many happy birthdays, though the pheasant is only three yars old (the number of candles next to the beating heart of truth). The five candles on the cake may indicate the many birthdays or the fact that the pheasant exaggerates his age a bit.

458 THE MYSTIC UNICORN OF THE MONTANA SUNSET. On 22 November 1922 Lindsay sent Untermeyer a translation of Akhnaton's "Hymn to the Sun" (UL-B). From this it is clear that the first two hieroglyphs in the signature to this poem represent sunset and the west respectively.

460 JOHNNY APPLESEED STILL FURTHER WEST. On 9 January 1920 Lindsay writes Untermeyer: "I have said for years that if almost everything that was said in praise of Whitman was rewritten with the names of Johnny Appleseed and Abraham Lincoln substituted, it would be much truer, in the eyes of the real open minds of America. And most everything said in praise of Thoreau had better be said for Johnny Appleseed, who was one of the great and beautiful and successful unconscious humorists of his day. He beat the game without knowing it . . . ," (Chénetier, pp. 193-194).

462 THE APPLE-BARREL OF JOHNNY APPLESEED. See AMP, p. 35.

465 THE COMET OF GOING-TO-THE-SUN.

465 THE BOAT WITH THE KITE STRING AND THE CELESTIAL EYES. For Lindsay and the United States map, see AMP, pp. 26-27.

469 SO MUCH THE WORSE FOR BOSTON: *1st* in *New Republic*, 6 December 1922; *London Mercury*, April 1923; GSu. Published by Braithwaite (1923) as one of the year's best works in a periodical; the title in *1st* and Braithwaite is "The Mountain Cat." Lindsay's datebook (V) reveals that he was thinking about the poem as early as May 1922, but his not-so-successful experience at Harvard in June 1922 (see "Bob Taylor's Birthday" below) was probably all the stimulus he needed for finishing the work. See Ruggles, pp. 300-302. The hieroglyphic signature at the bottom of the drawing of the rat is one of the more interesting ones in GSu: 'The living truth about the big-eared rat as described by the writer, who "marvels at" a number of big-eared Boston rats.' VARIANTS 13, 16 *not in LM* 15 *And ... sunshine not in 1st, LM* 17 big-eared] Boston *1st, LM* 25 I . . .

rat] Not in all of Boston are there hunting scenes like that *1st* 54-55 I . . .
crudities] He reads his rainwashed Shakespear on horseback, in the dawn.
/He has made me quite a college cat. My western ways *1st* 58 Hawthorne]
fierce John Brown *1st* 66 spout and leap,] huff and puff *1st* 67 trail] path *1st*
107 In the wood-lot] Their laughing, *1st* 112 lecherous] merry *1st* 121 bats]
fish *1st* 136-137 *not in LM* 137 fall in] turn to *1st* 147 dim] grey *1st* 171
speaking] listening *1st* 178-180 *Boston . . . your*] So much the worse for *1st*
182 at . . . wild] the cat had ended his great *1st* 188 Boston] mountain *1st*
EMENDATION 58 has] had

480 THE ROCKETS THAT REACHED SATURN. Manuscript title (V):
"The Weeds of Saturn."

482 MEDITATION. EMENDATION 5 lost (as corrected by Lindsay in his
own hand in the copy of GSu he gave to Mary Humphrey — LH)] rest

483 ELIZABETH BARRETT BROWNING. The hieroglyphic signature
indicates that, whereas Mrs. Browning has found one page, the writer
admires many books of Robert Browning's work.

484 SOME BALLOONS GROW ON TREES. On 8 and 9 April 1922 Lindsay
writes in his datebook (UDB-V): "I ought to make this rule: — Read no
poem I am used to reading. . . . *Omit* every familiar poem and refuse *every*
request. Read untouched verses till they are the most popular — including
verses for pictures; advertise pictures in this way, Some Balloons Grow on
Trees — etc. Make several drawings for this poem. To avoid internal
conflict, take audience into workshop — like Amy [Lowell]. Tell them my
rule is to recite *no* poem I have already recited 1,0001 [*sic*] times. It is
rough — but my only salvation. I have now completely covered America in a
sort — once, into every corner of the Union. Every college & university in
the country contains at least one instructor in English or member of the
faculty who has heard Congo, Booth, the Trail, etc. Unless I am to go
crazy — I must stop reciting these, must interest the public in my new
verses and pictures." The hieroglyphics indicate the writer's great
admiration for the fanciful balloons of children, though he also admires the
practical boots of adulthood, which outnumber the balloons. "Betsy
Richards" is the daughter of George Mather Richards (see the note to JA
below).

485 BABYLON'S GARDENS ARE BURNING. Compare the fires of
materialism burning in "The Firemen's Ball' (*q.v.*). See also AMP, pp.
12-13.

487 IN THE BEAUTY PARLORS

488 PEARLS. The hieroglyphics emphasize the writer's admiration for
oysters!

489 CONCERNING THE MOUSE WITH TWO TALES. Manuscript title
(V): "Concerning a Cat's Hallucination of the Apparition of a Mouse with

Two Tales.'' A note at the bottom of the manuscript reads: ''(See if you can draw this picture, by writing the words cat and mouse, and turning them upside down.)'' If one turns the drawing so that the animals are on their backs, one should be able to see Lindsay's entertaining attempt at picture-writing. The late Lillian Scalzo, former President of the Springfield Art Association and one who drew with Lindsay, remembered how he would write a name on a full sheet of paper and then proceed, Spencerian style, to create a picture from and with that name.

490 WORDS ABOUT AN ANCIENT QUEEN. The large hieroglyphics are another Lindsay attempt to adapt Egyptian hieroglyphics to what he termed the United States language. The first hieroglyph and the overall form are reasonably authentic reproductions; the first hieroglyph means, literally, 'the King (here Queen) of Upper and Lower (in other words, all) Egypt.' The Queen's name is in the first cartouche and this Lindsay invents; if we follow an Egyptian grammar, her name seems to be 'One-quarter-true-and-pious'! After the first cartouche is then an adaptation of traditional Egyptian naming: Queen One-Quarter-True-and-Pious is the 'hair-netted daughter of.' And her ancestor's name is in the second cartouche and is reasonably authentic: 'the revered Amenhotep.' The last hieroglyph, which I have translated 'revered,' seems to be idiomatic for royal names of Egypt's Middle Kingdom; however, the seated figure holds a flagellum, not a pyramid as Lindsay has drawn it. Perhaps the pyramid suggests Amenhotep is dead. The standard hieroglyphic signature, which follows, suggests that the writer has ''marvelled at'' a great number of hair nets in his day. On 27 December 1922 Lindsay writes Armstrong (pp. 91-92) that he is planning a long poem on his mother ''called *Hat shep sut*, who seems to have been remarkably like her.'' Clearly, though, he has changed his mind, for this little poem satirizes, not Mrs. Lindsay but rather the pompous club women the poet was growing to hate (see Armstrong, p. xiii). Debunking the ''great,'' of course, is what Lytton Strachey (*Eminent Victorians*, 1918) is famous for. The stimulus for the poem may be in a pun on the Queen's name, which, with a little slurring and imagination, sounds like 'hat shuts up.'

491 *From* THE VILLAGE MAGAZINE (3rd Edition, Springfield, Spring, 1925), [VM 3 adds approximately forty-five pages to VM 2. Lindsay reprints PA and *War Bulletins* 1, 2, 3, and 5, adding: ''These Tracts are reprinted as a matter of record. They were my opinions in and about 1909. They are not my opinions in 1925. For my 1925 opinions, read my 1925 poems.'' Lindsay also includes those poems from RB and TE (which was officially *War Bulletin* 4) that had not already appeared in his nationally published books. The concluding work is ''The Map of the Universe'' (from TE), the second edition of which serves as the frontispiece to the revised CP (see below).]

493 IN MEMORY OF A GOOD PRINTER: in VM 4. The first draft of this poem is in Lindsay's 1925 datebook (V), beginning January 2. Naylor worked for Jeffersons Printing Company, which printed most of Lindsay's privately published Springfield works, obviously to the poet's satisfaction.

495 *From* COLLECTED POEMS (2nd Edition, New York: The Macmillan Company, Spring, 1925) [The illustrated edition of CP adds forty of Lindsay's drawings, nearly all from the three editions of *The Village Magazine*; a second preface — "Adventures While Preaching Hieroglyphic Sermons"; a section of poems (all previously published) under the title "Invocation for 'The Map of the Universe'"; nine new poems (all below) in a section entitled "Songs Based on American Hieroglyphics, Cartoons, and Motion Pictures"; and a concluding poem — "The Trial of Cleopatra" — in a section by itself, with the title "A Song Based on Egyptian Hieroglyphics" (also below).]

496 THE MAP OF THE UNIVERSE: in PP (28 February 1926); CP. Lindsay's letters reveal that this second edition of the "Map," which serves as frontispiece for the illustrated CP and has its own 'explanation,' was completed in the fall, 1924. We can only conjecture what Lindsay's American-Egyptian hieroglyphics around the border mean, but they seem to tell a story that begins in the upper righthand corner and, Egyptian fashion, reads from right to left. The Eastern sun god Ra or Re — creator of the heavens and the seas, the light, and the soul — controls the rain and guides the soul through the rain and the god's own heavens and seas by means of a boat. The journey begins in the morning — at the top left — when the soul joins other souls and journeys through the hours of the day, across seas of blood (the secular blood shed in the efforts of materialism?), finally reaching the night (of the day and the soul) — in the lower righthand corner. Here, through crucifixion, the soul's blood, along with seas of blood from other martyred souls, causes the ship of the universe — and the ship of the soul itself — to return to a purer East (or Beginning of Beginnings), thus redeeming the soul and the universe through blood and sacrifice. The hieroglyphics (not in CP) at the bottom of the 'explanation' are clear: 'the living truth about the East as told according to the judgment of the scribe of Thoth, who uses the words of the West.' For Lindsay on hieroglyphics, see the note to GSu above; also see the "Explanation of 'The Map of the Universe'" in the Appendix.

497 ROOSEVELT: *1st* in *New Republic,* 14 May 1924; PP (4 April 1924); CP. The headnote is not in *1st*; the end note is not in *1st*, PP. The title in PP is "When the Stuffed Prophets Quarrel." As 1924 was an election year and April was a month of several primaries, the papers are filled with stories of political feuds, any one of which could have been the stimulus for the poem. My guess is that Wisconsin's Robert M. La Follette, who had refused to support Roosevelt in his Progressive bid for the Presidency in 1912 and now (1924) planned to run for President himself on the Progressive Party ticket, was one of the involved principals. The *St. Louis Post Dispatch* (4 April 1924), the day Lindsay claims to have written the poem, reports that Minnesota Governor Preus has warned of La Follette's third-party intentions. On 18 March 1923 Lindsay writes in his datebook (V): "It is assumed to be orthodox to tell small boys in the third grade they may reach the presidential chair. But it is also assumed to be fantastic to stimulate the ambition of the real leaders of America toward that office. Therefore it goes to dubs. Why not confess it a noble occupation to

stimulate the ambition of our real leaders of all types, toward the
Presidential Chair?'' For Lindsay on Roosevelt, see the note to ''In Which
Roosevelt Is Compared to Saul'' (above); also see Massa, pp. 217-219.
VARIANTS 26 that] the pride *1st* 29 Confucius, the] a brainy man *1st, PP*
38 tight] hot *1st, PP* 39 bark] howl *1st, PP* 61 Must . . . fade] They faded
1st, PP 63 *not in 1st* 65 Or by] On the phonograph—on the *1st, PP* 69-103
not in 1st 76 Yes,] In *PP* 81-90, 99 *not in PP* 97 *Extra line follows in PP:* Oh
poets, friends, and companions!

500 BABYLON, BABYLON, BABYLON THE GREAT: *1st* in *New York
Evening Post*, 25 May 1923; PP (17 November 1923); CP. In PP the
hieroglyphic picture is entitled ''Babylon, Babylon, Babylon, Babylon'';
the title of the poem is ''So Keep Going to the Sun: So Keep Going to the
Sun!'' A headnote in PP reads: ''But forever stands Babylon, fresh in the
sunrise, Foam upon the ocean---'' Lindsay's letters to Sara Teasdale
(UL-Y) reveal that the poem was completed in April 1923; two manuscript
versions (Y) indicate that the poet initially planned to chant some of the
lines to the tune of ''The Farmer in the Dell.'' VARIANTS 1 the jazz—]
Babylon *1st, PP* 7-14 *not in 1st, PP* 16 jazz—] proud *1st, PP* 22 bore . . .
sand] haunt the ruins *1st* 24 forever] always *1st* 24 fresh] there *1st* 31
Troubadour!—] Poet, you must *1st* 32 *not in 1st* 36 *not in 1st, PP* 37
against], once more, *1st, PP* 37 city's music,] city. *1st* 39-43 *not in 1st* 40
improvise] settle on *PP* 44 Improvise a] Sing the *1st, PP* 44 cactus] freedom
1st 45-56 *not in 1st* 52, 54 *not in PP* 57 clean] brave *1st* 61-62 *not in 1st* 66
old duster flapping] grey duster cutting capers *1st, PP* 67 prairie] eternal
1st, PP 68 *not in 1st, PP* 69 mighty] prairie *1st, PP* 70 *not in 1st*.

502 BOB TAYLOR'S BIRTHDAY. Lindsay's letters reveal that he began
the poem in December 1921, shortly after accepting the invitation of
Harvard's Professor G.H. Palmer to deliver the Phi Beta Kappa
commencement poem (the letter of acceptance is at Wellesley
College—dated 19 November 1921). The poem was read on 19 June 1922
and, in Lindsay's own words, it ''was a mess'' (UL to Katharine Lee Bates,
5 November 1923, at the New York Public Library, Henry W. and Albert
A. Berg Collection, Astor, Lenox and Tilden Foundations). In fact, ''So
Much the Worse for Boston'' (*q.v.*) was completed soon after. An entry in
Lindsay's datebook (UDB-V, 9 February 1923) reveals the poet's
awareness of the structural weakness of the poem: ''Bob Taylor poem
called: 'Two Poems in one—or Two Songs in One—the Song of Bob Taylor
and the vision of the coming of Avanel Boone.' '' During the summer of
1924, Lindsay undertook a revision of the poem; by September 28 the work
is finished and he writes Elizabeth Mann Wills(UL-P): ''You are the Fairy
Child Tennessee, who holds out her white hand and works miracles when
Bob Taylor plays. I wrote the Poem for the Harvard Phi Beta Kappa
Society, 1922, and she was Avanel Boone then. But in the last revision this
spring I remembered you at the Jackson Fair and changed her to The Fairy
Tennessee, and you must *now* prepare real blushes and get ready to be
sweet and enjoy it, for it's just about you, and more than one Tennessee
person will guess as much. You are described as the incarnation of your
state. . . .''

518 A SONG FOR ELIZABETH. The Elizabeth is Elizabeth Mann Wills; manuscript title (V): "The Psyche-Butterfly."

519 THE FLYING HOUSE, AND THE MAY QUEEN ETERNAL: *1st* in *New York Evening Post*, 13 June 1923; CP. Lindsay's mother died on 1 February 1922; in December of that year he writes in his datebook (V): "Write Dec. 21, 1922 to the bunch to sell the house if ready." Then, on 3 January 1923, we find this entry in his datebook (V): "I will live in Springfield in an invisible House, a flying house, that camps first on this corner and then on that. I will be the Flying Dutchman of the Prairie." Three months later—15 April 1923—he begins the poem. The May Queen is again Elizabeth Wills. In *1st* there is an extra stanza at the end:

Although you swoop off, alien and far
Smiling one smile a day, or maybe two,
So, once or twice, life comes, and better light.
Even that cautious smile, has hints of you.

520 BILLBOARDS AND GALLEONS: *1st* in *New Republic*, 10 September 1924; *London Mercury*, December 1924; CP. Although published later, the LM version is earlier than *1st*. The title in LM is "The Wrecks of the Galleons of Spain"; the headnote reads: "An improvisation, after reading Stephen Graham's 'In Quest of El Dorado.'" The LM version is very different from that in *1st* and CP; it does not include the first thirty lines or the last twenty-three; and there is no reference to the ancestral "Don Ivan." Other changes are relatively minor and too numerous to itemize; the following are from *1st*: VARIATIONS 49 glory wakes] my soul re-awakes 53 *not in 1st* 90 scorning] scaring 128-134, 144, 151-163, 175-176, 225-226 *not in 1st* 252 *Extra line follows in 1st*: Haughtily, patronizingly there, EMENDATIONS 61, 79 Came] Come 78 stare] store

526 HOW DULCENIA DEL TOBOSO IS LIKE THE LEFT WING OF A BIRD: in SP. Manuscript subtitle (V): "A reminiscence of the old Spanish Trail, Biloxi, Mississippi." A note in the margin reads: "This poem to be read aloud rapidly, till it becomes a song with its own vowel-tune, watching every vowel." See Ruggles, pp. 316-320.

527 THE PEARL OF BILOXI. Manuscript note (V): "After Swimming Into the Sunrise this morning, I Write this Song to My Lady, Who Just Would not Wake Up and Swim With me, But Was With me anyhow." On 29 June 1923 Lindsay writes in his datebook (V): "I want to write more physical poems: (1) about Riding Horseback, (2) about Modern Dancing, (3) about Swimming, (4) about Vaudeville Acts [that] might be offered to Indians."

528 DOCTOR MOHAWK: *1st* in *New Republic*, 5 December 1923; CP. For the significance of the poem vis-à-vis Lindsay's father, see Ruggles, pp. 33-34, 315, 432; Masters, pp. 10-11. On 5 November 1923 Lindsay writes Armstrong (p. 112) about "a most fierce poem called *The Mohawk*. Just a terrible poem to make timid ladies afraid." The poet's interest in his Mohawk ancestor begins to appear in his datebook (V) during the summer

of 1922, although the poem itself was not begun until the following year. The poem is not in SP, probably because Lindsay's letters to Sara Teasdale (UL-Y) reveal that by 1931 he considered the work a bad piece of writing. The version in *1st* is considerably different from that in CP; the following lines are not in *1st*: 2, 5, 10-17, 20, 28-32, 39-44, 50-53, 58-59, 65-66, 73, 75, 78-79, 88, 90, 92-93, 98-99, 105-115, 118, 120-121, 126, 129, 131, 133-134, 136-138, 155, 157-159, 162. There are also numerous verbal changes; the following are very selective: VARIANTS 19 snow] grave- 23 dawn] night 24 every] the front 60 Proud] Strange 60 a dream] vain 74 pillow] curls 80 white . . . and] roof open, and I saw the clouds 84 roared] said 96 I . . . all] But I cried, and held hard to her ribs 124 murder] desire 135 sky] sun Finally, there are six extra lines at the beginning in *1st:*

> You can tell any Englishman, the next time you see one
> Thus much of my undressed, delicate history: —
> I am no Anglo-Saxon. I am more of a mystery.
> As I woke in this world, singing and tingling,
> There were rumors in Springfield of a scandalous changeling
> Of a changeling who came with Fauntleroy curls.

533 THE TRIAL OF THE DEAD CLEOPATRA: *1st* in *American Mercury,* August 1924; SP. Fragments of this, the longest of Lindsay's poems, begin to appear in his datebook (V) as early as summer, 1922, and continue through all of 1923. The version in *1st* is very different from that in CP and SP, largely because Lindsay revised the work during the fall of 1924, after reading Arthur Weigall's book. On 26 October 1924 he writes Katharine Lee Bates (UL-V): "Cleopatra is now *much better* than in the American Mercury, being corrected by Arthur Weigall's splendid book about Cleopatra just published by Putnams, written on exactly the same point of view as the poem. It was a slow job—inserting *precise* history, yet *preserving* the poem." His efforts, though, must have pleased him, for on 3 February 1925 he advises Amabel Williams-Ellis that "a living, breathing Egyptologist, who can read hieroglyphics . . ., will testify that every line is good hieroglyphic idiom, whether it is good poetry or not, and in the light of this testimony which I cheerfully anticipate, I maintain it is the first verse in the English language which attempts to put the Egyptian idiom of the Book of the Dead into the Anglo-Saxon grand style" (Chénetier, pp. 341-342). Similar sentiments are expressed to John Drinkwater a few days later (16 February 1925), in Chénetier, p. 346. A study of *1st* reveals that Lindsay adds many details about Caesar, the Book of the Dead, and hieroglyphics in general. He also adds "The Terrace of a Million Years" and "the terrible lotos" (1. 457). The most significant change, however, is in the emphasis on Cleopatra as mother and on Caesarion as her son and the heir to Caesar. Overall *1st* is a shorter, less detailed poem. The following, all from CP, demonstrate that Lindsay continued to revise the work even after 1925: VARIANTS 47 Roman] Rome 59-60 *not in CP* 170 Assyrian] Hyksos 219 legions] regions 277 strong] iron 281-282 *not in CP* 316 shoulder,] heart. 386 nine] twelve 565 terrible] terrified

551 *From* THE VILLAGE MAGAZINE (4th Edition, Springfield, December 1925) [VM 4 is only a slight revision of VM 3. Several handlettered poems in VM 3 are here set in print, and two poems are added.]

553 FOR A "SOCIETY" GIRL: *1st* in *New Republic,* 2 September 1925; VM 4. The headnote is not in *1st.*

553 A SONG WHEN THE MAY QUEEN WAS ANGRY AND WICKED: *1st* in *New York Evening Post*, 29 June 1923; VM 4. The title in *1st* is "Written When the Eternal May Queen Was Angry." At the end of his 1923 datebook (V), Lindsay writes: "A man makes the choice between being the slave of a vain and tyrannical woman, and being the slave of his own outrageous egotism. He had infinitely better be the slave of the woman." About a year later, in a less charitable mood, he scrawls in a large hand: "Exactly why do some women turn into vinegar barrels?" (UDB-V, 3 October 1924).

555 GOING-TO-THE-STARS (New York: D. Appleton and Company, May 1926) [On 16 October 1924 Lindsay writes John L.B. Williams, his editor at Appleton, that he could send material for a new book, but that he wants to wait until Macmillan's *Collected Poems* is "clear off our hands, and off the market." He adds that he wants to make the Appleton book "an effervescent, light-hearted book, with some new material that is well considered and well thought-out, and it will require time and hard labor to do this" (UL-V). A letter from Elizabeth Lindsay, the poet's wife, to Sara Teasdale (UL-Y, Summer, 1926) confirms that the poems in GSt are largely from Lindsay's last bachelor days (they were married in May 1925). Elizabeth adds that the drawings were completed in two days, during the summer of 1925. For Lindsay on the Spencerian style of drawing, see "A Note by the Poet and Artist" in the Appendix; the preface to GSt, written after the poetry, is also in the Appendix.]

557 THESE ARE THE YOUNG: *1st* in *New Republic*, 25 March 1925; SP. Fragments of the poem begin appearing in Lindsay's datebook (V) in November 1922 and continue into January 1923. A headnote in GSt reads: "Dedicated to the Reverend Charles Pease: Minister of the Unitarian Society, Spokane, Washington"; a manuscript version (V) adds: "because of a recent sermon on giving the young their way and how Youth must be served." VARIANT 42 now *not in 1st, GSt.*

559 "OLD, OLD, OLD, OLD ANDREW JACKSON": *1st* in *New Republic*, 9 September 1925; SP. The title in *1st* has one less "Old"; the headnote and end note are not in *1st*. This, of course, is the "more serious rhyme about Jackson" that Lindsay planned after he completed "The Statue of Old Andrew Jackson" (see above). His datebooks reveal that he began thinking about the new poem as early as 1921, and then with increasing interest through all of 1922. On 8 May 1922 he writes: "I could have followed Andrew Jackson to the world's end: saying 'Lead on Old Blasphemer, Swear your way through stone walls'" (UDB-V). On 18

October 1922 he adds: ''The message of Jackson was simple, and old as the world—that is—that a man shall stand on his native worth and valor and the courage of his tongue, that he shall choose his own rank and no man but himself shall rank him. Most soldiers are cowards in thought and afraid of every comrade's opinion'' (UDB-V). Then, on 14 February 1925, Lindsay informs Sara Teasdale that he is about to begin a Jackson poem (UL-Y). A little more than a month later—20 March— he reports to Harriet Moody that his poem is finished (UL-V), and three days later he sends a draft version to Sara (UMs-Y). The version in *1st* is 185 lines shorter than that in GSt and SP; Lindsay probably began revising even before the publication of *1st*, since he advises Sara on 5 October 1925 that the version coming out in GSt is superior to that in *1st* (UL-Y). Besides numerous minor verbal changes, Lindsay considerably expands the roles of Rachel and John Calhoun in Jackson's thoughts, increases the specific detail relating Jackson's age, and gives much more vivid descriptions of Jackson's inaugural night and the appearances of his backwoods friends. The following are both from GSt: VARIANTS 186 young] so young 303 that] the

569 VIRGINIA: *1st* in *Spokane Daily Chronicle*, 25 December 1924; SP. A week after publication Lindsay writes Sara Teasdale that he feels the poem is the best he has ever done; he glories in it and advises her that it is his 'apologia pro vita sua' (UL-Y, 2 January 1925). A rough draft of the work appears in Lindsay's datebook (V) during the third week of April 1924. For Lindsay on Virginia, see ''The Virginians Are Coming Again'' below, and *The Litany of Washington Street*.

572 THE FLOWER-FED BUFFALOES: *1st* in *Saturday Review of Literature*, 7 March 1925; SP. The poem appears in rough form in Lindsay's datebook (V) on 18 April 1924. VARIANT 15 *not in 1st*.

572 THREE HOURS: in SP.

573 THE ANGEL SONS: *1st* in *New Republic*, 3 February 1926; GSt. VARIANTS 5 any we see] you or me *1st 30 extra line follows in 1st*: These earthly sons with weapons from heaven,

574 SUNRISE. In a manuscript version this work is clearly a sequel to ''Rain'' (below), and is entitled ''Sunrise Song in the High Mountains'' (UMs-V).

574 RAIN. See above; manuscript title is ''Rain in the High Mountains'' and the date is 26 April 1923 (UMs-Y).

574 WHAT THE WILD CRANE BROUGHT.

575 NANCY HANKS, MOTHER OF ABRAHAM LINCOLN: *1st* in *Spokane Daily Chronicle*, 18 January 1925; *New Republic*, 25 March 1925; SP. A headnote in *1st* reads: '' 'Nancy Hanks,' now published for the first time, was written by Vachel Lindsay, the poet of international reputation who is making Spokane his home. It was begun last year in Shreveport, La., and finished here recently. Mr. Lindsay is an authority on Lincoln,

having lived most of his life at Springfield, Ill. He says few people realize
the hardships of the life of Lincoln's mother and that people are apt to
forget the poverty from which Lincoln came. When Lincoln's mother was
alive they lived in the rudest sort of hut, a three-sided affair with a fire on
the fourth side to keep out wild animals and the cold.'' Fragments of the
poem appear in Lindsay's datebook in May 1924 (V). On 5 October 1925 the
poet writes his Princeton friend, Frances Charles Macdonald, sending a
copy of the poem with a note at the bottom: ''Do you remember I
improvised this as a toast, one of the few times I was allowed to sit next to
you at Gulf Park [Gulfport, Mississippi]?'' (UMs-P). Early manuscript title
(V): ''They Were Mothers.'' VARIANT 24 of] at *1st*.

576 THE JAZZ OF THIS HOTEL: in SP. Lindsay's datebooks reveal his
constant effort to shed the epithet 'jazz poet.' On 8 March 1923 he writes:
''To call me the Jazz Poet is to confuse the Yale Yell with the Yale Press
and the Yale Review; any reciting I have done has exactly the same relation
to my ten books that the Yale Yell has to the Yale Press and the Yale
Review'' (UDB-V). On 30 October of the same year he writes: ''The word
Jazz now means something—flip, snippy, 'fresh and smart alecky'—and I
wish no such mood read into my work. It is not an objection to a technical
description to musical experiments. It is the determination to wish on me
the Jazz attitude toward life. I do *not* believe in or follow people in the Jazz
state of mind'' (UDB-V). This poem and ''A Curse for the Saxophone'' (see
below) were written while Lindsay was staying at Spokane's Davenport
Hotel in the winter of 1924-1925.

576 A CURSE FOR THE SAXOPHONE: *1st* in *Spokane Daily Chronicle*, 16
December 1924; *Chicago Daily News*, 13 January 1925; SP. On 5 February
1925 Lindsay writes Henry Seidel Canby (UL-V): ''The cleverest man I
know, of first-class standing in the world of verse, who has no recognition
at all to fit his merit, is the local columnist here, Stoddard King. I wish you
fellows would all combine and discover him with a rush. I can furnish you
with all the evidence you want. The Chicago people would not believe he
cooperated with me in producing my recent 'Curse For The Saxophone,'
which started a series of interviews in the Chicago Daily News two columns
long, lasting more than a week. It has now slopped over into many middle
Western papers. They say I am abolishing the saxophone. I do not believe
it, but I somewhat resent the elimination of Stoddard King's name as
collaborator in producing the 'Curse For the Saxophone'. . . . He did his
full half in producing this rhyme. This 'Curse For The Saxophone' has been
one of the delightful surprises of my life in one way—that is, the great
sport the Chicago boys had out of it.'' VARIANTS 10 marched] went *1st*,
News 53 None . . . this] Let us forget this horrible *1st*, *News* 57 of . . .
seraphim] slow Romance and the slow great *1st*, *News*, *GSt* There is an
extra stanza following 20 in *1st*, *News*:

> When Joshua marched around the walls of Jericho,
> He gave his soldiers saxophones and ordered them
>   to blow,
> And the great walls shimmied, they shook their
>   shoulders
> Until they were heaps of second-hand boulders.

578 WHEN I WAS A TREE: in SP.

579 CELESTIAL TREES OF GLACIER PARK. For the hieroglyphics, see the note to GSu above; also see "The Time When Things Had Better Names" below.

581 THOSE CLOUDY RIDERS.

581 JACK-IN-THE-PULPIT.

582 LADY LONDON.

582 THE PANSY WEDDING. In April 1909 Lindsay was invited to the wedding of Laura and Willard Wheeler, his friend and fellow artist. At the time he did not have money enough to attend but sent, instead, a book of poems and drawings. This and the following are from that book, a copy of which is at LH.

583 THE FOUR SEASONS. See above.

583 THE SPOKANE APPLE FAIRY. Manuscript title (V): "Out of the Apple."

583 WARMING UP THE MOON.

584 THE MOTH AND THE UNICORN.

585 TWO POEMS GEOGRAPHICAL. Each is treated separately below.

585 HIEROGLYPHICS ON THE GULF OF MEXICO. For the hieroglyphics, see the notes to GSu and the second edition of "The Map of the Universe" above.

591 SASKATOON, SASKATCHEWAN. An early manuscript version (V) is dated "November, 1922"; a later manuscript (V) has the following headnote: "Suggested by the Christmas Tree on the Roof of the Davenport Hotel Spokane."

592 GEOLOGY.

592 THE MOUNTAIN ANGELS: in *Nature Magazine*, November 1926; GSt.

593 THE BLOSSOMS THAT HAVE CHERUB'S WINGS.

593 CELESTIAL FLOWERS OF GLACIER PARK. Lindsay's letters to his wife from 1928 to 1931 (V)—written while he was on recitation tours—refer to this work several times. The poem and the drawings were apparently completed on one obviously idyllic afternoon during their

honeymoon in Glacier Park, Summer, 1925. For an account of the honeymoon, see ''Going-to-the-Stars'' in the Appendix; for the drawings, see ''A Note by the Poet and Artist'' (also in the Appendix), especially the closing paragraph, and compare the drawings in CC below. The poet's letters also reveal that he was pleased with his audiences' reaction to his recitation of this work.

603 THE CANDLE IN THE CABIN: A WEAVING TOGETHER OF SCRIPT AND SINGING (New York: D. Appleton and Company, Fall, 1926) [On 29 November 1926 Elizabeth Lindsay writes John L.B. Williams at Appleton (UL-V): ''The copies of THE CANDLE IN THE CABIN have arrived, and we are very much pleased with them. They have the authentic Lindsay flavor, and our gratitude is due you for preserving it so faithfully. The pictures have come out really very well for the most part; and we have had a delightful two days gloating over the result of our summer before last in the Park.'' She adds that their interest in the book ''is by no means inconsiderable, as it is the first book written since our marriage.'' Indeed, nearly all of the poems and drawings in CC were completed during the summer of 1925: see ''Going-to-the Stars'' in the Appendix and Ruggles, pp. 345-347. Also see the preface of CC—''A Note by the Poet and Artist''—in the Appendix and ''Celestial Flowers of Glacier Park'' above.]

605 THE MOUNTAINS WITH STORMS FOR WAR-BONNETS: *1st* in *Pan, Poetry, and Youth*, April 1926; CC.

606 RISING WOLF: in *Saturday Evening Post*, 18 December 1926; CC.

608 THE HUNTING DOGS.

609 CONCERNING HIS INSIGNIA.

609 WORLD-MAPS.

610 THE HOUSE OF BOONE.

610 THE RANGER'S CABIN.

610 THE SNOW BY RISING WOLF PEAK.

612 THE CHILD-HEART IN THE MOUNTAINS.

612 THE BRIDE'S BOUQUETS.

613 BONNETS.

613 THE LADY-SLIPPERS.

614 THE PENNANT.

614 ''COEUR d'ALENE.''

615 THE HALL OF JUDGMENT.

616 THE PIGEON DRAGON-ROSE.

617 THE TWIN WATERFALLS. Compare the drawing and hieroglyphics
for "We Start West for the Waterfalls" above.

617 THE CURLING WAVES.

618 THE MOUNTAINS ARE THE MEMBERS OF OUR FAMILY.

618 THE BABBITT JAMBOREE: *1st* in *Pan, Poetry and Youth*, April
1926; *London Mercury*, January 1928; *Literary Digest*, 11 February 1928;
KMR, March 1928; *Christian Century*, 19 April 1928; CC. On a manuscript
copy (V—n. d.), Lindsay indicates to Harriet Moody that the poem is
"much misquoted." He explains: "Half-breed Indians, quarter breeds,
eighth breeds, sixteenth breeds, thirty-second breeds, are all referred to in
Western parlance as 'breeds.' Pure-blooded Indians are referred to as
'bloods.'" VARIANT 7 breeds] broods *LM,LD* EMENDATION 23 bred (as
in 1st, LM, LD)] bread

619 THE MOUNTAIN WITH WINGS: in *Saturday Evening Post*, 18
December 1926; NV; CC. The title in the *Post* and NV is "Red Eagle—The
Mountain with Wings." VARIANT 6 display . . . fantastic] keep saying
"Hooray! Hooray!" *Post*.

620 THE RED EAGLE LOVE SONG.

621 THE PARABLE OF DEEPNESS: *1st* in *Lyric West*, November 1925;
London Mercury, July 1927; CC.

623 THE BEE.

623 THE DRAGON FLIES.

624 PATHFINDER OF THE AIR. Captain Lowell H. Smith was one of two
Americans to complete the first flight around the world, leaving Santa
Monica, California, in mid-March 1924 and returning on 23 September—
shattering the then world's record. Manuscript title (V): "Circumnavigator
and Pathfinder of the Air."

624 BY THE MOHAWK'S BUCKSKIN DOOR. This is the first of the
poems in "The Mohawk Section" of CC; Lindsay's note for this section
reads: "I have used 'The Mohawk' in many previous poems, in other books
as a total symbol of all the Red Indian Tribes and all the Red Indian Gods
from the beginning to the end of time." The poet's letters to his wife from
1929 to 1931 (V) show that more and more he thought of his father and,
consequently, himself as manifesting Mohawk characteristics; also see
"Doctor Mohawk" above and "What Is the Mohawk?" below.

625 THE MOHAWK COMES.

626 CONCERNING THE MOUNTAIN IN GLACIER PARK CALLED "ALMOST A DOG."

627 THE RED INDIAN BRIDE. Manuscript title (V): "What the Forest Ranger Said about His Indian Ancestry."

628 THE FLYING PAPOOSES.

629 THE FOURTH RETURN TO SUN-MOUNTAIN: *1st* in *Pan, Poetry, and Youth*, April 1926; CC.

629 IDOL OF THE DEER.

630 THE GOLDEN ORCHIDS: *1st* in *Poetry Magazine*, April 1926; CC.

630 TO THE TALLEST ASPEN OF GLACIER PARK: *1st* in *Poetry Magazine*, April 1926; CC. The title in *1st* is "To the Tallest Aspen." On 4 August 1926 Lindsay writes his wife from Gunnison, Colorado: "Well the whole place is *Colorado*, which has a 'lost boom' character all its own in the back villages. And out in the country beautiful camping places, and above all the aspen tree—the aspen—the aspen—as only Colorado knows it. Some day I will sing the Colorado aspen. It is a thing all to itself. Elizabeth—I just *adore* aspens" (UL-V).

630 THE OLD MAIL COACH TO BELTON: *1st* in *Poetry Magazine*, April 1926; CC. See "Going-to-the-Sun" in the Appendix.

631 THE FAWNS AND THE STRANGER: *1st* in *Poetry Magazine*, April 1926; CC.

631 THE DEER OF QUARTZ RIDGE: *1st* in *Poetry Magazine*, April 1926; CC. Title in *1st*: "The Deer of Quartz Lake."

631 THE WRITHING, IMPERFECT EARTH: *1st* in *Poetry Magazine*, April 1926. See Ruggles, p. 347. VARIANTS 11 Standing] Naked *1st* 12 Yet] Yet now *1st* 13 wither] chance to wither *1st*.

632 BEGGING PARDON: *1st* in *Poetry Magazine*, April 1926; CC.

633 I SAW A ROSE IN EGYPT. Compare with the ending of "The Trial of Cleopatra" above.

633 WHEN YOU AND I WERE SINGERS IN THE MOUNTAINS: in *Saturday Evening Post*, 18 December 1926; CC.

634 THE HOUR OF FATE. See Ruggles, p. 347.

634 BY AN OLD UNLIGHTED CANDLE.

635 FINDING THE MYSTERIOUS CABIN. A manuscript note (V) indicates that this poem is "Prelude" to "The Journey to the Center of the Earth" below.

636 THE JOURNEY TO THE CENTER OF THE EARTH: *1st* in *Pan, Poetry, and Youth*, April 1926; CC. See above.

639 THE CANDLE IN THE CABIN. Manuscript title (V): "The Candle in the Shack."

642 BY THE OLDEST TRAILS: *1st* in *Pan, Poetry, and Youth,* April 1926; CC.

642 THE DRAGON FLY GUIDE: *1st* in *Poetry Magazine*, April 1926; CC. VARIANT 20 *repeated in 1st.*

643 WHY DO WE RETURN?

644 THE INDIAN GIRL—MY GRANDMOTHER.

644 BEHIND SUN-MOUNTAIN.

645 THE FOG COMES AND GOES.

646 A GREAT SHADOWY DAY: *1st* in *Poetry Magazine*, April 1926; CC.

646 THE BREATH OF THE WIND.

647 THE QUAIL RECEIVES A GUEST.

647 THE BABY THAT CAME FROM THE FERN.

647 THE TIME WHEN THINGS HAD BETTER NAMES: *1st* in *Pan, Poetry, and Youth*, April 1926; CC. This poem is, perhaps, the key to many of the little poems and drawings in Lindsay's last books. His interest lies in creating a United States hieroglyphic.

648 THE BAT.

651 ONCE MORE.

651 THE WHIRLWIND.

653 THE SUMMER ARROW OF SUNSHINE.

653 THE CRYSTALLINE CROWN.

654 THE RAT-SOULED FOE THE CITY FEARS: *1st* in *Poetry Magazine*, April 1926; CC. Compare with "The Firemen's Ball" above.

655 A MEMORY OF BOYHOOD.

655 THE CITY OF GLASS: *1st* in *Poetry Magazine*, April 1926; CC. On 2 May 1926 Lindsay writes to his wife from the interurban train to Racine, Wisconsin, where he is to recite. He is in a good mood and is reminiscing over the happy days of their honeymoon. He then concludes: "Those were sweet days, to remember and to be true to. They were clean like this May-day rain, all kisses. We *must* find ways to be gay the minute we get together again. I feel just like the afternoon and night on Flattop [mountain]—by the Lake Called the 'City of Glass,' etc." (UL-V).

655 THE PICTURE OF THE HEART-BOAT.

656 THE FISH WITH THE BRACELETS.

657 THE FIR-TREE.

657 THE APPLE TREE.

657 THE MUSICAL WIND.

658 THE DRIFTWOOD BED. Manuscript title (V): "The Little Driftwood Bed."

658 LIKE THEIR FATHERS OF OLD.

659 THE ASPEN LEAF LOVERS.

659 THREE LITTLE FLOWER-SHIPS.

660 THE MUSICAL BUTTERFLY.

660 THE STORM-BLOWN BUTTERFLIES.

661 THE PRAIRIE BUTTERFLY.

661 THE BUTTERFLY CITIZENS: in *Saturday Evening Post*, 18 December 1926; CC.

663 THE PROCESSION POLITICAL.

663 THE PRESIDENT.

663 SNOW-BORN BUTTERFLIES.

664 SEPTEMBER ENDED.

665 THE LEAVES FALL.

665 THE MOHAWK WAR-BONNET. Compare the poem and drawing with "The War-Path" in "The Five Seals in the Sky" below.

666 BUBBLES FROM BLACKFEET GLACIER FALLS.

666 ONE MORE SONG: *1st* in *Poetry Magazine*, April 1926; CC.

JOHNNY APPLESEED AND OTHER POEMS (New York: The Macmillan Company, December 1928) [The "Foreword" advertises this volume as "the first official selection from Lindsay for boys and girls" and as "an unusual record of a rare friendship." For, although JA offers no previously unpublished poems, the volume is illustrated with drawings and three color plates by George Mather Richards, Lindsay's close friend throughout his life, from the days they met at art school in New York. Richards also illustrated several of the poems in ESC (see below).]

667 EVERY SOUL IS A CIRCUS (New York: The Macmillan Company, October 1929) [The poems and drawings for ESC were largely done during the summer and fall of 1928. The story of the book involves the poet's wife, as a letter of 19 February 1929 reveals: "When I went through 'Every Soul is a Circus' last Sunday at New Canaan and found all your little faithful marks all through the book, and realized how much of it was the record of our combined blood, and not a single person, I was touched most deeply. I will *never* forget how you pulled that book through. I went down town about 3 P.M.—about Oct. 5 or 8—in as black despair and exhaustion as I have ever known. And I staggered back home about seven and found you had put *every inch* of the book in order, had been through it from end to end three times, and the sense of your *power to rescue* poor me was put into me for all time by that afternoon of vigil and returning to you. I was able to pack up the book and mail it at once. And if you *remember*, I was able then to go straight through the book for a final look-over myself as I packed it" (UL-V). Once at Macmillan the work was largely in the hands of two of Lindsay's close friends: George Mather Richards (see note to JA above) and Hazelton Spencer, who would edit *Selected Poems* (New York: The Macmillan Company, 1931). Their combined effort led to Lindsay's best printed volume; his pleasure is evident in a second letter to his wife, this one on 31 October 1929 (UL-V): " 'Every Soul is a Circus' arrived today, and Richards surely brought out a cracker jack of a book, including better paper and paging than in all my history, and the end-papers and the paper jacket and the design for the cover are whirlwinds. *I am delight-ed.*" Richards also provided many drawings for the work; the ones re-produced here, however, are all Lindsay's. The preface to ESC—entitled "Inscription for the Entrance to a Book"—is in the Appendix.]

669 EVERY SOUL IS A CIRCUS: *1st* in *Poetry Magazine*, October 1928; SP. Technically, the publication of this work in *Poetry Magazine* was not its first appearance in print, since it had been already published in the Kansas City *Star*; see Ruggles, pp. 380-381. The headnote and end note are not in *1st*. Lindsay's attitudes toward Barnum in the 1920s reflect the poet's

different moods. At one point he writes: "I hate Barnumism. I hate jazz" (UDB-V, 28 October 1924). In more playful moods, he loves to pun on the name, spelling it "Barnumb." But he also saw a seriousness in Barnum's show: "It seems to me Barnumb's live animals and three ring circus and band playing for the chariot races—are nearer to Emerson's Self-Reliance and American Scholar than Whitman's poems. A bridge can be built to the Ringling-Brothers and Barnumb and Bailey circus from The American Scholar—that approximates prophecy—and which gives the American Psychology [its] Rhythm—Chivalry and Rhyme—and Humor" (UDB-V, 15 May 1924). Fragments for a poem on Barnum and Jenny Lind begin to appear in Lindsay's datebooks as early as April and May 1924, but the poem was not finished until March 1928. On 27 March 1928 Lindsay writes William Lyon Phelps (UL-Y) that he has just completed his "bran new long poem Barnum and Jenny Lind." A manuscript version (V), with the title "Jenny Lind in Chicago," has the following headnote: "P.T. Barnum, creator of the U.S.A. unique three ring circus and the U.S.A. circus parade, had nevertheless for his chief glory something quite the opposite, that was taken in a far loftier spirit. He was the manager of Jenny Lind's marvelous popular singing triumphs clear across the United States in the forties and fifties." At the end of yet another manuscript (V), the poet notes: "Take Walk on Michigan Ave., till everything is precisely located." VARIANTS 62, 209 Victoriously] Dominantly *1st* 72 See,] Then *1st* 107 caves] souls *1st, ESC* 157-158 *in lieu of these lines 1st reads:*

> With his feet on the ground in Chicago,
> Invent those blatant stunts, undreamed of in the past,
> And would invent his own parade, and strut for
>   his little Yankee maid,
> And stand beside his mansion,
> In his own special wedding-animal-skins arrayed,
> Though he thinks he holds in his possession
> New tin Lizzies past description or expression . . .

181 Run, run,] We will hike *1st.*

675 A CHRIST CHILD BOOK: *1st* in *McCalls*, December 1927; ESC. The title in *1st* is "A Wild Fantasy about Christmas Moons." This work is one of several in ESC that reflect Lindsay's distaste for others' attempts or even requests to set his poems to music. Some of his reasoning is apparent from an entry in his datebook in late December 1925: "To ask to set my poems to music is like asking to saw off my leg and add a wonderful wooden leg of the composer's own invention. It utterly disregards the fundamental that words and music come to me at once—and are inseparable in my mind, and should be in the mind of the listener or reader. He who is unable to get these tunes with the words is so utterly insensible to the poem he should have nothing to do with it" (UDB-V). See also Ruggles, pp. 376-378.

676 RIGAMAROLE, RIGAMAROLE: in *The Poetry Quartos* (New York: Random House, 1929). The title in ESC is "Excuse Me if I Cry into My Handkerchief"; a headnote in ESC reads: "A story for mature infants and

immature older people." In revising the poem for the poetry quarto pamphlet, Lindsay adds the entire theme of "rigamarole" and all names except "Psaffonoff." VARIANTS 12 squall] fall *ESC* 47 song of adultery] sugared cacofony *ESC* 85, 90-91, 101-104 *not in ESC*.

680 A SWAN IS LIKE A MOON TO ME. In a letter to Harriet Moody on 2 April 1925, Lindsay indicates that this work is his "newest poem game" (Chénetier, p. 353). For this and the other poem games, see "The Poem Games" and "Inscription for the Entrance to a Book" in the Appendix.

681 THE RIM ROCK OF SPOKANE, PART I: *1st* in *Spokane Daily Chronicle*, 4 June 1928; PP (16 March 1929); ESC. The title in *1st* and PP is "Under Spokane's Brocaded Sun." PP is one of Lindsay's several rhyme sheets.

682 THE RIM ROCK OF SPOKANE, PART II: *1st* in *Spokane Daily Chronicle*, 5 June 1928; ESC. The title in *1st* is "For All the Youngsters in Spokane"; a headnote in *1st* reads: "To be hummed and chanted, but not to be set to music." VARIANT 42-43 *not in 1st*.

682 BUTTERFLY PICTURE-WRITING: *1st* in *Spokane Daily Chronicle*, Fall, 1924; ESC. The title in *1st* is "Butterfly Hieroglyphics"; see Ruggles, p. 330.

683 THE VOYAGE: *1st* in *Spokane Daily Chronicle*, Fall, 1924; ESC. See Ruggles, p. 330.

683 WHAT THE BEACH HEN SAID WHEN THE TIDE CAME IN: in *Christian Science Monitor*, 2 November 1929; *World Review*, 14 December 1929; ESC.

684 WHEN THE SUN ROSE FROM THE MARIPOSA LILY. Manuscript title (V): "When the Sun Rose from the Lily."

684 QUITE ENCHANTED.

684 ADDRESS TO A CANOE-BIRCH.

685 THE RED INDIAN WITCH GIRL.

685 WHAT IS THE MOHAWK? On 16 December 1928, when Lindsay was struggling to support his wife and his two children with yet another recitation tour, he writes home: ". . . you better believe the husband of your *bosom* (so to speak) is the son of old *V.T. Lindsay* [his father]. *He's* the buckaroo *who will pull us through*— The Mohawk, The Mohawk! I wish you had known the old boy. He sits inside my bones and smiles at these others! A buck with horns!" (UL-V). See "Doctor Mohawk" above.

686 THE MOHAWK IN THE SKY: *1st* in *Palms*, March 1928; ESC.

Manuscript note (V): "To be chanted very softly and very slowly and danced very slowly." VARIANT 13 *extra line follows in 1st*: A war of dreams on high!

686 BEHIND MOUNT SPOKANE, THE BEEHIVE MOUNTAIN. Headnote in manuscript (V): "(Directions just how to rear children)."

687 THE VIRGINIANS ARE COMING AGAIN: *1st* in *American Mercury*, July 1928; PP (c. 1929); NP; SP. PP is one of Lindsay's rhyme sheets; a headnote reads: "This song is to be chanted to your own unwritten troubadour chant, invented by yourself after reading it many times yourself aloud out-of-doors." On 27 March 1928 Lindsay advises William Lyon Phelps (UL-Y) that the work "is representative among my later pieces. It is from the heart! It looks like rhetoric on paper, but you will find an audience takes it well. It is in antithesis to 'So Much the Worse for Boston' [*q.v.*] and much simpler for the platform." Also see "Virginia" above. VARIANTS 39 Foreigners] Pitiful *1st* 98 Scribble] Set down *1st*.

690 THE LOCOMOTIVE DRAGON-HIPPOGRIFF: *1st* in *Spokane Daily Chronicle*, 1928 (reprinted 14 January 1931); ESC.

691 THE CLOCKS THAT I LIKE BEST.

691 THE MOON IS A FLOATING SEA-SHELL.

691 THE RANGER'S HOUND DOG. A manuscript title (V) is "The Hound Dog"; a note at the bottom indicates that Lindsay intended a drawing of the dog. The couplet is in Lindsay's datebook (V) under 28 March 1924.

691 A HIGH-SCHOOL NATIONAL SONG. See Graham, pp. 172-174.

693 THREE RED INDIANS. For Chief Joseph, see note for "The Song of My Fiftieth Birthday" below.

693 ON PORCUPINE RIDGE: *1st* in *Pan, Poetry, and Youth*, April 1926; ESC. This is the first of the poems that comprise "Part Two"—entitled "Every Mind"—of ESC; the final poem of the part is "The Flying Papooses Are Boys and Girls with Wings" below. A note for the part reads: "Containing a discussion of the clowns of the mountains, the deep-woods clowns, and the funniest part of the forest menagerie." The shorter verses were all accompanied by drawings, some of which were rejected by Macmillan and are apparently lost. Whereas many of the drawings for GSt and CC are based on letters of the alphabet (see note for "Celestial Flowers of Glacier Park" above), these drawings in ESC are based on names (see the note for "Concerning the Mouse with Two Tales" above). Manuscript notes (V) indicate, for example, that the "picture-whimsy" parrot in "Mike Whaler and the Parrot" (below) was originally intended for "'How' and 'How'" (also below) and is based on the name "Elizabeth" turned upside down. Other likely names for the drawings in ESC are the names of the poet-artist's children: Susan and Nickey. Generally, the drawings were made first and the verses written as imaginative interpretations after.

694 THE CALICO CAT.

695 THE WICKED POUTER PIGEON.

696 FRIEND FOREST-HORSE.

696 INTERLUDE: DO NOT STUFF THEM WITH CHILDREN'S SONGS: in SP. An early version of this work is written on both sides of an envelope (V) postmarked "July 30, 1927."

697 "HOW" AND "HOW." Manuscript date (V): "1927."

698 IF YOU ARE A MOUSIE.

699 THE PET ELK.

699 THE WILD FOREST DUCK.

700 MIKE WHALER AND THE PARROT. See the note for "On Porcupine Ridge" above.

701 THE FUR-BACKED SKATE FISH.

701 THE BREAKFAST AND DINNER TREES.

701 THE EAGLE HEN.

702 THE WHISTLING MARMOT.

703 THE FERN CALLED: "THE GRASSHOPPER'S GRANDMA."

703 ROBINSON CRUSOE'S PARROTS.

703 THE INFORMATION BUREAU. A manuscript (V)—with the title "Tourist Information Bureau"—indicates that this work once had an extra stanza:

> "The glaciers brought all the rocks to this place,
> This picnic place on the mountain's face."
> "Where are they now?"
> The old girl sighed.
> "Gone back for more rocks,"
> The cowboy replied.

703 THE THIRSTY PUPPY'S DREAM.

704 A SNAIL PARADE.

706 THE WOOD-SQUEAK.

706 THE TREE-CLIMBING FISH.

706 MY TREE TOAD.

707 THE WATERFALL THAT SINGS LIKE A BACCHANTE.

707 THE POWERFUL SQUIRREL.

707 THE WICKED OLD TREE.

707 HOW WE PAPOOSES PLANT FLOWERS.

708 THE WHALE WE SAW.

708 BEWARE OF THE SILVER GRIZZLY: in *Spokane Daily Chronicle*, 2 February 1931; ESC.

708 MISTER CHIPMUNK: *1st* in *Pan, Poetry, and Youth,* April 1926; ESC. The title in *1st* is "The Powerful Chipmunk."

710 THE SMOKE LION.

710 THE GLACIAL FLEA.

710 THE CAULIFLOWER WORM.

711 ROBINSON CRUSOE'S MONKEY.

711 CONCERNING A WESTERN MOUNTAIN SHAPED LIKE A WHALE. Manuscript title (V): "Concerning Whale Creek and Whale Butte."

711 THE FLYING PAPOOSES ARE BOYS AND GIRLS WITH WINGS. See note for "On Porcupine Ridge" above.

712 ON ENTERING A MORE SOLEMN FOREST. This is the prefatory poem for the final part—entitled "Every Heart"—of ESC; a headnote for the part reads: "This section is for Campfire girls, for Boy-Scouts and for us all."

712 WHEN WE PLUNGE INTO THE WILDERNESS.

713 MEETING OURSELVES.

714 MY LADY, DANCER FOR THE UNIVERSE. Manuscript titles (V): "Education as a Pleasure and a Culture and a Source of Fantasy" (in this version the lady's name is Elizabeth); "The Circus Called 'The Universe'"; and "My Lady, Hostess to the Universe." Manuscript date (V) is "December 1927." On 1 May 1926 Lindsay interrupts a letter to his wife, indicating that he is going to "investigate" the May-day revel in Chicago, where he is to give a recitation. Upon returning to his hotel room and again taking up the letter, he reports: "Well—I sat around an hour

waiting for 'em to revel, and they didn't, so I came up stairs. I sat there
alone thinking of you and how you are the only girl I ever knew who cared
enough about me to sweetly flatter me into dancing whether I could or not''
(UL-V).

715 THE SICK EAGLE: in *Spokane Daily Chronicle*, 28 January 1931;
ESC.

716 THE SONG OF MY FIFTIETH BIRTHDAY. Manuscript title (V):
''Apocalypse of the Davenport Roof''; a shortened version of the poem
(UMs-V) is entitled ''The Song of Spokane (and the Return to Springfield
Illinois).'' Sacajawea was the Indian woman who accompanied Lewis and
Clark on their famous expedition (1804-1806); Chief Joseph, leader of the
Nez Percé tribe, led his people on an unsuccessful campaign against the
United States in 1877. See ''My New Singer, Sacajawea'' below.

724 TWENTY YEARS AGO: *1st* in *Palms*, December 1928; SP. An end
note in *1st* reads: ''While this poem was only recently finished, it is a
record of the mood in which I gave up art study in New York, 1908.''
Manuscript titles (V) are: ''I Will Certainly Do as I Please'' and ''My Letter
to the Earl of Chesterfield.'' A headnote in the latter reads: ''Remember-
ing February 7, 1755''—the date of Samuel Johnson's famous letter on
patronage addressed to the Fourth Earl of Chesterfield. Lindsay then
quotes the final paragraph of Johnson's letter at the end of the manuscript,
signing his own name. For the story behind the 200 building blocks, see
Fowler, pp. 184, 194-195; Lindsay returned the blocks to the Wines family
in October 1909. ''Loami'' (1. 19) is a small community just west of
Springfield. VARIANTS 5, 105 in due time] half a lifetime *1st* 6, 106
Remembering] Not before *1st* 23 to make] of small- *1st* 34, years . . . ago].
It seemed good to me *1st* 36 know] see *1st* 44 how *not in 1st* 63 You] But you
1st 81 You] Or *1st* 87 two *not in 1st* 117 I reject] And I damn *1st*
EMENDATION 29 shake; (as in *1st*)] shake

728 THE FIVE SEALS IN THE SKY. The five drawings appear at the
bottom of several of Lindsay's late rhyme sheets: ''Under Spokane's
Brocaded Sun'' (see ''The Rim Rock of Spokane, Part I'' above) and ''The
Virginians Are Coming Again'' for example. The five poems are treated
separately below.

728 SUNRISE.

729 THE WAR-PATH: in *Spokane Daily Chronicle*, 8 November 1930;
ESC.

729 THE BOOK-PATH: in *Spokane Daily Chronicle*, 13 November 1930;
ESC. VARIANT 1 wolves] squirrels *SDC*.

730 SUNSET: in *Spokane Daily Chronicle*, 17 November 1930; ESC.
VARIANT 8 sing the] wake with *SDC*.

730 THE MOON-PATH: in *Spokane Daily Chronicle,* 20 November 1930;
ESC. VARIANTS 2 dream] lie in *SDC* 7 swift] their *SDC.*

SELECTED POEMS OF VACHEL LINDSAY (New York, The Macmillan
Company, January 1931) [Edited with an introduction by the poet's friend,
Hazelton Spencer, SP is part of "The Modern Readers' Series." The
"Introduction" indicates that the text of the volume "incorporates the
poet's latest revisions" (p.x). A letter to Sara Teasdale (UL-Y, 21 March
1931) reveals, however, that Lindsay himself did not read the proof
sheets—to his regret, it would seem. There are no previously unpublished
poems in the volume.]

733 OTHER PUBLISHED POEMS [The poems that follow were published
or were intended for publication by Lindsay himself; none, however, was
included in any of his books.]

735 AT NOON ON EASTER-DAY: in *Critic,* April 1905. The poem is
hand-lettered—all in capitals—and incorporated into a drawing, much like
"The Queen of Bubbles" (*q.v.*).

735 THE DANCE OF UNSKILLED LABOR: in AL; PP (November 1908). In
early summer, 1903, Lindsay mailed a copy of the poem to Springfield's
Mary Humphrey. The manuscript title (LH) is "A Poor Orchestra" and the
date given is "Sept. 1902." A note on the manuscript reads: "Poor
stuff—except the last two lines. I had *not seen* any such dancers till last
Saturday night. So the poem is at last made good." PP is for Lindsay's
YMCA lectures on "composite citizenship" (see "On the Building of
Springfield" above). The lectures began on 14 October 1908 and dealt with
what Lindsay felt to be the inherent qualities and values of each race and
how these are perverted in American society. The opening lecture on "The
Indian," for example, contrasted "His Native Genius: War Paint and
Feathers" with his "American Calling: Farming and Football." Lecture
five, on 11 November, compared the black's "Native Genius:—Sorrow
Songs; Folk Lore; Oratory; Sense of the Picturesque; Minstrelsy" with his
"American Calling: Professor of the Whisk Broom." "The Dance of
Unskilled Labor," called a "Vision" in PP, was printed for the 25
November lecture on "The Italians," with the further title: "Will These
People, the Greatest Painters of History, Do Nothing Here But Sell Fruit?"
A note with the poem reads: "Our unskilled laborers, though they come
from nations with a mighty past, are coarse revellers after business hours.
How they work! How they drink! How they save! How squalid they are! Yet
they have future civilizations hidden in them seven times better than
ours." Several of Lindsay's watercolor posters for the series are extant
(V).

735 THE MOON IS COMPARED TO A CITY: in *Poetry Magazine,* July
1913.

736 THE MOON IS A KNIGHT IN ARMOR: in *Poetry Magazine,* July
1913.

736 THE RECREANT QUEENS: in *Poetry Magazine*, July 1913.

737 WHAT THE YOUNG RHYMER SAID: in *Poetry Magazine*, July 1913.

737 THE MOON IS A BOOK: in *Reedy's Mirror*, 12 June 1914.

738 THE CHANDELIER: in *Reedy's Mirror*, 12 June 1914.

738 WHAT THE MISER SAID: in *Reedy's Mirror*, 12 June 1914.

738 THE MOON IN FOREIGN COUNTRIES: in *Reedy's Mirror*, 12 June 1914.

739 GIRL, YOU SHALL MOCK NO LONGER: in *Little Review*, June 1914. Lindsay's letters to Sara Teasdale (Y) reveal that the poem was written in the winter of 1912-1913, after Lindsay broke with Octavia Roberts. The original title was "The Proud Lady." Compare "A Song When the May Queen Was Angry and Wicked" above.

739 MY MIDDLE NAME: in *Chicago Herald*, 26 August 1914; *Little Review*, September 1914. VARIANT 3-4 *not in Herald*.

740 THE GOODLY, STRANGE LANTERNS: in *Chicago Herald*, 27 August 1914. A Lindsay letter to Sara Teasdale (UL-Y, 7 August 1914) mentions a new poem on the movies. Also see AMP, Chapter XV.

741 THE WOMAN-VOTER COMES: in *Chicago Herald*, 30 August 1914.

742 SATURDAY NIGHT IN THE PARK: in *Chicago Herald*, 5 September 1914. The 7 August letter to Sara Teasdale (see "The Goodly, Strange Lanterns" above) indicates that this poem was written about the same time as "General William Booth Enters into Heaven" (*q.v.*); the original title was "The Band Playing in the Park Saturday Night." Also see "The Village Improvement Parade" above.

743 THE ANGLO-SAXON LANGUAGE: in *Chicago Herald*, 9 September 1914. A manuscript copy of the poem was sent to Sara Teasdale on 13 April 1914 (UL-Y).

744 ST. FRANCIS: in *Chicago Herald*, 11 September 1914. See "The Voice of St. Francis of Assisi" in Vol. 1, p. 397.

744 THE MAGGOT, THE HYENA AND THE JACKAL: in *Chicago Herald*, 13 September 1914. This and the following poem were written in the rush of war poems that Lindsay produced in the late summer and early fall, 1914; see the note to Cg above. The following is from the author's own corrections on a copy of the poem in a scrapbook (V): EMENDATION 8 others follow] other fellows

745 BUDDHA WAS A PRINCE: in *Chicago Herald*, 14 September 1914. See above. The following is from the same scrapbook: EMENDATION 7 touched . . . austere] cleansed men's hearts with austere love

745 THE CHRISTMAS SHIP: in *Chicago Herald*, 27 September 1914. In the fall of 1914, James Keeley, editor of the *Chicago Herald*, organized a Christmas ship to carry presents to the unfortunate children of war-ravaged Europe; the ship sailed on 10 November. Several months later Henry Ford made plans for his famous Peace ship, which was to have sailed in the fall of 1915. Lindsay was one of the many invited to go; he declined. See "We Cannot Conquer Time" above.

748 WHAT THE BURRO SAID: in *Chicago Herald*, 7 May 1915.

748 WHAT THE SAILOR SAID: in *Chicago Herald*, 7 May 1915. The following are Lindsay's own (see note to "The Maggot, the Hyena and the Jackal" above): EMENDATIONS 2 Jezebel] street wench 7 gal] Sal 8 them . . . sorrowful] midnight wonderful 10 By the house] This child

748 WHAT THE COURT JESTER SANG: in *Chicago Herald*, 7 May 1915.

749 WHAT THE CLOCK-MAKER SAID: in *Chicago Herald*, 7 May 1915. Lindsay's scrapbook (see above) indicates that he considered deleting the second stanza; other changes: EMENDATIONS 9 wheat] corn 12 the race] all men

749 "OH WISDOM IN THE WINTER": in *Christian Century*, 10 April 1919. In ChC the work is untitled; on 1 August 1914 Lindsay informs Sara Teasdale that he has written a new road poem for her (UL-Y).

750 WHY IS A MOUSE WHEN IT SPINS?: in *New York Evening Post*, 20 July 1922. This and the following poem were printed in Christopher Morley's column, "The Bowling Green," which began in the *Post* on 9 February 1920 and ran through 1923.

750 I LIKE NANCY BOYD: in *New York Evening Post*, 22 July 1922. See above. On 22 April 1926 Lindsay writes his wife (UL-V): "I see this whole land as a unit. I have traveled over it so much — and a thousand songs and drawings have almost reached the surface about it. There is something in me that *is* patriotic, I just can't help it, and I see the whole land as a unit from the very beginning. Patriotism, like love, is a most imperfect passion, and surely I have it, with all its imperfections."

753 THE NAVY AND MARINE MEMORIAL: in *Literary Digest*, 7 March 1925. The editor of LD indicates that the poem was first published in the New York *Herald Tribune*.

754 THE RHINOCEROS AND THE BUTTERFLY: in *New Republic*, 25 March 1925. The "butterfly child" is Elizabeth Mann Wills; see "A Song for Elizabeth" above.

754 THE DOVE OF NEW SNOW: in MsAP, 1927.

755 WE WILL SAIL IN HENDRIK HUDSON'S HALF-MOON FOR SINGAPORE: in MsAP, 1927. This work reflects the poet's trip East with his new wife—in the fall of 1925.

756 WHEN LINCOLN CAME TO SPRINGFIELD: in MsAP, 1927.

756 MANHATTAN, 1927: in MsAP, 1927. Despite the date, this poem could very probably have been written in late 1925.

757 WHERE MY LADY SLEEPS: in MsAP, 1927. One of Lindsay's first poems to his wife Elizabeth; manuscript date (V): "1925."

757 RETURNING TO SPRINGFIELD: in MsAP, 1927. Lindsay and his wife spent the Christmas holidays, 1925, in Springfield.

758 BLOWING UP HELL-GATE: in MsAP, 1927. The original poem (V) is written on the "Beverage" menu of the Hotel Brevoort in New York City. Lindsay's cup of coffee cost him twenty-five cents!

758 A REMARKABLE STORY FROM KOKOMO, INDIANA: in MsAP, 1927. A note on the original manuscript (V) indicates the poem was written in Toronto on "December 8, 1925."

759 THE FREER GALLERY, WASHINGTON, D.C.: in MsAP. Manuscript title (V): "The Whistler Art Gallery, Washington, D.C."

759 THREE ROOSTERS: in MsAP, 1927.

760 WILD CATS: in MsAP, 1927. A manuscript note (V) indicates that the poem was written on the Lindsay's first Thanksgiving together (1925).

761 OUR LITTLE NEW CAVE-MAN: in PP (September 1927); *Illinois State Register,* 13 November 1927. Written for the poet's son—born in Spokane, Washington on 16 September 1927. "Cave" is an old Lindsay family name. PP is another Lindsay rhyme sheet.

762 THE TALL FIFTH MONARCHY MAN: in *Forge,* Fall, 1929. This late poem, with several images that suggest "The Map of the Universe" (*q.v.*), manifests Lindsay's continuing love for Milton. Indeed, his letters show that he was studying *Paradise Lost* in the very last months of his life. See Masters, pp. 327-329.

766 THE EZEKIEL CHANT: in PP (October 1930). An end note on a manuscript version of the poem (V) reads: "First read at the installation of President Kenneth I. Brown, Hiram College, October 10th, 1930, Hiram, Ohio." Upon the occasion, Lindsay was awarded the honorary degree of Doctor of Literature. On a copy of the poem sent to his wife (V), Lindsay

writes: "I wrote, typed and mailed this before rereading the first chapter of Ezekiel, which I had not seen for years. I was afraid I would put too much in if I read him."

768 THE DUNCE-CAP ON THE GHOST: in *Nation*, 26 November 1930.

768 POP SPINK AND THE MICE HAVE A CHRISTMAS: in *New York Evening Post*, November 1930; *Literary Digest*, 6 December 1930. On 25 October 1930 Lindsay advises his wife that he has written a Christmas poem for Susan and Nickey, their two children (UL-V). The next day he informs her that he is revising the poem and adds: "It is the first time in my life I have caught the mood of Susan and Nickey, but I think I have it" (UL-V, 26 October 1930). "Pop" or "Mr. Spink" seems to have been a pet name the poet used for himself in relation to his children.

770 THE JAZZ AGE: in *Liberty*, 21 February 1931; KMR, June 1931. On 1 February 1930 Lindsay writes his wife that *Liberty* has asked for a one-page poem on the jazz age (UL-V). In December 1930, after *Liberty* purchased the poem for $250, Lindsay's letters reveal that he is well aware that his poem is not exactly what the editors of the magazine expected. Manuscript title (V): "All Hail—Jazz Age."

772 BALLAD OF THE ARIZONA SHERIFF: in Macmillan's *News Review*, 2 March 1931. Manuscript note (V): "First draft written at Flagstaff, Arizona—Dec. 12, 1930"; a headnote reads: "A Talkie Scenario." When the poem was sent to the publisher, Lindsay gave the option of including or deleting a last line: "Chicago, do you understand?" The publisher's decision is obvious.

774 BALLAD ON HOW TO WRITE A POEM: in *Illinois State Register*, 8 March 1931; *The Writer's 1931 Year Book and Market Guide*. For Stoddard King, see the note to "A Curse for the Saxophone" above. The poem may have been written for the occasion of King's visit to Springfield, in January 1931. Manuscript title (V): "Write Your Poem if You Can."

776 FASHION PLATES FROM WHIMSYLAND: in *Child-Life*, April 1931. Compare "Fashion Plates from Fairyland"—see the note for "The Tramp's Excuse" above.

776 THE TEENSEY WHALE: in *Child-Life*, April 1931.

777 THE MAGNANIMOUS SUN: in *Child-Life*, April 1931.

777 THE PHILOSOPHER: in *Ladies' Home Journal*, October 1931. Except for sporadic periods of dissatisfaction and despair—most of them quite understandable and nearly all, it seems to me, quite normal—Lindsay's "philosophy" remains remarkably consistent throughout his creative life. It is perhaps best stated at the close of a letter to his wife: "I *believe* in the human race, in the perfectibility of mankind, in the virtue of keeping a

tender and innocent heart, and I will *not* be downed by cormorants and croakers. I am going to love the heart of the world to the end, and whoever tries to make a cynic of me is wasting his breath'' (UL-V, 4 March 1930). Also see "Time Gives Me Strength Each Hour" below.

780 MENTOR GRAHAM: in *Illinois State Journal*, 8 November 1931. A headnote for the poem reads: "Lincoln arrived in New Salem, a very young man, one hundred and one years ago. Mentor Graham was there before him, and remained after he left for Springfield in 1837. As Lincoln progressed in his studies in New Salem, Graham tutored him in subjects from grammar to surveying, and Lincoln was a frequent caller at the school house." The poem is, of course, a revision of an early Lindsay work: "The Lamp in the Window" (*q.v.*). See also "When Lincoln Came to Springfield" above.

781 EPITAPH FOR HENRY FORD: in *English Review*, March 1932. As "Mentor Graham" above, this work is an early poem revised—see "We Cannot Conquer Time" above.

781 IS WISDOM SUCH A THING?: in *Poetry Magazine*, July 1932. This and the following five poems were published together, under the title "Poems He Left Us." In the "News Notes" of the issue, probably written by Harriet Monroe herself, we read: "We are fortunate in being able to present this month a group of unpublished poems by the late Vachel Lindsay, whose sudden death last December, in his fifty-third year, was a profound shock to his friends and a serious loss to the art. While none of the poems we offer will ever rank with some that we published and gave him prizes for during the first five years of our history, yet they throw side-lights upon his personality and his development as an artist." One of the "side-lights" may be seen in this poem: Lindsay's letters in the latter years manifest a hatred for psychoanalysis, and it is very probable that this is what the "Wisdom" in the work is meant to be.

782 TO A GIRL IN A SUN SUIT: in *Poetry Magazine*, July 1932.

783 WHEN I GAVE MY LADY A DOUBLE ROSEBUD: in *Poetry Magazine*, July 1932. This work probably dates back to Lindsay's Gulf Park years, in which case the "lady" is Elizabeth Wills.

783 THE POET IN THE ORCHARD OF ART: in *Poetry Magazine*, July 1932. Since publication of volume two, I have seen a manuscript (Hiram College) that dates this work 1901-1903, Lindsay's art school days in Chicago.

784 IN MEMORY: in *Poetry Magazine*, July 1932. Manuscript note (V): "To Frances Frazee Hamilton, his mother's youngest sister."

784 EPITAPH FOR JEB STUART: in *Poetry Magazine*, July 1932. James Ewell Brown—"Jeb"—Stuart, famous Confederate cavalry officer during the Civil War, was wounded by Sheridan's men at Yellow Tavern, 11 May 1864, and died the next day. The poem reflects Lindsay's love for the

rebellious South — a love that is expressed more and more in the poems and letters of his later years. Manuscript title (V): "Epitaph for This Violet."

785 UNPUBLISHED POEMS AND JUVENILIA [Poems included here are largely of biographical interest; except for a few late works, Lindsay himself had no intention of publishing any of these.]

787 COME. The manuscript (V) is done in the careful, shaky hand of a child, signed "Vachel" and dated "July 31, 1890." The poem is printed exactly the way it is written; the spelling and punctuation are young Lindsay's.

787 THE EASTER-PRAYER OF A WHITE ROSE TO AN EASTER LILY. A manuscript copy (LH) is signed "Nicholas Vachel Lindsay" and dated "Spring, 1897."

788 THE NONSENSE TREE. A manuscript copy owned by Catharine Ward, Lindsay's niece, is dated "1898." The version of the poem here is from an undated drawing and poem (V) given to Arthur Paul Wakefield, Catharine's father, perhaps in 1904, on the occasion of his marriage to Olive Lindsay, Vachel's sister.

789 ASTARTE. The manuscript copy (LH) is signed "Nicholas Vachel Lindsay, Stamford, Colorado" and dated "August '98." An end note reads: "Notice — this is unmendable: it is such an intricate mixture of good and bad."

789 WHEN LIFE GREETS LIFE. The manuscript (LH) is signed and dated "Summer 1900."

790 SONG OF THE MICHIGAN WAVES. The manuscript (LH) is signed and dated "Chicago 1901."

791 THE GREAT SUPPER. A typescript of the poem (LH), obviously from Lindsay's older sister, Olive Lindsay Wakefield, has an authorial end note: "The proudest passage of The Great Supper, copied to inspire my sister on her birthday, October 10th 1901. It may not inspire, but it represents the most inspired effort of her brother to be inspiring."

791 FAREWELL TO CHRISTMAS. The manuscript (LH) is signed and dated "February, 1902."

791 THE IDOL AND THE GHOSTS: in AL. A manuscript copy (LH) has the following authorial note: "Copied for Miss Humphrey April 6, 1902." Mary Humphrey was the daughter of Springfield's Judge J. Otis Humphrey.

792 THE MYRAPOSA LILY. The manuscript (LH) is signed and dated "Nov. 2, 1902."

792 THE SONG OF THE TEMPLE SPARROWS AFTER THE TEMPLE
FELL: in AL. Two authorial notes read: "Written by the Painter, vexed by
flabby, practical, cheap-minded, pious co-workers"; and "Vexed also by
the inert conventional commercialists who have enough religion to make
them hypocrites." A manuscript copy (LH), with the title "The Song of
Devout Sparrows and Swallows—After the Temple Was Last Overthrown"
and dated "Jan. 20, 1903," also has an authorial note: "I rather like the
next to the last line. The rest is rather dull, though I think I will like it some
day." The next-to-last line then read: "That are sweetest after Springtime
Showers!"

793 TO MARY OF BETHANY. The manuscript copy (LH) is signed and
dated "January 1903." An authorial note reads: "I think this is about what
I meant by recommending Morris to you.—As to Christ being a Romeo—I
am rather fascinated by my own shocking heresy—by the *originality* of its
form, rather than its heresy and in my unpoetic hours I continue
orthodox!" The "you" is Mary Humphrey (see above).

794 SONS OF THE MIDDLE WEST: in AL. An authorial note reads: "It is
fitting that Arnold be called *Almost Forgotten*, that Lincoln be called
Always Remembered" (see Lindsay's poem "To Matthew Arnold"). A
manuscript copy of "Sons of the Middle West" (LH), signed and dated
"Feb. 2, 1903," has the following note: "I have marked the line I like [10].
Otherwise the sentiment and not the treatment interests me. And *of course*
such a poem marks the *first stage* of an ultimate surrender to the better
things the East has for us!"

794 THE SOUL OF LINCOLN. The manuscript (LH) is signed and dated
"1903." A note reads: "This poem was written for a picture of the Son of
Freedom hurling down a censer—while Freedom and her two daughters
remain in the background shading their eyes." Apparently, the picture is
lost.

796 LET US RISE AND SING. The manuscript (LH) is signed and dated
"Jan. 1, 1904."

796 MIDNIGHT ALLEYS. The manuscript (LH) is signed "Nicholas
Vachel Lindsay, 345 West 57—New York City" and dated "January 17,
1904."

797 THE FIVE DRAGONS. The manuscript (LH) is undated, but a letter to
Sara Teasdale reveals the poem was written in 1909 (see Carpenter, p.
299). Lindsay wrote the poem to accompany five large oil paintings of the
dragons; four of these are extant (V). One of the four is reproduced as the
frontispiece for volume two of this edition.

798 PARENTS. The manuscript was sent to poet Anna Hempstead Branch
during the summer of 1911, as part of a "home-made book." A copy is in
the Lindsay home.

799 I TURNED MY HEAD AWAY. The manuscript (V) is undated.

799 WRITTEN FOR THE EUCALYPTUS TREES. These verses are included as an example of a typical Lindsay book inscription. They are from the front endpaper of a copy of *The Chinese Nightingale and Other Poems* (LH) and follow a note in the poet's hand: "To Miss Hope Traver with the good wishes and admiration of Nicholas Vachel Lindsay, San Francisco, 1920." A headnote for the poem reads: "Where we held our Sunday Picnic: April 25, 1920."

800 THE MASSACRE. The manuscript (V) is undated, but the poem probably reflects the aftermath of Lindsay's love for Isadora Bennett.

802 GOING TO THE SUN. WATERFALLS, REMEMBERED LONG AFTER. The manuscript (V) is undated, but the work was obviously intended for GSu, perhaps as the introductory poem (see "We Start West for the Waterfalls" above). The "sermon" "at the Book's far end" is probably "Avanel Boone Flies from the Hearthfire with an Escort of Flying, Flaming Books" below.

802 "NOW COMES A CARTOON LETTER." The manuscript (V) is undated and untitled, but the work reflects Lindsay's pride in the drawings for GSu, his first nationally published, illustrated book. The poem's significance, it seems to me, lies in its portrayal of Lindsay's friends and teachers at his New York art school. See "Adventures While Singing These Songs" in CP.

804 AVANEL BOONE FLIES FROM THE HEARTHFIRE WITH AN ESCORT OF FLYING, FLAMING BOOKS. The manuscript (V) is not dated, but the poem seems once to have been designed as the conclusion of GSu. Since Lindsay uses this same title for other manuscript poems, he may for a time intended it as the title for the volume. For the cat and the mouse, see "Concerning the Mouse with Two Tails"; also see "Fantasy of The Golden Book and Its Escort."

806 THE SUN IS A SPHINX. The manuscript (LH) is hand-lettered but undated; the work may be a product of Lindsay's increased interest in Egyptology during 1922-1923.

806 THE PEACOCK'S DAUGHTER. The manuscript (V) is undated, but the work reflects Lindsay's Gulf Park College days.

807 THE STARS FOR CHANDELIERS. Undated manuscript (V) but, again, from Gulf Park.

808 MY BITTER RIVALS. Undated manuscript (V): the work reflects Lindsay's troubled love for Elizabeth Mann Wills.

808 I AM TRAVELLING TOO FAST TO VOTE. The manuscript (V) is not dated, but the fragment (which is untitled) seems to reflect Lindsay's feelings following the death of his mother (1922) and before his marriage

(1925). The fragment is included because of its biographical significance.

809 YOUNG DAUGHTER OF THE ANCIENT SUN. Undated manuscript
(V) but probably a late poem to Elizabeth Wills. On 26 June 1917 Lindsay
writes Arthur Davison Ficke (UL-H): "For years I was a maniac on things
Japanese. When we were very little children my mother chanced to buy a
history of Japan when we were all laid over from missing a train, at a
railway station—Decatur [Illinois] it was. Well that Child's history of
Japan, in words of one syllable has stayed with me ever since, and I know
who Jimmu Tenno was. . . ." See "The Jingo and the Minstrel."

810 BEFORE THE ORATION. The manuscript (V) is dated "Thursday—
November 5, 1925"; the poem was written for Elizabeth Conner Lindsay,
the poet's wife, just before he took the platform for a recitation.

812 TODAY THERE IS A MARKET FOR PINK BUBBLES. On 29 January
1926, Elizabeth Lindsay writes Henry Seidel Canby, sending a copy of the
poem and informing him: "You will find herewith a verse which Vachel
wrote last night, and in which he hopes you may be interested. He wanted
to call it 'Munsey,' but it would seem to be clear enough without that"
(UL-V). Frank Andrew Munsey, the renowned but controversial publishing
mogul, owner of the *New York Sun* and the *New York Evening Telegraph*,
died after a short illness on 22 December 1925. The version of the poem
here (UMs-V) is a later revision; a headnote reads: "For the Bulletin of the
Author's League of America."

813 NEW FASHIONS. Manuscript date (V): "1930."

813 IN PRAISE OF WIT. The manuscript (V) is undated, but the verse is
undoubtedly late. The epigraph is the final stanza of Longfellow's "The
Day Is Done"; for Stoddard King, see the note to "A Curse for the
Saxophone."

815 REMARKS BY THE CAPTAIN OF A TRAMP STEAMER. The
manuscript (V) is not dated, but the verse, it seems to me, is obviously late.

816 MY NEW SINGER, SACAJAWEA. A note on the manuscript (V)
reads: "Accepted by a British Mag." However, I have not been able to
determine which magazine and whether or not the poem was ever
published. For Sacajawea, see the note to "The Song of My Fiftieth
Birthday."

816 TIME GIVES ME STRENGTH EACH HOUR. This manuscript (V) is a
rejected stanza of "The Philosopher" (*q.v.*).

APPENDIX

PREFACE to *The Tramp's Excuse and Other Poems*

Early in 1897, though I scorned verses, I began to write them, "The Battle" first of all. It woke me at midnight. I rose and put it down, not in sadness, but great joy, because I was making a picture drama in words. In the morning I drew a pen and ink illustration to embellish it. After that I generally drew the pictures first and wrote the poems to fit. Most of the pictures have been given to friends. I have here reproduced a few drawings, and the elect can imagine the rest.

Walking has been a mania with me. I have often, from my earliest days, walked myself into a sort of intoxication. But it was not until nineteen hundred and one, as a student in the Chicago Art Institute, I wrote my first poem of pilgrimage, "Star Of My Heart." In nineteen hundred and four, while a student in the New York School of Art, I wrote "I Want To Go Wandering". In the summer of that year I produced a foolish, three volume mystery-tale "Where is Aladdin's Lamp?" since consigned to the flames. It was an illustrated story of three tramp-magicians who searched through the Universe for that Wizard's plaything, Aladdin's lamp. I mention these dates to show how I gradually became a tramp by conviction.

It was not until March, nineteen hundred and six, that I made the plunge, being stranded in Florida with malice aforethought. I tramped. I rode freight cabooses two hundred miles, then tramped again eight hundred miles through Macon and Atlanta, Georgia; Ashville, North Carolina; Greenville, Tennessee; and Cumberland Gap to Frankfort, Kentucky. My baggage was a razor, tooth-brush, comb, soap, bandanna, and my poem, "The Tree of Laughing Bells". I found an extraordinary responsiveness in cultured and uncultured. It seemed the only time I had ever lived. I will never forget those log houses of the Blue Ridge, those rings of faces lit only by the fire on the hearth.

In the spring of nineteen hundred and eight, my lecture season closing in the West Side Y.M.C.A., New York, I encountered the same divine hospitality, walking through New Jersey and Pennsylvania to Hiram, Ohio. I carried two booklets of verse: "The Last Song of Lucifer" and "God Help Us To Be Brave."

Thus the poems of the road are based on life itself, good reader. Whether you be in Kamakura, London or Moscow, sometime I may pass your way.

One more word. In September, nineteen hundred and six, on the boat returning from Europe, about two o'clock in the morning I was awakened by the overwhelming vision of Christ as a Shepherd, singing on a hill. The first three stanzas of the poem, "I Heard Immanuel Singing," were half-formed in my mind before I awoke, and I said aloud, "I have found my God." I felt at the time that this experience had more right to authority over me than any previous picture in the air. It came with terrible power. It came after years of struggle between the Hebraism and Hellenism in my universe, and set that struggle forever at rest. It shows how after Christ sets up the Moral Order he sings a requiem for all the beauty destroyed by the Judgment Day. Then he begins to live the pure Art Life.

—NICHOLAS VACHEL LINDSAY.
1909

At my home in Springfield, Illinois.

EXPLANATION OF THE MAP OF THE UNIVERSE from
The Tramp's Excuse and Other Poems

In the summer of 1904 I began to have some noteworthy experiences. It is plausible, I think, that for one who had so long co-ordinated drawings and poems for drawings, his religious experiences should paint themselves before him in the air. Had I been an Arabian I might have drawn the sword on the authority of the visions that came in cataracts. Even yet I cannot disabuse my mind of the faith that they were sent. I believe they were inspired, but by no means infallible. They were metaphors of the day, consolations of the hour. I determined to make them the servants, not the masters of my religious life. Though I understood mysteries and knowledge, and had not charity, I was nothing.

Being taught by that admirable practical but unimaginative master William M. Chase never to draw a thing till I saw it on the blank paper before me, it was only the terrible power and blaze of the pictures that came that made them unusual. In a certain corner of this room, one night, I saw the Prophets go by in gorgeous apparel. Then I wrote "A Prayer in the Jungles of Heaven." At another time, in the day by the elm in the front yard, they went by in the same robes. Yet when I wrote a story about them, I clothed them in rough penentential raiment. All through the summer I took similar liberties in the face of Hell and Heaven, determined not to be conquered by pictures in the air; I built a universe, half my own, half revealed, and put it all in a book I have destroyed, entitled "Where is Aladdin's lamp?"

The Map of the Universe, here given is the stage of that lost drama. It deepens the metaphors of several poems. Let it be like the stage plan of **Every-man**, dear reader. Do not despise this, my little Mystery Play, all that is left of six wonderful months of eating of the flower of the Holy Ghost.

The Throne Mountains were once the dwelling place of the Trinity; but they are desolate. Only the vine of the Amaranth, the flower of the Holy Ghost, grows about his mountain throne, bearing luminous inflaming honey-flowers. Around this mountain gather the boats of the prophets. The ancient men eat this flower only. It makes them hope against hope. They prophecy a New Universe. On the plateau below are the Jungles of Heaven, empty of souls, a region of fallen palaces, rotted harps, broken crowns, swords of rusted gold. The Angels are the Missionaries of the Universe. They have gone forth to the stars to be crucified, and to be forsaken of God. Their shed blood, by transubstantiation enters the Wine jars carried by the boats of the prophets. This wine is poured as a purple mist in the paths of men. It becomes the light that never shone on sea or land, the gleam, the still small voice, the cloud of glory.

Some day Hell shall be redeemed by a storm of this wine poured down. This is just; because it was by a leaping flame from the Harp of the great Singer Lucifer, that the angels fell in love with suffering, and went forth to the stars to be forsaken of God. Thus was Lucifer King of the Universe the moment before he was cursed with eternal silence and sealed in his tomb.

Beneath the walls of Heaven is the soul of the Butterfly, which is the soul of the Earth redeemed, and on the edge of Hell is the soul of the Giant

Spider, who is Mammon. East of the Universe is the Palace of Eve, whence come the perfect Brides; west of the Universe is the Star of Laughing Bells, only to be reached by the Wings of the Morning. One bell will quench all memory, all hope, all borrowed sorrow. You will have no thirst for yesterday or for the future. Wizards and witches and fairies say that by finding Aladdin's Lamp, which sleeps somewhere in the myriad treasure-pits of the jungles of Heaven, the new Universe can be built, and all the cities of the Wise. The Genii of the lamp can be commanded to carry the Laughing Bells to every soul in the Universe, and thus redeem them all. The angels and prophets say that the New Universe comes by the power of the Wine of God, the blood of the crucified Angels. But however it come, I have a faith in the most treasured metaphor of my life that the day after the Millennium, Immanuel will sing.

THE SOUL OF THE CITY RECEIVES THE GIFT OF THE HOLY SPIRIT
AND A NOTE from
A Letter About My Four Programmes For Committees in Correspondence

The pictures of certain public buildings that follow are used as hieroglyphics of the body and soul of the place. They come in the following order: Abraham Lincoln's Residence; The Lincoln Monument; The Immaculate Conception Church (Catholic); The First Presbyterian Church; The Central Christian Church; The Sangamon County Court House, which was the State House in Lincoln's time; the present State House; The High School Building; The Hall of Horticulture at the State Fair. The institutions enshrined in these buildings and many others are becoming wonderful in their inner spirit. Soon the city shall be rebuilt in splendor.

The picture of the Horticultural Building stands for the prairie school of art that is rising in Illinois, whose symbols are the Hawthorn Tree, the Compass Plant and the Prairie Rose. This school will include landscape-gardeners, painters, sculptors, masters of pageantry and the like. This school, this great movement, will unite the spirit of the ploughed land and prairie with the spirit of the city streets.

There are modernists in the Catholic and Protestant churches and in the synagogues of Springfield, and in the Church of Christ, Scientist. Whatever the dogmas of their brotherhoods they are forward-looking, vision-seeing people. These, in especial, are the hope of the town. The vision they see of a place that serves God in simplicity without creed, dogma or superstition as though it were one congregation under the open sky, this vision will make Springfield the high altar of civic religion.

The buildings associated with Lincoln stand for the most precious tradition in America. The greatest use of these buildings is in giving our citizens spirit-pictures of the future, when the slaves of special tyrannies of the twentieth century shall be set free. These citizens feel assured that Springfield is going to be the place where arrogant idleness and the caste system and the wicked notions that go with them are to be abolished. They feel assured that this is to be the town where the bodies and thoughts of men shall be glorified, where no man's soul shall be chained or thwarted or put to shame.

The new State House stands, in this book, as the representative of that handfull of legislators, constantly growing in influence who for many sessions in the future are destined to triumphant battle for a Socialist Illinois.

Meanwhile many hearth-stones in Springfield are being transfigured. And young lovers, just beginning to plant their little cottages, are dreaming of homes of permanence. Their thoughts are of future generations, who shall return here with real family pride, and in this city carry forward the glories of Art, Liberty, Americanism and Socialism.

Springfield, Illinois, 1913.

(Note.—The tract: The Soul of the City Receives the Gift of the Holy Spirit, forms the basis of programme one, and is, perhaps, the index to all my writing. It was issued a year after the trip across Kansas described in the Adventures While Preaching the Gospel of Beauty, and has a relation to the proclamations with which that book closes.

Several thousand copies of this tract were distributed in Springfield, Illinois. People were so good as to ask me to make speeches to divers organizations about it. I remember the Avonian Club was particularly courteous, both in giving me an audience in the library and in distributing copies of the work. The pastor of the First Methodist Church, Rev. A.C. Piersel, turned over to me his Sunday evening service and a large audience, gathered by his exertions, that I could not myself have assembled. I spoke of the poem, read it, and gave away the last thousand.

The tract is here a little revised in this first reprinting since that time.

About a year after the tract was issued, by no means as a result of it, but indicating a kindred feeling had been at work in other citizens in a more practical way, the movement for a Springfield Survey culminated in a cooperative arrangement with the Russel Sage foundation. A Springfield welfare exhibition was held, recommendations offered, many thick reports printed, and permanent plans undertaken. Now the city and state, working toward the centennial celebration of Illinois in 1918 are undertaking to make that the basis of certain permanent changes in the city plan and policy.)

THE HISTORY OF THE ROSE AND LOTUS RHYME from
A Letter About My Four Programmes For Committees in Correspondence

The Rose and the Lotus was written when international peace seemed the general rule forevermore. It was written upon the completion of the Panama canal, and in anticipation of the Panama-Pacific Exposition. On the opening days it was distributed at the Exposition and in Washington, D.C., through the co-operation of Secretary of the Interior Franklin K. Lane and Mrs. Lane, who were particularly generous friends of the poem and its intention. I here take opportunity of again acknowledging their courtesy and that of Assistant Secretary of Agriculture, Carl Vrooman and Mrs. Vrooman, who had a liberal hand in the distribution of the poem.

About the same time that I wrote The Rose and the Lotus I composed The Jingo and the Minstrel, a poem of friendship with Japan, and was beginning The Chinese Nightingale, a poem of friendship with China.

But friendship is not the fashion now, June, 1916. Japan is darkly suspected by some because she is alleged to be preparing too much for war, and China is held out as a horrible and contemptible example, because she is alleged to be preparing too little. But I still must champion my verses of friendship, and show their meaning as I can.

All these sorrows may be but the birth pangs of international government. Above the conflict there is a spiritual internationalism yearning for the dawn. As it says in the first chapter of Genesis: "And the Earth was without form and void, and darkness was upon the face of the deep. And the spirit of God moved upon the face of the waters."

But as to this poem. The rose has been the favorite flower of the west from the beginning. Christ is spoken of as the Rose of Sharon. In many a church picture of Mary, His mother, her burning heart is surrounded by a wreath of roses, and it is with a rosary that she is invoked by those who love her. In the medieval time Dante went through Hell and Purgatory and entered Paradise and found it one great rose. The Gothic cathedrals developed the rose-windows, wonderful flowers of art and devotion, windows so large that the cathedrals might be described as celestial lanterns. We could speak endlessly of the rose in western religion.

But the rose has been in turn a symbol of every passion of the west. There was the Romance of the Rose. There were the wars of the Roses. And to this hour every tragedy, every funeral, every love song, every bridal has its tempest or shame or glory of roses.

In like manner the lotus has been the characteristic eastern flower from the beginning. Its mood is that of the regions of opium and hasheesh and quiescent philosophy. Homer and Tennyson have spoken of the land of the lotus eaters as philosophers speak of all Asia. There is magic in every line of the lotus. In Egypt to build the temples there were the lotus-bud capitals and the lotus-bloom capitals. Horus, god of the sun, is depicted as born from the original ocean of night rising like an exhalation from an opening lotus flower. The lotus is in the hands of many a reveller and of many a worshipper in the inscriptions.

In India the lotus has had a like domination. And in the vast regions of Buddhism that are outside of India the lotus rules above all other blossoms. A typical title for a Buddhist sacred book is: "The Lotus of the true Law." The Thibetan, turning his prayer-wheel, invoking Buddha, cries: "O Mani Padme Hum:—**O the jewel in the lotus**." In Japan the various Buddhas are enthroned in open lotus flowers.

The lotus is Asia. It represents everything Asiatic from opium and hasheesh and slavery to Nirvana and freedom and victory.

Columbus and all his kind pushed west away from Asia. Now for the first time in history east and west with all their cultures and sins and glories meet in the Pacific. These that have been separated from the beginning of time are face to face till the end of time. There may be in prospect endless wars among the peoples and the statesmen. Let us pray that it be not so. The sages at least are destined to read each other's books, and eastern and western poets will sing each other's songs, eastern and western mystics seek the infinite together. Let us pray that the governments may reflect this unity and understanding.

The rose and the lotus grow equally well in the East and the West. I humbly suggest that all those who may chance to read this poem who have large gardens at their command, be they florists, private citizens, landscape architects or park commissioners, do take these two flowers for friends. Let such of them as hold international good-will as a darling hope plan their grounds accordingly. I have dared to dream of lotus ponds the world around, with rose-gardens beside them, and men in like friendship.

THE POTATOES' DANCE from
A Letter About My Four Programmes For Committees in Correspondence

The Potatoes' Dance is printed in this fashion to indicate one phase of
the Higher Vaudeville method, which is in this case an exaggeration of the
phonetic qualities and the metrical form after the poem is written, rather
than the developing of the subject and sound scheme to fit an old tune. The
chanting of this piece is based upon a development of the traditional
timbre and color effect of the English Language, and upon the distinct
enunciation of the musical elements inherent in each word. In combining
the words the chanter should bring out every hint of assonance and
alliteration. The verses were written with the intention of making the
metre so close to the meaning that any exaggeration of the metre would
only make the story clearer from the dramatic standpoint. Professor
Hamilton Macdougall of Wellesley, hearing the piece given in this way,
has put it down elsewhere in a musical transcript to be used as a delicate
accompaniment, written music based on the English language rather than
on musical tradition. Of course neither musical nor printed transcript is an
adequate substitute for the instinctive individual method any reader may
develop.

THE POEM GAMES from
The Chinese Nightingale and Other Poems

In the summer of 1916 in the parlor of Mrs. William Vaughn Moody; and in the following winter in the Chicago Little Theatre, under the auspices of Poetry, A Magazine of Verse; and in Mandel Hall, the University of Chicago, under the auspices of the Senior Class, — these Poem Games were presented. Miss Eleanor Dougherty was the dancer throughout. The entire undertaking developed through the generous coöperation and advice of Mrs. William Vaughn Moody. The writer is exceedingly grateful to Mrs. Moody and all concerned for making place for the idea. Now comes the test of its vitality. Can it go on in the absence of its initiators?

Mr. Lewellyn Jones, of the Chicago Evening Post, announced the affair as a "rhythmic picnic." Mr. Maurice Browne of the Chicago Little Theatre said Miss Dougherty was at the beginning of the old Greek Tragic Dance. Somewhere between lies the accomplishment.

In the Congo volume, as is indicated in the margins, the meaning of a few of the verses is aided by chanting. In the Poem Games the English word is still first in importance, the dancer comes second, the chanter third. The marginal directions of King Solomon indicate the spirit in which all the pantomime was developed. Miss Dougherty designed her own costumes, and worked out her own stage business for King Solomon, The Potatoes' Dance, The King of Yellow Butterflies and Aladdin and the Jinn. In the last, " ' I am your slave,' said the Jinn" was repeated four times at the end of each stanza.

The Poem Game idea was first indorsed in the Wellesley kindergarten, by the children. They improvised pantomime and dance for the Potatoes' Dance, while the writer chanted it, and while Professor Hamilton C. Macdougall of the Wellesley musical department followed on the piano the outline of the jingle. Later Professor Macdougall very kindly wrote down his piano rendition. A study of this transcript helps to confirm the idea that when the cadences of a bit of verse are a little exaggerated, they are tunes, yet of a truth they are tunes which can be but vaguely recorded by notation or expressed by an instrument. The author of this book is now against instrumental music in this type of work. It blurs the English.

Professor Macdougall has in various conversations helped the author toward a Poem Game theory. He agrees that neither the dancing nor the chanting nor any other thing should be allowed to run away with the original intention of the words. The chanting should not be carried to the point where it seeks to rival conventional musical composition. The dancer should be subordinated to the natural rhythms of English speech, and not attempt to incorporate bodily all the precedents of professional dancing.

Speaking generally, poetic ideas can be conveyed word by word, faster than musical feeling. The repetitions in the Poem Games are to keep the singing, the dancing and the ideas at one pace. The repetitions may be varied according to the necessities of the individual dancer. Dancing is slower than poetry and faster than music in developing the same thoughts. In folk dances and vaudeville, the verse, music, and dancing are on so simple a basis the time elements can be easily combined. Likewise the rhythms and the other elements.

Miss Dougherty is particularly illustrative in her pantomime, but there were many verses she looked over and rejected because they could not be rendered without blurring the original intent. Possibly every poem in the world has its dancer somewhere waiting, who can dance but that one poem. Certainly those poems would be most successful in games, where the tone color is so close to the meaning that any exaggeration of that color by dancing and chanting only makes the story clearer. The writer would like to see some one try Dryden's Alexander's Feast, or Swinburne's Atalanta in Calydon. Certainly in those poems the decorative rhythm and the meaning are absolutely one.

With no dancing evolutions, the author of this book has chanted John Brown and King Solomon for the last two years for many audiences. It took but a minute to teach the people the responses. As a rule they had no advance notice they were going to sing. The versifier sang the parts of the King and Queen in turn, and found each audience perfectly willing to be the oxen, the sweethearts, the swans, the sons, the shepherds, etc.

A year ago the writer had the honor of chanting for the Florence Fleming Noyes school of dancers. In one short evening they made the first section of the Congo into an incantation, the King Solomon into an extraordinarily graceful series of tableaus, and the Potatoes' Dance into a veritable whirlwind. Later came the more elaborately prepared Chicago experiment.

In the King of Yellow Butterflies and the Potatoes' Dance Miss Dougherty occupied the entire eye of the audience and interpreted, while the versifier chanted the poems as a semi-invisible orchestra, by the side of the curtain. For Aladdin and for King Solomon Miss Dougherty and the writer divided the stage between them, but the author was little more than the orchestra. The main intention was carried out, which was to combine the work of the dancer with the words of the production and the responses of the audience.

The present rhymer has no ambitions as a stage manager. The Poem Game idea, in its rhythmic picnic stage, is recommended to amateurs, its further development to be on their own initiative. Informal parties might divide into groups of dancers and groups of chanters. The whole might be worked out in the spirit in which children play King William was King James' Son, London Bridge, or As We Go Round the Mulberry Bush. And the author of this book would certainly welcome the tragic dance, if Miss Dougherty will gather a company about her and go forward, using any acceptable poems, new or old. Swinburne's Atalanta in Calydon is perhaps the most literal and rhythmic example of the idea we have in English, though it may not be available when tried out.

The main revolution necessary for dancing improvisers, who would go a longer way with the Poem Game idea, is to shake off the Isadora Duncan and the Russian precedents for a while, and abolish the orchestra and piano, replacing all these with the natural meaning and cadences of English speech. The work would come closer to acting, than dancing is now conceived.

A WORD ON CALIFORNIA, PHOTOPLAYS, AND SAINT FRANCIS from
The Golden Whales of California and Other Rhymes
in the American Language

In *The Art of the Moving Picture*, in the chapter on California and America, I said, in part:

"The moving picture captains of industry, like the California gold finders of 1849, making colossal fortunes in two or three years, have the same glorious irresponsibility and occasional need of the sheriff. They are Californians more literally than this. Around Los Angeles the greatest and most characteristic moving picture colonies are built. Each photoplay magazine has its California letter, telling of the putting up of new studios, and the transfer of actors with much slap-you-on-the-back personal gossip.

". . . Every type of the photoplay but the intimate is founded on some phase of the out-of doors. Being thus dependent, the plant can best be set up where there is no winter. Besides this, the Los Angeles region has the sea, the mountains, the desert, and many kinds of grove and field. . . .

"If the photoplay is the consistent utterance of its scenes, if the actors are incarnations of the land they walk upon, as they should be, California indeed stands a chance to achieve through the films an utterance of her own. Will this land, furthest west, be the first to capture the inner spirit of this newest and most curious of the arts? . . .

"People who revere the Pilgrim Fathers of 1620 have often wished those gentlemen had moored their bark in the region of Los Angeles, rather than Plymouth Rock, that Boston had been founded there. At last that landing is achieved.

"Patriotic art students have discussed with mingled irony and admiration the Boston domination of the only American culture of the nineteenth century, namely, literature. Indianapolis has had her day since then. Chicago is lifting her head. Nevertheless Boston still controls the text-book in English, and dominates our high schools. Ironic feelings in this matter, on the part of western men, are based somewhat on envy and illegitimate cussedness, but are also grounded in the honest hope of a healthful rivalry. They want new romanticists and artists as indigenous to their soil as was Hawthorne to witch-haunted Salem, or Longfellow to the chestnuts of his native heath. Whatever may be said of the patriarchs, from Oliver Wendell Holmes to Amos Bronson Alcott, they were true sons of the New England stone fences and meeting houses. They could not have been born or nurtured anywhere else on the face of the earth.

"Some of us view with a peculiar thrill the prospect that Los Angeles may become the Boston of the photoplay. Perhaps it would be better to say the Florence, because California reminds one of colorful Italy, more than of any part of the United States. Yet there is a difference.

"The present day man-in-the-street, man-about-town Californian has an obvious magnificence about him that is allied to the eucalyptus tree, the pomegranate. . . .

"The enemy of California says the state is magnificent, but thin. He declares it is as though it were painted on a Brobdingnagian piece of gilt paper, and he who dampens his finger and thrusts it through finds an alkali valley on the other side, the lonely prickly pear, and a heap of ashes from a deserted camp-fire. He says the citizens of this state lack the richness of an aesthetic and religious tradition. He says there is no substitute for time. But even these things make for coincidence. This apparent thinness California has in common with the routine photoplay, which is at times as shallow in its thought as the shadow it throws upon the screen. This newness California has in common with all photoplays. It is thrillingly possible for the state and the art to acquire spiritual tradition and depth together.

"Part of the thinness of California is not only its youth, but the result of the physical fact that the human race is there spread over so many acres of land. "Good" Californians count their mines and enumerate their palm trees. They count the miles of their sea-coast, and the acres under cultivation and the height of the peaks, and revel in large statistics and the bigness generally, and forget how a few men rattle around in a great deal of scenery. They shout the statistics across the Rockies and the deserts to New York. The Mississippi valley is non-existent to the Californian. His fellow-feeling is for the opposite coast line. Through the geographical accident of separation by mountain and desert from the rest of the country, he becomes a mere shouter, hurrahing so assiduously that all variety in the voice is lost. Then he tries gestures, and becomes flamboyant, rococo.

"These are the defects of the motion picture qualities. Also its panoramic tendency runs wild. As an institution it advertises itself with a sweeping gesture. It has the same passion for coast-line. These are not the sins of New England. When, in the hands of masters, they become sources of strength, they will be a different set of virtues from those of New England. . . .

"When the Californian relegates the dramatic to secondary scenes, both in his life and his photoplay, and turns to the genuinely epic and lyric, he and this instrument may find their immortality together as New England found its soul in the essays of Emerson. Tide upon tide of Spring comes into California, through all four seasons. Fairy beauty overwhelms the lumbering grand-stand players. The tiniest garden is a jewelled pathway of wonder. But the Californian cannot shout 'orange blossoms, orange blossoms; heliotrope, heliotrope.' He cannot boom forth 'roseleaves, roseleaves' so that he does their beauties justice. Here is where the photoplay can begin to give him a more delicate utterance. And he can go on into stranger things, and evolve all the *Splendor Films* into higher types, for the very name of California is splendor. . . . The California photoplaywright can base his *Crowd Picture* upon the city-worshipping mobs of San Francisco. He can derive his *Patriotic* and *Religious Splendors* from something older and more magnificent than the aisles of the Romanesque, namely: the groves of the giant redwoods.

"The campaigns for a beautiful nation could very well emanate from the west coast, where with the slightest care, grow up models for all the world of plant arrangement and tree-luxury. Our mechanical east is reproved, our tension is relaxed, our ugliness is challenged, every time we look upon those garden-paths and forests.

"It is possible for Los Angeles to lay hold of the motion picture as our national text book in art, as Boston appropriated to herself the guardianship of the national text book of literature. If California has a shining soul, and not merely a golden body, let her forget her seventeen year old melodramatics, and turn to her poets who understand the heart underneath the glory. Edwin Markham, the dean of American singers, Clark Ashton Smith, the young star-treader, George Sterling . . . have, in their songs, seeds of better scenarios than California has sent us. . . .

"California can tell us stories that are grim children of the tales of the wild Ambrose Bierce. Then there is the lovely unforgotten Nora May French, and the austere Edward Rowland Sill. . . ."

All this from *The Art of the Moving Picture* may serve to answer many questions I have been asked as to my general ideas in the realms of art and verse, and it may more particularly elucidate my *personal attitude toward California.*

One item that should perhaps chasten the native son, is that these motion picture people, so truly the hope of California, are not native sons or daughters.

When I was in Los Angeles, visiting my cousin Ruby Vachel Lindsay, we discussed many of these items at great length, as we walked about the Los Angeles region together. I owe much of my conception of the more idealistic moods of the state to those conversations. Others who have shown me what might be called the Franciscan soul, of the Franciscan minority, are Professor and Mrs. E. Olan James, my host and hostess at Mills College. Another discriminating interpreter of the coast is that follower of Alexander Campbell, Peter Clark Macfarlane, to whom I owe much of my hope for a state that will some day gleam with spiritual and Franciscan, and not earthly gold.

When I think of California, I think so emphatically of these people and the things they have to say to the native sons, and the rest, that if the discussion in this volume is not considered conclusive, I refer the reader to these, and to the California poets, and to motion picture people like Anita Loos and John Emerson, people who still dream of things that are not gilded, and know the difference for instance, between St. Francis and Mammon. For a general view of those poets of California who make clear its spiritual gold, turn to "Golden Songs of the Golden State," an anthology collected by Marguerite Wilkinson.

ADVENTURES WHILE SINGING THESE SONGS from
Collected Poems

I have had many adventures while singing these songs. Now I have had
the adventure of collecting them, and deciding for the first time the natural
sequence of them all.

Section One of the collection, called *Nightingales*, and Section Two,
Orations, College War-Cries and Olympic Games, are obviously in
contrast, as songs differ from orations, and I have put the songs first,
because I somewhat prefer them. In these two sections, as in the whole
book, many sentences may be found which run parallel to the opening
chapter of *The Art of the Moving Picture* (1922). That book, as this one,
champions my favorite notions of Painting, Sculpture, Architecture and
Hieroglyphics. I have been an art student all my life, in the strictest sense
of the word. I have been so exclusively an art student, I am still surprised
to be called a writer.

Section Three, *Litany of the Heroes*, is an "Outline of History," written
in 1906-7-8, still in process of development. The litany was projected with
the active aid and choice of heroes, and other accompanying discussions by
a group of fellow-students of art. We decorated a restaurant together, and
the restaurant used this song for a souvenir. We gloried in that place. It
was there we held some of our midnight arguments. We were grander than
Greenwich Village, long before there ever was such a thing on the art map.
We were Paul Burlin, George Mather Richards, Pierre Laird, Earl H.
Brewster, Leighton Haring Smith, and some brilliant girls, among whom
were Margery Torrey Hood, now Torrey Bevans, and Achsa Barlow, now
Mrs. Earl H. Brewster. The restaurant was called *The Pig and the Goose*,
and has since disappeared. Brewster is painting the lives of St. Francis and
of Buddha, in Sicily and Ceylon, and winning his due meed of laurels and
friends. Those two heroes are in the song. The rest of our group are
following our various gods over the world, and I have added a few new
heroes and villains since we scattered. I hope some day to write the
delectable story of our Pig and Goose Restaurant, which was half-way
between history and tradition, being on Fifty-ninth Street, between
Columbus Circle and the beautiful Paulist Fathers' Church.

Section Seven, *Runes of the Road*, runs parallel with the prose work,
Adventures While Preaching the Gospel of Beauty. This might also be said
of Sections Four, Five and Six. And the last two sections of the book run
parallel to *The Golden Book of Springfield*.

In the Table of Contents I have made a running commentary that the
unity of thought, such as it is, may now have a better chance.

I have just completed two national reciting tours, and am this month
starting on another, covering again every state in the Union. If to my
fellow-art-students and fellow-larks, with whom I have spent much time
for many genial years, there seems an over emphasis on some points in the
present method of editing, please let them remember that this whole book
is a weapon in a strenuous battlefield; that practically every new copy will
be first opened on the lap of some person in a new audience of mine, trying
to follow me as I recite, as one follows the translation of the opera libretto.
Let them remember that these new friends are stuffed with hasty
newspaper accounts of what it is all about. Night after night I step forth, a

gently but altogether misrepresented stranger, and therefore separated from new audiences that I love at sight, and dearly desire to win, for a simple lifetime friendship.

My favorite long poem in this collection is "The Chinese Nightingale," and therefore the first section is named for it. My favorite short poem is, "My Fathers Came from Kentucky." This answers the question I am oftenest asked in new towns.

If there is one fact in regard to my verses of which I am proud, it is that they have been danced. "The Chinese Nightingale" has been used for several seasons in a special production evolved by the students of English at the University of Chicago. When she was twelve years of age, I petitioned Miss Ruth Lovett to undertake the matter. She was even then a wonderful dancer, severely trained, no mere improviser pinned up in a sheet. It was not long till I had heard that that infant Pavlova had grown up, and had danced the poem in the spacious Mandel Hall, with all the University of Chicago in her train. This production has been reproduced and imitated in other parts of the country.

The singing and dancing of poetry is based on the twenty-six letters of the United States and British alphabet, and on the way they are pronounced in the dictionary and in clear conversation. Poems to be danced are to be made musical in the same sense that classic dramas are to be made musical by good actors. The exact pronunication of the letters of the alphabet should prevail over the tune. It always disturbs me when people write asking for permission to set my verses to music. It shows such a misapprehension of the point of view from which they were written. It is like asking permission to rewrite the poems entirely, while pretending they remain the same. Sheet music, piano music, orchestras and the like should not be in the same room with verses, as a general rule. No musical notation ever invented can express the same musical scheme as the twenty-six letters of the alphabet. Stringed instruments destroy the value of vowels. Music might be played between lines or stanzas.

But back to the University of Chicago version of "The Chinese Nightingale." Having had faithful friends in that University for years it was easy, even before the "Nightingale" event, to try an experiment there on a large scale. The first "Poem Games" were given with the aid of Miss Eleanor Dougherty, a graduate of the University of Chicago, who had there an enviable record in the acting of the Elizabethan drama. She also was a dancer, trained in severe schools, and equally a careful technician with her brother, Paul Dougherty, the marine painter, and Walter Hampden, the Shakespearian actor.

The Eleanor Dougherty "Poem Games" were first put on, on a large scale in Mandel Hall, at the University, in the autumn of 1916. This work was accomplished in many of its stages with the moral support of active promoters of the *Poetry Magazine* in Chicago: Mrs. William Vaughn Moody, Miss Harriet Monroe, Carl Sandburg, and others. Llewellyn Jones of the Chicago *Evening Post* Literary Review called the affair a rhythmic picnic. Maurice Browne backed us at the Chicago Little Theatre, and gave suggestions.

And with the whole Chicago Poetry group I had argued pro and con for several seasons the question of dancing poetry.

The substance of the Mandel Hall event was this: I chanted the poems, by the side of the stage, and Miss Dougherty occupied the entire stage for the evening, dancing to the syllables of the verses. She used her own interpretations of "The King of Yellow Butterflies," "The Potatoes' Dance," "Aladdin and the Jinn," "The Rose and the Lotus," "King Solomon and the Queen of Sheba," and others. The stage directions of King Solomon are hers. Miss Lovett and her group, having witnessed Miss Dougherty's dancing in public and in private many times, evolved the present University of Chicago production of "The Chinese Nightingale."

Every English Department that I visit insists that I discuss the matter of rhythm. I have chosen my old "Song of Lucifer" as the key to such rhythm as I understand. I wrote this chant at Hiram College in 1899 when I was re-reading John Milton. I presume I read "The Last Song of Lucifer" to fifty fellow-students throughout that year, correcting immediately by their suggestions, making it all casual and conversational. It was one of the Hiram courtesies to read orations to one another, and take criticism endlessly, much as in art school we criticise each other's drawings systematically and with interest. The Hiram custom goes back all the way to the famous orator and statesman, James A. Garfield, who was a student of Hiram, and President thereof, and creator of its spirit. The Garfield influence so prevailing, the college undertook to make every student a trained public citizen, capable of holding for the length of an oration the student and village and faculty assembly, four hundred strong. We had great speaking field days with all the victors heroes. There was as keen oratorical competition as there is athletic competition in less classical schools. Yet Hiram had the astringent New England mind, with the astringent, non-rhetorical standards of speaking. I submit the poem as one which has suffered if not survived this test, and being as full of the rigid Hiram rhythms as I and my fellow-students knew how to fill it and also as containing all the tunes and rhyme-schemes which are supposed to have first appeared in later work.

I have paid too great a penalty for having written a few rhymed orations. All I write is assumed to be loose oratory, or even jazz, though I have never used the word "jazz" except in irony. I knew and loved in infancy the lines of Keats:

"Heard melodies are sweet but those unheard
Are sweeter; therefore, ye soft pipes, play on."

I, who have spent scraps of many winters lecturing on the Doric and Ionic elements in the evolution of the Parthenon, and the austere prehistoric gold ornaments and cups of Greece, I, who have drawn endlessly and with great admiration the casts of the Elgin Marbles am assumed to hate the classics and champion their destruction. I, who have spent delightful years alone in the corridors of cool museums, am assumed to love noise and hate quiet. I read it in every newspaper in every town to which I go.

"How then? How about the Kallyope Yell?" asks the skeptic. We will now discuss the Kallyope Yell.

In my speaking tours I appear almost altogether before high-school, university or college assemblies, and I adore them. They are The United

States in its gorgeous youth, and I love them like my own soul. I love their customs. They generally welcome me with the high-school, university or college "yell" and I generally reply with the Kallyope Yell. The literati of Great Britain do not seem to have realized it, but yell-writing is as steady an occupation of bright youths here, as the writing of sonnets was in England in the Elizabethan age. I take it that "sonnet" is Sanskrit for "yell," and "yell" will some day be Sanskrit for "sonnet." It can be music, just as is the music of bagpipes or flutes, or the Shouts of the Valkyries in Wagner, and is in fact the beginning of a Natural United States Opera, and United States Russian Dancing. Many of the yells are already danced, especially after victory.

But let it be noted that the *Kallyope Yell* is marked to be given in the manner of the University of Kansas or Jay Hawk Yell. Let all students of the University of Kansas teach the tune of the Jay Hawk Yell to the world, especially to those inclined to true United States poetry. That yell, as all who have heard it know, contains no strain, jazz, spasm or vulgarity. It is actually whispered, slowly and beautifully, by about four thousand students, in spiritual unison, all soul-children of William Allen White of Emporia. It sounds like a glorified editorial from the Emporia *Gazette*. The least whisper of that village paper may creep over America like a wind or leap like wireless.

All my verses marked to be read aloud, should be whispered, however contradictory that may seem. All poetry is first and last for the inner ear, and its final pleasures are for the soul, whispering in solitude. Even the University of Kansas war cries have not served their full use till the graduate takes his walk alone through the wheat, whispering to himself its secret battle-cry, in meditative warfare arming himself for the soul's long solitary Pilgrim's Progress to the sun.

As the best comment on Section Four, *Verses of an Especially Inscriptional Character, Being Songs of My Art-Student Days*, let me say that, of course, my early drawings are of no interest except as a matter of record and a statement of method. Any one interested in full sets can get them secondhand, from Coe's Book Store, Springfield, Illinois, or Barker's Art Store, by writing a letter. Each of my acquaintances in Springfield has one or three copies of my portfolio humorously named *The Village Magazine*. There was an issue of 1910 and an issue of 1920, it being a decade magazine, instead of a monthly magazine. There will probably be a 1930 issue. The 1920 and 1910 issues were generously reviewed by the late Edward J. Wheeler, creator and long president of the Poetry Society of America. It is one of the many debts I owe that generous spirit that he took more interest in this portfolio than it deserved. I dedicated the second issue to him. *The Village Magazine* is expounded by him in *Current Literature*, March, 1911, and in *Current Opinion,* September, 1920. Those reviews are preliminary to what I would now more emphatically point out, the difference between poems to be danced and chanted, and poems written for pictures. Poems written for pictures are to be judged by a Philosophy of Hieroglyphics. If the friends of this book care to go further into my notions here, I invite them to glance through the Egyptian chapters in *The Art of the Moving Picture*. Poems to be danced and chanted are to be judged by standards of oratory and music, and come in through the imagination of the inner ear, rather than the imagination of the inner eye.

I have had many adventures while singing these songs. One type has been straightening out extraordinary biographies, such as the statement that I have spent all my life as a box-car tramp. An interesting life, but alas, not mine.

I was stuffed with family history in my helpless infancy. The last of my tribe to reach this land arrived in Baltimore in 1800. An aunt of mine once told me she suspected that there was one Red Indian among the ancestors, and if that is true, there were millions of them, of course, if one goes far enough back. I take an increasing interest in my aunt's suspicion.

I was born in Springfield, Illinois, in the house where I now live. Everything begins and ends there for me. Ours happens to be an old house. When it was new, long before my people bought it, it was owned by Mr. and Mrs. C.M. Smith, early builders of Springfield. Mrs. Smith was a sister of Mrs. Abraham Lincoln. As I knew from my earliest days, our front parlor was a place of distinction. Parties had been given to Abraham Lincoln there by his sister-in-law, especially one grand party, before he started for Washington.

My uncle, Johnson Lindsay, lived next to the Lincoln home, four blocks away from our house. His daughter, Ruby Vachel, was my favorite playmate. We made a Christmas tree of the lilac bush in the shadow of that home, and we kept it up all the year round. At that time the well-known collector, Mr. Oldroyd, was the custodian of the "Lincoln House," and he was on good terms with all the children. I used to play through the rooms of the "Home" with Ruby Vachel, while the G.A.R. veterans who were entertaining out-of-town visitors from all over the world, conducted them from picture to picture. The walls were covered with the Oldroyd collection of Civil War cartoons, since removed to Washington, D.C. These cartoons were from Northern and Southern papers, immediately preceding the Civil War, and from London *Punch* and the like. Those who hate the George Gray Barnard statue of Abraham Lincoln seem to think their hero has always been a steel engraving of a man in a Prince Albert coat and decorously trimmed whiskers. They have seen this so often on the back of the dollar bill that they believe it. But Ruby and I knew better than that about Lincoln. He was a profound volcano, producing, incidentally, ferocious debate. We saw the cartoons of his enemies, showing the alleged rank, slack, ungrammatical, sweating, thieving person. We saw the cartoons of his friends which expressed every kind of devotion to the rail-splitter and lawyer from the vast prairie circuit. But there was no Prince Albert dollar-bill hero dominating the devotion of his friends. Meanwhile Ruby at her school and I at mine were taught "The Battle Hymn of the Republic," and "Marching Through Georgia," and "John Brown's Body" and "Shouting the Battle-Cry of Freedom." We loved these songs, and marched to them in our games.

And the Grand Army of the Republic, the American Legion of that time, was marching through the streets to these songs, on all occasions, carrying the elections for the Republican Party under John A. Logan, and investing the State House of our little capital like a fortification. Visitors to the city were taken to the State House Memorial Room, dripping with Northern trophies, captured "rebel" battle flags, and the like.

And the same visitors who were taken to the Lincoln residence, and the

State House, were taken to the Lincoln Tomb. The Lincoln Tomb is a little north of the town, at Oak Ridge, where all the Springfield dead are laid away. The Lincoln Tomb is cold and strange as the legendary tomb of Osiris at Abydos must have been. And there is an obelisk over it, to give us Egyptian thoughts.

Ruby and I, though personal acquaintances of the Oldroyds, remained Southerners. The inexplicable Mason and Dixon line, deep-dyed and awful, ran straight through our hearts. We were made conscious of this by all our Lindsay kin. They were Breckenridge Democrats, remaining for the most part in Kentucky, but they came visiting us in our Ishmaelite loneliness in this flaming and arrogant G.A.R. state capital. Ruby and I told fairy stories, most of the time. We made them up, Ruby one sentence, then I one sentence, till Aunt Emma made us quit. But when we were not telling fairy stories we were having Democratic parades among ourselves, since the G.A.R. seemed to monopolize the streets most of the time. Our fathers helped manfully in the event when Grover Cleveland was first elected. My father went to the nominating convention, and on the night of the parade ratifying the election the streets were really ours for the first time. Our papas rode in that torchlight parade that was millions of miles long. Our papas had on big sashes, and the Democratic hats of that time, and their horses cavorted splendidly. Next day Ruby and I were still called rebels by the other children in the school yard. Springfield is still a Republican state capital, and I am still a kind of intrusive Kentuckian, though it was long before I saw Kentucky.

At home my mother's favorite tale was how one of her pioneer grandfathers in Kentucky taught Daniel Boone's children to read. She was full of such stories as are found in the autobiography of Peter Cartwright, but she told them with the literary accent of her idol, Jane Austen. But if you think we followers of Alexander Campbell and the Methodists were the same, read Peter Cartwright and get yourself enlightened. Our precise, pedantic, frigidly logical Campbellite scholars were the dearest foes of the wild Methodists. The "Campbellites" were the enemies of all the religious ecstatics of their time, and I still resent being called a Methodist. I remember my mother's frequent report of the legends of the "Cane Ridge Meeting." Imagine them told by a disciple of the much-mentioned Jane Austen, and then read Peter Cartwright's report. There was always a cold second thought, a double consciousness, among the "Campbellite" theologians. They breathed fire, but they thought in granite. Scotch heads, Red Indian and Kentucky blood.

In infancy I never heard of New England. I heard of Europe every day. History, tragic and awful, was a straight path in war and cartoon and politics and pioneering and preaching, and fighting the Methodists in debate, and University building and all similar activities along the Daniel Boone trail, from a Scotland we left millions of years ago. One of the multitude of books brought from Kentucky was the little blue volume of the Poems of Edgar Allan Poe. Another of my personal treasures was a gift from my father of Rawlinson's *History of Egypt*, two thick volumes, of which I knew every picture by heart, and the substance of every line, when I was very young indeed. I was even then moved to awe and curiosity by the strangely cartooned face of Amenophis Fourth, that archeology has of late so glorified and refined. He has been made a hero of antiquity like King Asoka. It is a matter of outrageous pride with me that I knew him, even in his cruder guise, when I was very young. Another heavy treasure was a battered *Chambers' Encyclopaedia of English Literature* that did not mention any Americans, and stopped about 1830. From it I knew Chatterton and Shelley and Byron and Coleridge and Dryden as very special discoveries, like the Kings of Egypt.

Poe was always a kind of Egyptian to me. In the gorgeous bridal chamber of Ligeia there is in each corner a great coffin, "From the Tombs of the Kings Over Against Luxor." There was not even a picture of Poe in the histories of American Literature taught in the High-School when I entered it. There was nothing to be found but the full-page portraits of a famous mutual-admiration society. I knew exactly Poe's opinion of these whiskered worthies. I had read his complete works, criticism and all, through and through, before I was fourteen. I could use his whip. I could quote his critical headlines, that brought blood. I was a kind of literary outcast, because I championed Poe and his view. I knew also George E. Woodberry's *Life of Poe.* In my egotism I thought that I and George E. Woodberry were the only people north of Kentucky venturesome enough to estimate Poe as a sage, and a high priest of every form of beauty, and not a jingle man. One of my great days was when the *Century Magazine* published a picture of the Zolnay bust which is at the University of Virginia.

But back to a far more remote infancy: My mother destined me, from the beginning, to be an artist. This seemed reasonable, for those were days of splendor. For instance, my mother staged two miracle plays, which were apocalyptic in color. These she had written and staged in a Kentucky college where she had taught painting and English literature.

These plays were written in a similar style to the *Litany of the Heroes*, and I suppose that is where I found the idea. Women's clubs write me a letter a day, asking me just where I get my ideas, and insist on something confidential, not imparted to the vulgar throng. Now there is something confidential.

One of my mother's plays was "Olympus," with the well-known characters, from Mercury to Father Time. My uncle, Johnson Lindsay, was Neptune, since he had a wonderful, long, beautiful red beard, and was exceedingly tall and handsome besides; a Neptune of Neptunes, when draped in seaweed. The Sunday School superintendent impersonated Bacchus. How they let him get into the pulpit with all those grapes on him I do not know. But he laughed hard, and Peter Paul Rubens would have been proud of him. I was too young to know what the church elders said about him. My mother was a riot in those days. How she did it in the midst of that rigor I do not know. Possibly she persuaded the elders it was like a Christmas or Easter Entertainment, which had by that time been accepted as primitive, Biblical and orthodox, and in no way violating the conditions of Saint Peter's platform on the day of Pentecost.

I know my mother called her show "Colloquy." It takes an epic poetess to call a heathen show a "colloquy" and have the associated elders and deacons openly approve. But my mother was already flushed with victory. She had recently read a famous paper on the great Italian Madonnas.

This had been before the Illinois Art Association assembled in annual conclave in the State House I have mentioned. She was flaming with many such great days in her youth, including many oratorical triumphs, which were, in their fashion, spoken epics, in frank imitation of her forensic and senatorial Kentucky and Virginia ancestors. It now becomes plain that I was pumped as full of ambition by this aggressive lady as my silly little hide could hold. But back to that colloquy. My mother was, in a way, like Woodrow Wilson, and trained me early to respect such a type of mind. Anything of which Wilson is accused, is to me a point for admiration rather than reviling. My mother wrote all the speeches for all the gods. She did it deftly enough, I have no doubt. Impersonating deity, or writing shrewd speeches for various divinities comes naturally with a certain ecclesiastical strain. My Sunday School teacher was chosen by my mother to be Venus in this colloquy. Venus was as voluminously robed and as magnificently crowned as is the Statue of Liberty in New York Harbor, and in my memory, would resemble that figure, if the bronze of the New York idol could be changed to perfect ivory.

I was six or seven years old at this particular time, and I was Cupid. To silence the thunders of my Grandfather Nicholas Lindsay, who was blind, and hated effeminacy in his namesake, and reviled my long curls every time he put his hand on my head, my mother had recently cut off those curls and cried all over me. But now she let my hair grow again. She put it up in papers for all one night, and when she took out the papers, I did not know myself. She took off most of my clothes. She put a pink slip on me, and sewed dove's wings to the back of it. I was given silver pasteboard arrows, and a silver pasteboard bow, and a silver quiver on my shoulder, under the wings. I climbed into that pulpit hand in hand with the beautiful Venus, my Sunday School teacher. She had discussed with me, heretofore, the story of the suffering saints of the Old Testament and what they endured in Egypt from my friend Pharaoh. She had spoken of the virtuous adventures of Joseph, and of Moses, and such-like matters. But now, in silence through most of the "Colloquy," she let her beauty speak for her. And when, at last, she addressed implacably the awestruck throng, it must have been something like a verse from the "Song of Songs" in which the Church, the Bride, speaks devoutly of the Bridegroom.

I said nothing, but held tight to one hand of Venus. In her other hand she carried a beautiful golden apple.

At this time my mother staged another colloquy, in which nations, rather than gods, were impersonated by the best and handsomest actors in Springfield. It was ostensibly to celebrate Washington's Birthday. It was given once in the Church of the Disciples, once in the Y.M.C.A. Hall. My mother was epic poet enough to write the speeches for the nations. She went on through her life, writing oracles and speaking them to audiences of thousands in the Middle West, oracles for the gods and for the nations. In a great many places where I go my crowds are rallied by those who once heard her. Sometimes even the nations and the gods seemed to listen to her oracles. Oftener they did not. If they would only live up to her "Speeches" as she humbly called them, it would be a kinder, a more literary, a more sapient, a wittier, a more motherly and a far more resplendent world.

As I have said, my mother destined me from the beginning to be an artist. My Grandfather Frazee had spoken rather contemptuously of poets in my self-important infant presence. He said they were clever men, and we like to memorize long passages from their works, and it was eminently desirable we should do so. But almost all of them had a screw loose somewhere. He said this in the midst of his much-read books, which began with Shakespeare and Addison, and ended with all of Mark Twain. And then, incidentally, there were all the established authorities on shorthorn cattle.

My Grandfather Frazee was a great man, so I stored this matter away in my infant mind, and decided, if one wrote poetry, one did it as a side-line, and agreed with my mother I was to be an artist. All the elegant young ladies in our family had always painted pictures. Some few could draw well. But in general their kind of craftsmanship has been characteristic of the accomplished daughters of pioneer families since the Daughters of Noah embroidered superfluous bibs for the elephants in the ark.

Before I went to the usual public school and met for lifetime friendship all the youngsters in our end of town, I was sent to a breathlessly exclusive private school, and was "taught drawing." My exercise book was called *The Aurora Drawing Book*, and on the back of it was an engraving of Guido Reni's Aurora. My mother and I were both quite fond of the picture. It was the fresco delineating Apollo and his chariot. The chariot is drawn by the horses of the dawn. The muses are dancing behind and around on lovely clouds, and Cupid or some other dimpled infant is flying before them with a splendid torch. Aurora herself, leading the pageant, is scattering flowers on the sleeping cities. It is a picture I still love, despite any cubists in the world, or drunk, disorderly and obscene painters and beachcombers, from the Pacific islands.

At Miss Sampson's drawing class I filled this book with pictures of peacock feathers, and of clover red and white, and all the strange grasses I could gather in the vacant lots of South Sixth Street. I am fond of clover and wild grass and peacock feathers to this day, and no man shall shame me out of it.

The way the easier gods had won authority over my father and mother was the romance of their lives. He, Doctor Vachel Lindsay, and she, school-marm, Kate Frazee, had done their courting in the galleries of Dresden, Saxony, and Florence, Italy, and in the gondolas of Venice. Between times Doctor Vachel Lindsay was taking a season of study at the Vienna hospitals. He had practiced medicine about nine years near Springfield. He was in Europe to brush up and perfect himself in the hospitals most approved by all the world for learned young physicians of his time. My mother and her chum, Eudora Lindsay, fellow teachers from the same Kentucky college, were taking their European year in art galleries and cathedrals and pagan temples from Scotland to Sicily. My Aunt Eudora subsequently put the studies into a book, *Wayside Notes and Fireside Thoughts*, which is one of the household gods of the tribe. Both girls were corresponding with Kentucky literary weeklies.

So all the stories of this trip were a thousand times retold and re-measured in my infancy. And my father and mother returned throughout their lives to Europe and came back with new improvised unwritten poems about the architecture and the pictures, reappraising the favorites of their youth. They divided their summer holidays between this sort of thing and camping like cinnamon bears on Mount Clinton, Colorado, and admiring the views from every peak within a day's climb. And once they went to China.

So it was natural that my infancy should be crowded with oracles about the nations, and the Italian painters, and when I was told I was to be an artist, that was final. Literature was taken for granted. For instance all we children were drilled in memorizing choice verses from King James' Bible. We had to recite three verses apiece before we could have our breakfast. Thus we memorized every Sunday School lesson, having it letter-perfect by the end of the week, for fourteen years. My mother took an especial pleasure in those poets who dealt also in art, and filled me full of the Brownings and the Pre-Raphaelites.

My little world still insists I am a student of phonetics. But it seems to me reasonable that, as one of my new adventures while singing these songs (if the technique of my verse is to be discussed at all from town to town by committees) that my verse be judged not as a series of experiments in sound, but for lifetime and even hereditary thoughts and memories of painting. Let the verse be scrutinized for evidences of experience in drawing from life, drawing architecture, drawing sculpture, trying to draw the Venus of Milo, and imitating the Japanese Prints and Beardsley, and trying to draw like Blake, and all such matters. Unless I am much mistaken, I shall sooner or later evolve a special type of United States Hieroglyphics, based on a contemplation of the borderline between letters and art, and the bridges that cross it. The theory of these hieroglyphics is already embedded in the text of *The Art of the Moving Picture*.

I have now, for eighteen years, walked the corridors of the Metropolitan Museum of Art, for the most part alone. Each room echoes like a mausoleum. Of all the university thousands I address in the winter, and have addressed since 1915, none turn up in that Museum that is my Princeton and my University of California. An art student is far more separated from the United States Civilization than is a speaker or writer. And this brings me to a curious story, which may serve as a symbol of this assertion.

When I was in the New York School of Art, William M. Chase gave us a lecture on drawing the beauties of the nude figure from memory. I had already drawn from life four years. I could put up the usual life drawing, and have it exhibited on the line in due place. So, bearing the words of Chase in mind, I made the conventional charcoal record of a most Olympian model, a most exquisite model, of whom I made a dull, accurate map.

That evening, far from school, and the thought of the day's work I pinned to the wall a sheet of the same size of paper as I used at school, and to my astonishment drew from memory a better picture of that model in an hour than the one it had taken a week to draw in class. It was one of the great adventures while singing these songs, to find it could actually be done. I brought the two drawings together next day and found that the memory drawing was as well measured, but more Greek than the other.

Then, again from memory, I did the picture in miniature, in pen and ink. Then I added, beneath the feet of the lady, a bubble-chariot, in which she was riding. Around her were stars and moons, turning to bubbles, and bubbles turning to stars and moons. Then I gave her a crown of bubbles, and the whole picture seemed to be ascending. Ascending to what? I put in the final bubble, a gigantic one, in the top corner of the picture. Then I gave it sunrays, and made it a sun. Then, and only then, did the poem occur to me, which was later accepted by Ridgely Torrence for *The Critic*, and has gone, with his generous endorsement, into anthologies. The picture of the Queen was turned down by *The Critic*, through the austere insistence of Miss Jeannette Gilder, Mr. Torrence's co-editor. She hated the nude, even when it was flying to the sun in blazing sunshine. In a perfectly friendly way, as it were, for argument's sake, I blame Mr. Torrence for not fighting like a desperate wild-cat for the picture.

Miss Gilder was the first of a long series of people in the world of letters quite sure a poet should not draw pictures. Now the newspaper editors that never scrutinize my books and who send their reporters to get hasty impressions at my recitals, are vowing I can recite, but cannot write. All that some newspapers are willing to leave of my infant and prenatal destiny is the Kentucky Orator. It is "Too Much," as Artemus Ward said, "Too, Too Much." At the risk of being accused of every kind of lavishness, I say "Back to the *Aurora Drawing Book*, and the pictures of Peacock Feathers and Clover."

Newspaper reporters of the sort who never read any man's books, and who do not expect to begin with mine, are fond of filling column after column, in town after town where I recite, with stories of how I have spent the most of my forty-three years in some form of deeply degraded beggary.

The reason my beggar days started talk was that each time I broke loose, and went on the road, in the spring, after a winter of Art lecturing, it was definitely an act of protest against the United States commercial standard, a protest against the type of life set forth for all time in two books of Sinclair Lewis: *Babbitt* and *Main Street*.

After I had been twice on the road, and proved my independence in a fashion, there were days in my home town when the Babbitts and their friends in the Country Club were about ready to send me to jail or burn me at the stake for some sort of witchcraft, dimly apprehended, but impossible for them to define. One of my crimes was a course of lectures at the Y.M.C.A. on Ruskin's famous chapters on the Nature of Gothic, from the second volume of the *Stones of Venice*. I went on lecturing, approving all Ruskin said, in spite of mutterings.

After I had been twice on the road, still the Babbitts insisted on my drawing purely commercial pictures, or quitting the business of drawing altogether. They insisted that I write purely commercial verse, that could be syndicated like crackers and cheese, and they brought their views to bear in every direct and indirect way. The only way out was a clean-cut defiance. I was told by the Babbitts on every hand I must quit being an artist, or beg. So I said, for the third time, "I will beg."

But I made this resolve after having had my pictures and verses turned down by every art editor and literary editor of New York for two years. And on two other desperate occasions named above, I thus broke loose.

It was because it was a three-times-loudly-proclaimed act of defiance, not the time spent on the road, that made the stir. As a matter of fact I came back temporarily beaten each time, at the end of less than four months. But each time I was fortified to try it again. I am not yet through, either. I have spent a total of only two springs and one summer as a beggar, less than a year. Because it was an act of spiritual war, I have written many bulletins and reminiscences.

As to my fourth extensive experience on the road, it was as a pedestrian, not as a beggar, as a companion, as a Franciscan of the more liberal observance. This is all too generously recorded by my good friend Stephen Graham in that book of his own verses and his own prose: — *Tramping with a Poet in the Rockies*. So here I give my poor thanks, and it comes with a full heart.

The United States Men of Letters in general have experienced a similar fraternity from other British Men of Letters, and they all appreciate it as a God-given thing. I hope that forever and a day, writers will walk with writers, politicians with politicians, statesmen with statesmen. I venture on the strength of this hope to suggest that British and United States Universities explore the world abreast. I urge students of California, Washington and Oregon, contemplating a University career, to go to England. With even more emphasis I urge the British to send all the sons they can spare, not to any eastern school, but to the University of the State of Washington, the University of Oregon, the University of California.

The poem called "General Booth Enters Heaven" was built in part upon certain adventures while singing these songs. When I was dead broke, and begging, in Atlanta, Georgia, and much confused as to my next move in this world, I slept for three nights in the Salvation Army quarters there. And when I passed through Newark, New Jersey, on another trip, I slept in the Salvation Army quarters there. I could tell some fearful stories of similar experiences. I will say briefly, that I know the Salvation Army from the inside. Certainly, at that time, the Army was struggling with what General Booth called the submerged tenth of the population. And I was with the submerged.

In the spring of 1912 the news went around the world that the great founder of the Army had gone blind. Every Sunday newspaper had a full-page picture of the blind General. Later came the announcement of his death, with elaborate biographies. Later in these same newspapers, all over the world, came the story of his life as told by himself. So much has happened since, such rivers of blood have run under the bridges of the world, that this succession of newspaper features has been forgotten. Meanwhile the fanatical Salvation Army, that was like the Franciscans of the Strict Observance in the very earliest days of St. Francis, has emerged as a prosperous rival of the Y.M.C.A.

By General Booth's own story, quoted incessantly by the papers the year of his death, he went into the lowest depths of London, with malice aforethought, with deliberate intention to rescue the most notoriously degraded, those given up by policeman, physician, preacher and charity worker. He reiterated in his autobiography that he wanted to find those so low there were none lower. He put them into uniform. He put them under military discipline. He put them in authority over one another. He chose their musical instruments, and their astonishing tunes. The world has forgotten what a scandal to respectable religion the resulting army was when it began. It was like the day St. Francis handed all his clothes to the priest, or the day he cut off the hair of St. Clara. In my poem I merely turned into rhyme as well as I could, word for word, General Booth's own account of his life, and the telegraph dispatches of his death after going blind. I set it to the tune that is not a tune, but a speech, a refrain used most frequently in the meetings of the Army on any public square to this day. Yet I encounter a great number of people who are sure they have never heard of the General, the army, or the tune, or who ask me if I wrote the poem to "make sport."

The verses in the section of this book called *Politics* remain as promises of more elaborate efforts in the future on that theme.

About the same time I was the tinseled infant Cupid that I have described in the early part of this discourse, my father had filled me with the notion that, way down in Kentucky, once upon a time a certain Abraham Lincoln came, with many soldiers. According to this tale they stole all the horses from my Grandfather Lindsay's estate, drove off all the negroes forever (my grandfather's personal property and mine), burned the crops, and then, in a way not mentioned, stole the farm, and left us all to begin again by studying medicine by a solitary candle. And as for Harriet Beecher Stowe, any one who would read her book was worse than an infidel. This general view of history was challenged by my mother, who, though having many Southern ideas, was all for Lincoln. And I have in many ways agreed with her, but not enough to alter the fact that Mason and Dixon's line runs straight through our house in Springfield still, and straight through my heart. No man may escape his bouncing infancy. I do not expect to get ten feet from my childhood till I die.

Elegant ladies ask me hundreds of times as I come to their towns as a reciter: "How did you get your knowledge of the 'neeegro'?" They put *e* in the word three times over. After profound meditation I now give my answer to them all. My father had a musical voice, and he used to read us *Uncle Remus*, and he could sing every scrap of song therein and revise every story by what some old slave had told him. He used to sing the littler children to sleep with negro melodies which he loved, and which negroes used to sing to him, when they rocked him to sleep in his infancy. We nearly always had a black hired man and a black hired girl. My father took us to jubilee singer concerts from Fisk or Hampton, and came home rendering the songs authentically, and from boyhood memory. Moreover, our negro servants did not hesitate to sing. One-fifth of the population of the town of Springfield is colored. I played with negro boys in the Stuart School yard. I have heard the race question argued to shreds every week of my life from then till now. We have so many negroes that we had race riots for a week in 1908. I took time off for months to argue the matter out with a good friend, a local negro lawyer, Charles Gibbs, who was just then beginning to practice law. Springfield is as far south as Maryland, Delaware and northern Virginia. Mason and Dixon's line goes straight east and west on Edwards Street. Lincoln's home is only two blocks north of it.

And it seems to me Mason and Dixon's line runs around every country in the world, around France, Japan, Canada, or Mexico or any other sovereignty. It is the terrible line, that should be the line of love and good-will, and witty conversation, but may be the bloody line of misunderstanding. When Graham and I climbed into Alberta, Canada, from Glacier Park, Montana, we crossed a Canadian-American line almost obliterated. Every line should be that way. We must have no Gettysburg of the nations. I still thrill to Andrew Jackson's old toast at the famous banquet: "The Federal Union, — it must and shall be preserved." But I would alter it to: "The League of Nations, it must and shall be preserved." And in my fancy I see Old Jackson rising to propose that toast to the world. Something like this is the implication beneath all the political poems, and the implication beneath the prose work, *The Golden Book of Springfield*.

Come, let us be bold with our songs.

VACHEL LINDSAY

October 15, 1922.

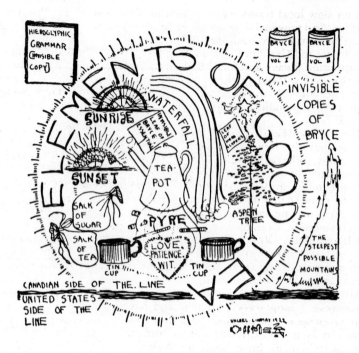

THE ELEMENTS OF GOOD TEA from
Going-to-the-Sun

This book is a sequel and a reply to a book by Stephen Graham, explorer-poet, and Vernon Hill, artist.

I had a splendid six weeks tramping with my lifetime friend, Stephen Graham, in the Rockies. We climbed northwest through Glacier Park, Montana, across the Canadian line into Alberta, Canada. There it is in two sentences.

It would take more than the *Encyclopaedia Britannica* to tell on how many points I differ from Stephen, and on how many points I agree with him. I had not the least idea that so much Lindsay was going into Graham's fireside notes — while I was asleep at noon, often recovering in an hour from ten hours of restless, sleepless freezing by night. I do not hold myself liable in court for any opinions of mine then recorded by Graham. My daytime strength was not all given to thought, however, but often to trying to keep Graham in sight when he was a quarter of a mile ahead of me climbing mountains absolutely perpendicular. As I remember our first fireside discussions, they were as to whether there was actually such a person as Patrick Henry. Graham had an idea he was a perverse invention of my own fancy. But he looked him up afterwards and found there was such a man. As I remember our conversations after that provocation, I kept trying to deliver to him from memory Bryce's *American Commonwealth*, unabridged, two volumes, one thousand pages each. I remember those volumes well. I read every page in lonely country hotels and on slow local trains while a Sunday field-worker for the Anti-Saloon League. And now invisible leaves of Bryce often made the chief ingredient of our tea. So I have indicated in the design.

I did not tell Graham I was quoting the great ambassador, and so many unsupported, heavy and formidable statements he quite properly hesitated to write out, without further confirmation, though he drank them down quite cheerfully. In the great blank spaces in Graham's narrative where he skips really splendid scenery, I was quoting Bryce—not always singing hymns!

The most authentic part of my book, the part Mr. Vernon Hill has left out, is that the mountains were as steep as I have drawn them. His mountains, otherwise quite correct, are not sufficiently perpendicular. Vernon Hill, of course, was not physically with us on the expedition. He was in London, drawing beautiful and famous Arcadian Calendars. When later he came to illustrate Graham's book in London, with Graham bending over him, no one mentioned the fact that the mountains were all like church steeples. Graham had not noticed it, and it did not occur to Vernon Hill by wireless. Otherwise Vernon Hill was in excellent communication with us, and every picture in Graham's book expresses exactly what Graham was talking to me about to make me forget the tumbles and the briers, and to drown out the Bryce.

After I had hunted for years and years to find an explorer-poet who would take a long walk with me, and had scared every one off by the elaborateness of the proposal, the first troubadour that took me up on it almost broke my neck. It was a grand and awful time. The sensible reviews of Graham's book have been by Walter Prichard Eaton. He does not discuss Graham's opinions or mine. But he is very plain about the fact that we almost slid into eternity. He has tried those mountains himself, and he knows. He should write several more reviews.

Stephen Graham is a lifetime friend, and I have assembled these drawings as a sign thereof. But because I have been studying Hieroglyphics in the Metropolitan Museum all this summer, and because United States Hieroglyphics of my own invention are haunting me day and night, this book is drawn, and not written. I serve notice on the critics—the verses are most incidental, merely to explain the pictures. And so, directly considered, it is much more a reply to Vernon Hill, the artist, than to Stephen.

The artist of the Arcadian Calendar discerned rightly. Graham and I were in Arcady, even if it was a bit rough.

Going-To-The-Sun Mountain is the very jewel of the mountains of Glacier Park. All the tourists love it, and they are right. Its name fits it.

Going-To-The-Sun Mountain is our American Fujiyama, as all testify who have seen it.

Obviously, an ingredient of good tea is talk on Egyptian Hieroglyphics. I had an invisible copy of an Egyptian Grammar with me and I put a leaf from it into every pot of tea. Graham did not take to the taste of it as much as he did to the pages of Bryce, but he was nobly patient, as one may say, with Egypt.

The Hieroglyphics in this work are based on two more British-Egyptian grammars he sent me after he reached London. Still, they may be

described as United States Hieroglyphics, and almost any Egyptologist will
be willing to describe them that way, having about as much to do with
Egypt as Egyptian cigarettes. The Egyptians were, briefly, a nation of
Vernon Hills, who drew their "Arcadian Calendar" for four thousand
years in red and black ink, or cut it in granite. *I keep thinking about them!*
A free translation of the hieroglyphic inscription at the bottom of the first
picture following is:

> *The beating heart of the waterfall of the*
> *double truth, as it appears to a scribe,*
> *a servant of Thoth—Thoth, who is god of*
> *picture-writing, photoplays and hieroglyphics,*
> *and an intense admirer of waterfalls.*

With this start, the reader can go straight through the book without a
mistake.

Now, a last word as to the seal, *The Elements of Good Tea.*

On the southern side of the Canadian-United States boundary, just as we
reached it, our coffee gave out. Most symbolical happening! There in the
deep woods, as we passed to the northern side, Graham said with a sigh of
insatiable anticipation: "Now we will have some tea." We had had tea all
along, alternated with coffee. But now Stephen, on his own heath, was
emphatic about it. So he made tea, a whole potful, with a kick like a
battering ram, and I drank my half.

Certainly the most worth-while thing in Stephen's book, and mine, is a
matter known to all men long before the books were written. That is, that a
Britisher and a United Stateser can cross the Canadian-American line
together and discover that it is hardly there; can discover that an
international boundary can be genuine and eternal and yet friendly. If
there is one thing on which Stephen and I will agree till the Judgment Day,
it is that all the boundaries in the world should be as open, and as happy,
as the Canadian-United States line. To many diplomats such a boundary is
incredible, and yet it exists, one of the longest in the world.

VACHEL LINDSAY

ADVENTURES WHILE PREACHING HIEROGLYPHIC SERMONS from
Collected Poems

Being about to start on a new national tour, it is my petition to my prospective audiences that they provide themselves with the illustrated edition of my COLLECTED POEMS before I arrive in town. I urge them to bring it to the lecture hall, not only to follow the texts as I recite them, but to follow the forty designs as I here discuss them. Begin with "The Village Improvement Parade," [pp. 258-264]; and follow it up with a careful study of "The Map of the Universe," frontispiece, and the poems which grew out of it.

The preface to the first edition of the COLLECTED POEMS is entitled "Adventures While Singing These Songs." This *might* be called "Adventures With the Bottle Volcanic" (see drawing [p. 97]), *might* be entitled "Adventures While Designing These Hieroglyphics." The first preface says that I am about to start on another reciting tour. I made the tour while the book was in the press, and being published. Later I toured the Western Capitals of Canada, as far north as Saskatoon, Saskatchewan. In the late winter the swing around the circle finally ended at Gulf Park, Gulfport, Mississippi, about which I have written many songs. This very preface is written at *The Studio of the Driftwood Fire*, at Gulf Park.

At Gulf Park College I have been teaching "The New Poetry Anthology," by Harriet Monroe and Alice Corbin Henderson, reading it through to my classes with the greatest joy. I have been revelling in poems most of them written by personal friends under circumstances fairly familiar. It has been a great luxury thus to pause and with the help of such shrewd editors as Harriet Monroe and Alice Corbin Henderson, make a reappraisal of all things that have happened in the United States and British Languages in Poetry since that mystic date of 1912. I anticipate interpreting for many years, to picked classes, these verses, and newer songs, for I am sure that the New Poetry Movement has but begun, and that this anthology will need to be enlarged again in a few years. These singers are young.

Harriet Monroe says in her preface:

"Indeed, many critics feel that poetry is coming nearer than either the novel or the drama to the actual life of our time. The magazine, *Poetry*, ever since its foundation in October, 1912, has encouraged this new spirit in the art, and the anthology is a further effort on the part of its editors to present the new spirit to the public."

I am always urging upon my classes the valor and efficiency and worth of Harriet Monroe and Alice Corbin Henderson.

But my present story is far from that story and almost all of it dates from before 1912, way back, when I drew "The Map of the Universe." Between October, 1912, and July, 1914, an astonishing number of events in the Poetry World can be chronicled. And to this general interest in poetry I attribute the fact that I, a speaker to whom not six persons were ever known to listen with patience, became a conventionalized "reciter" of my own verses almost instantly, and have since that time recited to about one million people.

I have put as much energy into reciting as a National League baseball player puts into grand-stand plays. It is not a bad fate, but this illustrated edition is a weapon in a strenuous warfare against that fate.

By the conservative estimate of all magazines that have a circulation of one million, I have a constituency of three million. I now address, as a body, my three million. May they enjoy it. The magazine of one million subscribers has a tragic limitation: which I am resolved to escape with the aid of this, my book of forty pictures, — forty mysterious ways for the grand-stand player to escape through the fence.

We will go back to the *Saturday Evening Post* of that much announced day when it reached one million subscribers and three million readers. Suppose on that occasion it had changed its entire formula, and taken on the aspects of *The Atlantic Monthly*. That million would, in two months have shrunk to one hundred thousand. Or suppose that it had taken on the aspects of a magazine I admire much more than either of these esteemed mediums. Suppose that it had suddenly become *Poetry, A Magazine of Verse*, published by Harriet Monroe, in Chicago?

Or suppose that the magazine *Poetry* with its present creditable circulation should suddenly publish forty poetical drawings, pen and ink experiments by a young artist. Probably many friends would be vexed. Yet life is an adventure with me, not a matter of professional standardization. I refuse to be put into uniform paraffin packages for the trade, like Uneeda Biscuit. Let me meet you, dear audience, as though you were an individual.

I want to come to your town. But I want to be judged, not by my speaking tours, but by what I did before October, 1912, even before *The Poetry Magazine* began, and before those tours began. So look at "The Village Improvement Parade" and "The Map of the Universe."

I have the notes on a long chant about my first long speaking tour. That tour was one of the great panoramas of my life. Never will I forget it. When I reached England and all the time that I was there reciting I was still remembering the thrill of California. When I was again in California, the English memory came in splendor. Life has been like a movie turned too fast, but even then a thrilling movie. Now I find the whole touring scheme hardening around me like a steel Pullman car, in the minds of the friendly committees. Even my oldest friends seem to want two expeditions to be as much alike as two bound volumes of *The Saturday Evening Post*. Against this deadly fate I now wage my warfare with these forty pictures. Also let me insist that I am teaching the Monroe-Henderson anthology steadily.

So look at "The Village Improvement Parade" and "The Map of the Universe."

The Mystic Springfield in which I always live, wherever I may happen to be, is not a place of recitals, of Pullman Car Welcomes and Pullman Car Farewells. It is a place dating before 1912 where one walks alone, from childhood, among historic structures (see text and hieroglyphic, page [199]) a place of clear visions. It is a place dominated in my mind by one harmonizer of all its history to the present hour, and a tiny group of devotees quite alien to her in their essential mood, but her practical allies. The friend was my English teacher in high school, Susan E. Wilcox. The group is a circle of the followers of Swedenborg.

Susan E. Wilcox is still the head of the very distinguished English Department of the Springfield High School. Half the poems in this book show her stern hand. Leaving out the members of my own family, she is, without doubt, both as a person and a teacher the noblest and most faithful friend of my life. She stood by me for years when I went through the usual Middle West crucifixion of the artist.

Early Hieroglyphics, like "The Shield of Lucifer" (page [72]), and early songs like "Lucifer" (page [362]), I submitted to her many times while she corrected everything. She worked on Johnny Appleseed with me the same way, much later. She will rise and testify that I am no improviser. By the time we were through with any one piece of writing she had not only the verse by heart, she had the commas by heart. My alleged theory of the jazzing of poetry, which I have never endorsed or agreed to, amounts to just this: I submitted the "Hieroglyphic," and then read and re-read the poem to Susan Wilcox. Week after week for six months I would read the verse till she was sure it was clear, grammatical and reasonable. Some of the British critics like neither my hieroglyphics, my spelling nor my punctuation. I refer them to the wrath of Susan E. Wilcox. She has a reply, if they care to write to the Springfield High School.

The Swedenborgian circle we found for friends much later, darkly suspected poetry and the reciting of poetry, as a work of the evil powers. Those who look for scraps of my alleged ragtime, vaudeville or jazz theory, in that circle, are doomed again to disappointment. But those Swedenborgians had ideas. Those critics who say that I have no ideas are casting reflections not on me but those Swedenborgians, for I listened to them with all my ears for years. I loved them because they could always talk me down. An egotist always likes an even stronger egotist to make him imagine he is humble. What did we have in common? We had in common what might even be called a "Swedenborgian Springfield," the Springfield of the "Map of the Universe"; a Springfield of Visions. But with the visions I was given the benefit of their intense hereditary intellectual Swedenborgian discipline, which let no man pass over hurriedly. It counts greatly in our villages. So look at "The Village Improvement Parade" and "The Map of the Universe."

The great and admirable Robert Frost said in *The New York Times*, in reference to his new work in Amherst: *"Philosophy, that's another subject I am going to teach. Philosophy of what? Of life. Of people about you. What's my philosophy? That's hard to say. I was brought up a Swedenborgian. I am not a Swedenborgian now. But there's a good deal of it that's left with me. I am a mystic. I believe in symbols,"* etc.

Springfield, without knowing it, was *"brought up a Swedenborgian,"* by this circle. Wherever I go I want to bring with me what might be called "The Swedenborgian Springfield." Johnny Appleseed, whom I recommend to all men who love visions, was a man of lonely walking, a literal Swedenborgian all his days, distributing tracts when occasionally he met a settler. For the most part he was consoled by his personal visions in the wilderness. I am for Johnny Appleseed's United States. Up to 1912, while I walked in Springfield for the most part silent as to literal vocalization, I tried to express this United States in cartoons. This Johnny Appleseed mood was our common ground.

The exquisite, sharp-edged Swedenborgian culture, though confined to an almost invisible sect, has brought some beautiful fruit that has been accepted the world over.

Howard Pyle was a literal Swedenborgian. His place as an old Master of American illustration is continually growing. William Dean Howells and Henry James and William James came of Swedenborgian stock. Their disposition to choose and fulfill a lifetime task with great severity to themselves and great kindness to their neighbors was typically Swedenborgian. The final act of the mind of Swedenborg was far from these three. They were unwilling to see their thoughts as splendid visions in the air. The most ordinary movie magnate goes further into this than Howells and Henry and William James. Swedenborg should be re-written in Hollywood. We want to know the meaning of all those hieroglyphics that they are thrusting upon us, for the present as unsolved, in many phases, as the hieroglyphic ruins of pre-historic Mexico and South America. The American mind has become an overgrown forest of unorganized pictures.

And this may be said to be true of the whole world, controlled in the end by the political cartoonists of *London Punch*, and the like. So look at "The Village Improvement Parade" and the "The Map of the Universe."

The Christian Century for September 27, 1923, says: *The members of the New Church, Swedenborgians, are much encouraged by the publication recently of a book called "New Light Upon Indian Philosophy." In this book D. Goupal Chetty, late editor of "The New Reformer," takes the position that it is the writings of Swedenborg which will make the necessary connection between Hindu Philosophy and Christianity. Mr. Chetty is a Tamil, and there are twenty millions of his race. His book will be given wide circulation in the English-speaking world by the Swedenborgians of England and of America.*

Howard Pyle always saw his pictures in the air, first, before he drew them. I see myself as the draughtsman of my own ideas only, and of those of my oldest and most intimate friends of our Swedenborgian Springfield before 1912.

These ideas I have had so long, I necessarily see them as pictures in the air. No doubt if they were all worked out they would be as poor philosophy to a real philosopher as Griffith's "Intolerance." Still they are with me in fancy, perhaps five hundred hieroglyphics, big and little, all of them differing from one another and all of them differing from anything that I have ever been advertised in the newspapers as doing. After I have written songs for them, you may pronounce these songs as being akin to the song of John L. Sullivan, if this is the truth. But I want the songs to have an even chance to be in contrast to that song, and the picture to be in contrast to the best liked drawing in this collection. I want it to be liked because it is a surprise. I claim the privilege of this versatility.

Up to 1912 I had been first, last and always, a cartooning adventurer and a cartooning preacher.

I consider all my cartooning in some sense hieroglyphic in the old Egyptian way. The principal towns of Southern Illinois are Cairo, Karnak and Thebes, and the swamp-bordered river moves southward past Memphis, Tennessee, named for the town of King Menes, first King of Egypt. There is a parallel between the psychology and history of the Mississippi delta and the famous delta of the old Nile. Africans roll cotton bales to steamships on wharves of both rivers. They sing the same tunes, ten thousand years old. Once I sang the Congo. Long before that I sang the

Nile. The forty pictures in this book, most of them dated before 1912, are in their own way, a part of the Egypt that is in me forever. And I beg all my readers to look into Swedenborg's theory of Egyptian Hieroglyphics. No one can read it without getting the notion that some fate is swinging us around to the moods of Egypt.

In anticipation of publishing this illustrated edition of my Collected Poems, I distributed in the summer of 1922 to many literary friends throughout the United States two grammars of Egyptian Hieroglyphics. One was Margaret A. Murray's delightful Elementary Grammar, published by Bernard Quaritch. The other was Gunther Roeder's Book, translated by Samuel F.B. Mercer, and published by the Yale University Press. Both grammars are simplified from Adolph Erman.

I thrust these books upon my friends as though they were candy. The while the Macmillan Company were reading the manuscript of the first edition of these "Collected Verses," and while my friends were carefully scrutinizing these grammars, and while I was way off in Saskatchewan, reciting for the British as well as I could, I read in the Saskatoon paper that Tut-Ankh-Amen's tomb had been opened by an Englishman and an American in friendly alliance. Such a roar went up to the sky that it swept from the hot Nile to the snow-buried plains of Canada.

Even the Egyptian Kings are on my side.

My friends opened their grammars again. It reminded me of the time in the "Adventures While Preaching the Gospel of Beauty," where the old "Duck-Pond-Diviner" told me I was a "Child of Destiny," and *also fond of sweets.* Part of my destiny is to issue "The Village Magazine" at intervals of years.

"The Village Magazine" is not a Monthly Magazine. It is a "destiny" magazine.

There is a new issue almost like the others for October, 1924.

I used "The Village Magazine" of 1910 and "The Village Magazine" of 1920, and all tracts allied to them in my Gospel of Beauty campaigns. These campaigns, begun in my days as a New York Art Student, became more intensive as I went back to my home town, expecting to settle and hide there forever.

I was suddenly hurled into a more conventional life almost against my will. In consequence of my having recited for a million people in their Sunday clothes, most of my friends have insisted on "jazzing" the motive of my life.

I have been looking out standardized windows of "The Flat-Wheeled Pullman Car." I have been living in standardized hotels, have been eating jazzed meals as impersonal as patent breakfast-food. It has been an amazing experience in "The Flat-Wheeled Pullman Car," "jazzed" and jerky.

But I suspected, when at the tender age of twelve, that the incessant orator blunts the edges of his brain. I have suspected it all along. I have tried to fight off all jazz. I have great sympathy with all those who share this same misgiving.

There is a secret to my travelling, oratorical life. So I begin to travel again with joy. The unstandardized thing is the overwhelming flame of youth that swept up and sweeps up from those thousands and hundreds of thousands of faces. It is a changing flame of far more subtle colors than the critic knows, a flame that still possesses me from this ten years' memory and eleven years' memory and twelve years' memory, and still burns on through my heart and mind and body and bone and soul. The critic hears my voice. He does not look down into those faces, into an audience of one thousand different dazzling hieroglyphics of flame, differing from one another as one star differeth from another star in glory. My mystic Springfield is here, also, in its fashion.

I have travelled so long it seems to me I have seen all young America and young Canada face to face. And each face is as it were a new word from Egypt, written by Hathor, goddess of young love.

I see the "Springfield Hieroglyphic," something akin to "The Village Improvement Parade," with the "Amaranth" above it, and "The Map of the Universe."

All touring appeals to me as a splendid and unending drunkenness, in spite of the flat-wheeled cars. But touring is not the innermost serious plan of my heart unless you help me bring "The Mystic Springfield" with me. What I want and pray for is a Springfield torn down and rebuilt from the very foundations, according to visions that might appear to an Egyptian or Shaw's Joan of Arc, or any one else whose secret movie-soul was a part of the great spiritual movie.

I believe that civic ecstasy can be so splendid, so unutterably afire, continuing and increasing with such apocalyptic zeal, that the whole visible fabric of the world can be changed. I believe in a change in the actual fabric, not a vague new outline. Therefore I begin with the hieroglyphic, the minute single cell of our thought, the very definite alphabet with which we are to spell out the first sentence of our great new vision. And I say: change not the mass, but change the fabric of your own soul and your own visions, and you change all. See "The Soul of the Spider," and "The Soul of the Butterfly," page [48]. This very precise new beginning of our life is something far more than the mere drunkenness of addressing enormous assemblies.

Every new high school auditorium is built to receive the whole school at once, generally two thousand students. It generally has a stage, almost as wide and high as the length of the auditorium the longest way. This is standardization with a vengeance. But there is an innocent and happy glory that goes with it. And there is a secret here, also, that remains unadvertised.

As he meets me in the office for the preliminary chat, nearly every principal says:

"We had eight hundred students in the old high school building. We built this new school and auditorium for fifteen hundred, and two thousand young men and women came the first day. Therefore they are sitting on the platform, stuffing the balcony, and in the aisles and standing up in the back, and crowding in there at the open doors, and some are out there in the yard trying to find a place to listen. We are now erecting a Junior High School building on the other side of town."

And so he continues in a matter of fact strain.

Yet I see the "Amaranth," the special "Springfield Hieroglyphic," in the air above him. This is the secret. It is a secret something akin to "The Village Improvement Parade."

Students who were leaving high school in 1912 and heard me then were university seniors in 1916 and heard me then, and are now the people sending for me as the heads of responsible faculty committees in universities. That is, I have seen these young Americans grow up, hundreds of them, all over the United States, unharnessed young Americans.

Those I spoke for, once, in one State, I meet again and then again in other audiences in other States. They are growing in gorgeousness and power. And they seem at first generalized types. But I see the special Springfield Hieroglyphic above their heads, and things like "The Soul of the Butterfly," and their own Hieroglyphics above their heads.

The fact that I am a part of this generation is a wonderful gift to me from the sky. The fact that I have had a voice physically loud enough to hold them, has spoiled their critical judgment, almost spoiled mine. Like the rest of the literati, they have at first a wholly jazz and oratorical notion of my ideas. But always a dozen of them speak to me about Springfield, in the handshaking afterward. As to the actual text of this volume, Percy Grainger has made the best appraisal of its intention (aesthetically).   The composer of "The Irish Tone from County Derry," and "Country Gardens" and "Colonial Song," approaches the verse as musical and not jazz composition. Please send for him, and add to his appraisal, "The Map of the Universe," the forty hieroglyphics of this book, "The Soul of the Butterfly," and "The Village Improvement Parade." My business is not jazzing, but Springfield and hieroglyphic and vision-seeing adventure. I claim the privilege of this versatility. I claim the privilege of issuing tracts, drawings of censers, such as are here in this book.

Even my enemies in Springfield know I want that city rebuilt. First of all I want a cathedral there. To that extent Theodore Maynard is right in saying I am a *"Catholic with a few fads."* But I doubt if Theodore Maynard or G.K. Chesterton would consent to have the statue of Johnny Appleseed or Prince Siddartha put up in their Cathedral, or that they would endorse the other prophecies of the Springfield Cathedral in "The Golden Book."

He is a Great Hieroglyphic, Prince Siddartha, seen in profile against the clouds of the ages. My Springfield will not be complete without him. His first virtue was humility. I hope in a thousand years to approximate his first teachings on that virtue. But I can say at least this thing humbly: That he is to me the supreme personality of history. There is something of this conviction back of my song of "The Rose and the Lotus," and the design — page [154].

I have been accused of having many heroes. Certainly the hero of the climax of the "Litany of Heroes" is Socrates, immediately approached through Wilson. Wilson is used as a modern follower of Socrates.

But setting that poem aside, remembering private studies of a lifetime, never put into rhyme, the hero having for me the greatest personal fascination is Prince Siddartha. And anything in any orthodoxy or high school ideal that runs counter to that admiration must be sacrificed. And this is but a hint of my cathedral, and the "Springfield Hieroglyphics," in which it is drawn for me.

Moving on toward my Cathedral, though maybe ten thousand years off, I started the march of "The Village Improvement Parade." I drew that series of panels in 1910. The marchers follow one another in varied succession and rhythm, as one might conjugate the Egyptian verb: *"To strut, or march."*

One need not have the Hieroglyphic grammars that I have mentioned to go into the understanding of such drawings. One need not have a phonetic theory. One need not to have read Swedenborg.

Another series, that might be compared to the conjugation of the Egyptian verb, "To Illumine," is the set of moon designs. See pages [41, 43]. The moon pictures have been scattered everywhere among my friends, done in many mediums. Practically all the moon-poems began with the simple picture of the moon, drawn with an ordinary high-school compass. But each one was separately developed by pen and ink or other medium to show a separate action of the moon. Some I did in Japanese embossed style, with cut-out papers of various hues and textures. I claim the privilege of this versatility. And the design called "The Moon Worms" (page [41]), was issued in Springfield about 1913, printed on a three-foot panel of gold and white. Some citizens liked these as an awful‾warning, some did not.

Next, let us look at the drawings of nine Springfield buildings, with censers swinging over them. These varying censers, shown in the pictures as though lowered by the hands of the angels, might stand for the conjugation of the verb: *"To have vision,"* see pages [197-212].

This set of drawings was first issued separately printed in gold, and these golden pamphlets I issued by the thousands in Springfield, Illinois, putting my last cent into them, as I did for every pamphlet, going broke over and over again for my pamphlets quite ostentatiously, greatly to the vexation of the wise. There were two seriously organized and promoted assemblies, nevertheless. One was given by the Avonian Club in the Library, and I addressed them on the meaning of these designs. Later, upon a Sunday evening, I was invited to preach my evangel in the largest church building: The First Methodist. The place was packed to the doors. A copy of the pamphlet was put into the hands of every person to look on, while I discussed the drawings, much as now, in your town, dear reader, this book will be open to those same drawings, and on the knees of those who welcome me, and want to know precisely my message. (Dear reader, either bring the book, or stay away!).

This Methodist evening was by the generous invitation of the pastor, A.C. Piersel, and I shall ever be grateful. He brought the book!

I have just read a brief biography in an Indianapolis paper which says: *"He has spent most of his life lecturing for the Anti-Saloon League."* I have spent most of my life doing most everything else.

Once I spent three months pushing a truck in the wholesale toy department of Marshall Fields, Chicago. Once I worked three months for a gas-tubing factory in New York City. Once I spent two weeks digging for the Springfield Illinois Department of Public Property, where they were installing a new boiler at the Water Works. Once I spent three days south of Springfield cutting corn for a silo, with as rare a gang of dollar-a-day thugs as ever remained unhung. Once I was offered the job of assistant town sanitarian (as it were) for the town of Raton, New Mexico, seventy-five cents a day, but I did not take the job. Once I spent a day painting signs in Tampa, Florida. It is a mistake to make me out a steady, orthodox established official Anti-Saloon-League worker. My precise experience and views on that subject may be found in the Chapter on "The Substitute for the Saloon" in "The Art of the Moving Picture." There is a certain type of dulcet and affetuoso Bacchanalian who would make me out the one and only dry in the United States, mentioning it rather bitterly in passing. But that imputes to me entirely too much personal influence on the constitution. I doubt if there is a Y.M.C.A. Secretary, member of the Salvation Army or Anti-Saloon-League worker who has ever opened one of my books. And when my pamphlets began to fly in Springfield, certainly those institutions were cheerfully hostile. I was dropped instantly from the rolls of the Y.M.C.A. and the Anti-Saloon League. They would not allow me any of the privileges of that versatility for which I am even now battling. Nevertheless I issued without their consent or approval, temperance tracts, such as the one inserted (page [23]). There is one consistent thread in my life. From first to last I have been an Art Student. I have spent the big part of my life in Art Galleries, Art Schools, and Art Libraries. From all the various adventures I returned to this study, and still return. No Y.M.C.A. man or Anti-Saloon-League worker likes an Art Student, even if he floods the town, gratis, with tracts like that on page [23].

The merry war with Springfield respectability, with the stereotyped United States in general, which any artist has to wage till death, is not a tragedy, but akin to one hundred Gilbert and Sullivan Operas, in long line, in continued performance, like Chinese plays that go on and on. Springfield is still a place of lifetime intimates who regret everything I have ever done, even the tract (page [23]), and everything up to October, 1912. They are sure I should pretend to have been born [in] 1912, and so ignore all my painful past. They are continually spatting me on the wrist, even yet, for things like the tract on page [23]. They deceive the stranger by talking as though they had written my books. And all this without opening the books, they are so sure that they contain statements deadly obscure, highbrow as German Philosophy at its worst, or else plain "*Russian Bolshevism.*" This is the exact reverse of the jazz slander. This type of old neighbor is one of the most valuable, infinitely better for my conceited soul than any advertiser with an ax to grind. Strangely enough, I see above his head "The Amaranth," the Springfield Hieroglyphic, and many solemn and splendid visions hover above the merry war.

I have definitely in mind a series of "*United States Follies*" in the mood of Percy Grainger's most light-hearted compositions, on the theme of the present essay, Gilbert and Sullivan affairs but with a Mohawk flavor, built on Middle West and Far West United States ideas, artistic, and anti-artistic. A friend of mine, of the old art student days on Fifty-seventh Street, New York City, is destined to do them if I do not. And these will contain the special Springfield Hieroglyphic in various outline, and fancies like "The Soul of the Butterfly," page [48], will hover above it all.

I am overwhelmed by people rising and testifying in New Towns that they are my intimate friends, just before I arrive. The papers are so full of jazz that my friends are forced in the end to believe, it comes in such a stream. I am now going to appoint official "old friends" familiar with drawings, hieroglyphics and tracts. Every fact should have their O.K.

before it reaches the point of a jail offense. One of them is the aforementioned Susan E. Wilcox of Springfield, Illinois, who really knows what I am about and has known since I was a very small boy. Another is this friend from Springfield with whom I first went to New York, Willard Wall Wheeler. He is full of plays and light operas, and the like. Both of us were boys together and chums when we were eight years old in Springfield. Both of us took lessons in English in high school under Susan E. Wilcox. We are still waiting in vain hope to deserve her stern praise. But we are still loyal, and glad that there is one firm and accurate standard of excellence in the world. A third is John Price Jones, of New York City and the world.

Willard Wall Wheeler is now a most active citizen of Cleveland, Ohio. But once upon a time, namely about 1904, we laid siege to New York City as though we were one Macedonian Phalanx. He had graduated from Williams College. I had spent the same period of time in The Art Institute, Chicago. We undertook to push the Flatiron Building over with the help of John Price Jones. It still stands. But we were in the same boarding houses on Fifty-sixth and Fifty-seventh Streets. The same crowd of newspaper men, artists, singers, actors, musical students and young writers were around us. Bill was the local center. He dug them out from everywhere. The pageant of the *"younger generation"* poured before us and past us.

We are going to write a "United States Follies" with John Price Jones, about the people of this period. Many of our crowd were rallied round a restaurant we decorated "The Pig and the Goose" (See page [940.). The two were cub reporters. I was a cub art student. Some of the cubs are tigers now; some of them fat bears. Many of the ideas Wheeler brought up from Williams College and I brought from the Art Institute were in the drawings and tracts I scattered in that region of New York. A member of the gang who has followed my work, every inch of it, till now, is George Mather Richards, still in New York. I accept his censorship absolutely.

It was with a head of steam still up after five years of grand free adventuring in New York with these that I went back to Springfield to continue my tracts and hieroglyphics.

In August, 1908, avowedly back in Springfield for good, renouncing "Babylon" forevermore, I began to issue certain "War Bulletins." They assembled all the heresies of the Columbus Circle region, the "Greenwich Village" of that time. According to my doctrine, which I had proclaimed in that "Greenwich Village," I had gone back to "Preach the Gospel of Beauty" in the admired home town. Akin to these "bulletins" was one of my first tracts, scattered in every yard in the town "The Building of Springfield" (page [168]), and I brought out my bulletins till Christmas, then declared a "Christmas Truce." I did it by handing out to any one who would take it on the street "The Sangamon County Peace Advocate."

The opening poem was:

"In this the City of my Discontent,
Sometimes there comes a whisper from the grass: —
'Romance, romance, is here. No Hindu town
Is quite so strange. No citadel of brass
By Sinbad found, held half such love and hate.
No picture palace in a picture-book,
Such webs of friendship, beauty, greed and fate.'"

The closing poem was: "The Springfield of the Far Future," page [75]. (See also page [71]). I mailed "War Bulletins" and "Peace Advocate" back to Willard Wall Wheeler, George Mather Richards, Gertrude Lundborg Richards, Earl H. Brewster, Ascha Barlow Brewster, Marjorie Torre Hood (now Torre Bevans), Leighton Harring Smith, John Price Jones, and others. I was at first happy with cheers from New York. Springfield did not hear those cheers. It was at this point that I was dropped from such Y.M.C.A. work and Anti-Saloon-League work as I was doing in the Springfield region. I was as near to the hieroglyphic as I will ever get, but far from the Sea at Sunrise. The rigors of that loneliness I will never again achieve, unless I consent to go to jail with Debs. And I do not agree with Debs. But there is a certain final clarity for the elect in tracts written amid stern conditions. I expect to fish out those tracts from the bottom of the Sangamon, one at a time, and republish them. Verses that paraphrase them may be found, pages [402, 140, 90, 156, 88, 129, 196, 194, 217, 314, 401, 123, 271, 75, 301, 89, 317, 286, 396]. And I refer the reader to "Adventures While Preaching the Gospel of Beauty," and such copies of "The Village Magazine" (privately printed) as are in the hands of the literati to indicate the mood of the tracts and see also the hieroglyphic and parable, page [399] — "The Fairy from the Apple-Seed."

There is just one way to convince citizens of the United States that you are dead in earnest about an idea. It will do no good to be crucified for it, or burned at the stake for it. It will do no good to go to jail for it. But if you go broke for a hobby over and over again the genuine fructifying wrath and opposition is terrific. They will notice your idea at least. I flooded Springfield with free pamphlets incessantly. And so I began to relish home-town controversy on its absolute merits: being conceited beyond all mortal toleration, being also *"a child of destiny and fond of sweets."*

Critics are still instructing me in elementary matters that they would find summarized in the bulletins if they went on the hunt. I, too, have been instructive (sarcasm).

"War Bulletin Number Four," brought out that fall of 1909, had for a sub-title: "The Tramp's Excuse." For appalling sentiments in this book I was proscribed by the Country Club and glared at by the Chamber of Commerce. It contained the drawings or ideas, on pages [19, 62, 48, 66, 53], and similar designs.

And so, for years, no one would have anything to do with me in Springfield, but Willis Spaulding and the Swedenborgians; Frank Bode and the Liberal Democrats; George and Maydie Lee and their daughter Virginia and the Single Taxers; Mr. and Mrs. Duncan Macdonald and the Socialists; Rabbi Tedesche and the Jews; Rachel Hiller and Susan Wilcox and the English teachers; and the Honorable James M. Graham and the Knights of Columbus.

I have never been in the least a literal Swedenborgian. But I back Willis Spaulding. All this time he was the Commissioner of Public Property, therefore the most powerful citizen in the City Hall. He was re-elected many times. He was continually trying to hunch the city nearer to Single Tax. The pleasant things said about him at The Country Club I will not here put down. I doubt if my tracts won a single vote for Willis. They won for me the opponents that fought him always in vain. They fought me to the point of getting the aforesaid "Peace Advocate" out of me and the poems such as those on page [71] and [75].

Stephen Graham is a lifetime friend of mine, but he has made one mistake. He says in one place that I am not for the Irish. I may have dropped a more impatient word in regard to the Irish than any Britisher is accustomed to drop. All of us are apt to show impatience with the theme at times. But, thinking it all over, I must say that I am for the Irish. I am for Padraic Colum *among* the Irish. And then I am for the *United States* Irish. Willis Spaulding could not carry a single Springfield election without them. Certainly I am for the *Springfield, Illinois*, Irish. I will never forget how Joseph Farris, a Single Taxer, as Irish as ever lived, stood by my "War Bulletins," in Springfield, when even some of the Swedenborgians were appalled. All things being equal, I get all my national and international views from Joseph Farris, out of pure gratitude. I like every political cartoon that he likes. His views, as man and politician, are close to the hieroglyphic, and close to the sea at sunrise. For years we were the two hottest readers in Springfield, of Reedy's St. Louis *Mirror*.

But to speak, even more seriously — the one ever-open church in the United States is built by the Irish. I am profoundly grateful for this Church. There it is waiting for me, the stranger, in Tucson or New Orleans or Bangor. I can step into that door from my hotel. There is instant peace and seclusion. There I can go back to my mysterious Springfield, even to my Swedenborgian Springfield, if you please. Other churches are marked most sentimentally *"Enter, rest and pray."* But generally the door is locked of a summer time. The only way to *"enter, rest and pray"* is to enter a church with the door open. And there I am a million miles from the Pullman car, the glittering hotel lobby, the loud lecture platform, the howling newsboys, the automobiles, the magazines. There Mary, Star of the Sea, always waits for the contrite. There too, I am close to the hieroglyphic, and close to the sea at sunrise.

Springfield surely will sometime have a great World University, and surely will take on the aspect after immemorial years of a great "University World's Fair." It will all go back to one cosy Swedenborgian cottage of that glowing and adventurous time that followed shortly after the period of the bulletins. The cottage that suddenly shone so brightly in our town was the home of George and Maydie Lee.

"Maydie" was only a pet name. Her solemn Swedenborgian name was Mary Thankful Spaulding Lee. Her consecrated heart was the mysterious heart of our mysterious Springfield. Twice my brother-in-law and my sister, Dr. and Mrs. Paul Wakefield, went to China and twice returned. Each time they joined the circle on their furlough. They found under that roof the seemingly contradictory ideas of the whole of active American citizenship, assembled in a tiny conclave. To this group the Wakefields brought news of Asia. They were a part of the circle 1908, and then again, on a second return, five years later.

The heroes of Maydie Lee's circle, among the living, were Joseph Fels, Herbert Quick, Woodrow Wilson, Robert La Follett[sic], Brand Whitlock, Frederick C. Howe (then newly famous for his book of disguised Single Tax — The City, The Hope of Democracy), Newton D. Baker, Mayor of Cleveland, Mr. and Mrs. Raymond Robbins, and Jane Addams. Dr.

Caroline Hedger was a close associate of Maydie Lee. Of our heroes was William Allen White, author of the series of bulletins entitled "The Old Order Changeth," which did more to make the fundamental thought of the Progressive Party, then forming, than any word or act of Theodore Roosevelt. White was the soul back of the Kansas chapters of "Adventures While Preaching the Gospel of Beauty."

The heroes of our circle, among the recently departed, were Tom Johnson, the great Single Tax Mayor of Cleveland, Golden Rule Jones, Mayor of Toledo, John P. Altgeld, Governor of Illinois, the most fearless user of the privilege of free speech since Jefferson. Among the great further back were Henry George, and, of course, Emmanuel Swedenborg.

These last two men seem to go together in the minds of many more Americans than our great universities realize. They furnish more austerity, fire, vision and relentless lifetime resolution to those who would make over our cities, than the heathen have ever dreamed. Thousands of folks of our purest, most valuable, oldest stock, go to the Swedenborgian church on Sunday and work steadily and silently for the Single Tax all week.

Catholic and Protestant, Jew and Greek were all brought to fine speaking terms by our great hostess. Her consecrated heart was indeed the very heart of Springfield. After his obvious victories, she kept her brother Willis Spaulding at the actual battle of bringing her ideals before the folks of the city, in some form that they could understand.

She it was who kept open house for the radical lobby that came down season after season to the State House, Agnes Nestor, Margaret Haley and the rest. She was the leading spirit of the local branch of the Woman's Trade Union League, and Mrs. Robbins' devoted lieutenant. Incidentally George and Maydie Lee gave one year of their lives to a state-wide campaign for "The Initiative and the Referendum," in which we all helped.

They circulated Progress and Poverty like a new Bible.

The spirit of this tide in American life is well set forth in Waldo R. Browne's "Altgeld of Illinois," published by B.W. Huebsh.

It was while all these activities were at their height that the *Mirror* brought out the "Spoon River Anthology." It was read instanter in Springfield. We followed its victories across the world as though they were our own. The father and mother of Edgar Lee Masters were old residents of Springfield. This of course greatly sharpened our interest.

Ours was what might be called "The Old Court-House America" (see hieroglyphic, page [207]), what might be called: "The Old Horse-and-Buggy America," the America that first put Woodrow Wilson into the Presidential chair. It was among this circle that I scattered my pen and ink drawings and cartoons and war bulletins with the most welcome. I fought my best to add to genuine Gospels of Democracy, my Gospel of Beauty, gathered in Life Classes and in Art Museums, and among Art Students, for many a day. And I had to fight every inch of the way with very stubborn, very earnest, very admirable minds. Wherever I go, as a lecturer and evangelist I find myself most wrongly interpreted, *and inconveniently fibbed about*. If you want to know the meaning of my life, my tracts and hieroglyphics from the beginning to the end, to the extent of three or five columns, interview my worst enemy in Springfield with whom I flooded these tracts, rather than my best friend discovered after October, 1912, from some other town.

The morning of June 1, 1912, when I started out on the "Adventures While Preaching," with a pack full of "Village Improvement Parade" posters, and "Rhymes to be Traded for Bread," George E. Lee was the man who walked out alone with me. He told me good-by and gave me his blessing. Ask those who hated and loved us just what we meant to the town. It was out of our warfare for Beauty and Democracy that most of the forty drawings in this book were born. It was out of the drawings and others like them, that the verses were finally born.

"The Map of the Universe," in the front of the book [p. 496], was one feature of *War Bulletin Number Four*, a "bulletin" which was actually a booklet which I called, *The Tramp's Excuse*. If examined closely the map will be discovered to be Miltonic: — as orthodox as Milton, certainly. It was the basis of a book that I wrote about the Millennium in Springfield. I afterwards destroyed it without publication, it seemed to provoke such amazing wrath. I called it *Where is Aladdin's Lamp*. The book was later reborn as *The Golden Book*. Sometimes I think the Millennium will come in ten thousand years, sometimes in one hundred thousand years. I have never had the delusion it will come immediately. But it is worth working toward. There is no sense in assuming we are hell-bent. I feel also, that the world war will somehow be made up to us by the powers invisible, and that civilization is on the edge of a new flowering that is far indeed from the millennium, but is a flowering, nevertheless. My hope in this matter has been called credulity. Still, please look at "The Village Improvement Parade," and remember that Florence, Athens and Venice once flowered. They flowered quickly, in one generation. The very edges of the Universe are nearer together than were the outer walls of Florence in her splendor; such is wireless and such is commerce to-day. It is not absurd to suppose the world will suddenly take on glory, as one city, as one compact Springfield, as one heroic village. "Hieroglyphic Marchers Here We Bring." (See text and Hieroglyphics, page [258].) And this will not be the millennium. Falstaff will riot in the taverns, when the world becomes for the first moment of its conscious life, one little Springfield, Athens, Florence, Venice.

If my friends will again examine the "Map of the Universe," in front [p. 496], along with the history of our Springfield circle, just outlined, they will have some of the material out of which *The Golden Book of Springfield* was written.

All my tracts have their bearing on *The Golden Book of Springfield*. They are, of course, out of print, or in the hands of Springfield people who hated or loved the circle that was around Maydie Lee's home. I have said in the preface: "Adventures While Singing These Songs," much about Lincoln (see text and hieroglyphic, page [198]), much about the South, Kentucky, Campbellism, and my own peculiar experiences as a tiny child in the Lindsay family. All this is far indeed from the Swedenborgian refrain I have now been singing. Between the events of my first preface and this there is the period of fifteen or twenty years of experience completely skipped. But already that first preface is being hardened into a plaster cast for me. So I write a new one. May the kind reader make the most of it. I claim the privilege of this versatility. And if this is not enough, there are other gods between my tenth and my thirty-second year I can invoke to overthrow any tyranny of Campbellite or Swedenborgian.

I was once introduced to a Canadian audience as having come from "humble and poverty-stricken antecedents." Then I said: —

"I am not only sophisticated, but all my ancestors were sophisticated. My people were not only important but they were self-important. The family conceit is hereditary from a long way back. It is the hardest thing I have to overcome."

"The Rose and the Lotus" is associated in my mind with one of the thrilling memories of my life when I was entertained in Washington by the Honorable and Mrs. Carl Vrooman. Carl Vrooman was then Assistant Secretary of Agriculture. The song I sang that seemed to mean the most in Washington was that of "The Rose and the Lotus." Franklin K. Lane, the then Secretary of the Interior, did me the honor to print it and send it to both Houses of Congress and to all those interested in a special way in the opening of the Panama Canal and the opening of the Panama-Pacific exposition at San Francisco. It is the nearest that my life has ever come to politics.

I drew the present design of "The Rose and the Lotus" from a sketch made when the poem was written. This I circulated on my own in Springfield, Illinois. The tract was issued with great faith in the good-will of the whole wide world. This faith I still maintain. The masses of mankind are in good-will toward one another. Only the old and silly are venomous.

Obviously the drawing of "The Rose and the Lotus" has a hieroglyphic and not a jazz meaning. I offer it here again as a visible symbol of good-will between all the races of mankind. It can be painted on the wall of every temple, shrine, tomb, state-house, court-house, and hut of the world, without destroying or interfering with any government, race integrity, religious prejudice or philosophic dogma of Buddha or Swedenborg or any saint between.

As to the Lotus: —

The lotus-eaters were the dreamers of classic allusion. They were those who had what might be called "The Asiatic Mind." The Egyptian used the lotus for revel, as we use the rose, and so it was used in India. Yet the lotus in great *solemnity* dominates Egyptian design. In India the lotus symbolizes the highest philosophic attainment of self-conquest. All the seemingly contradictory things that mean Asia are poured into the lotus-cup. The Thibetan invocation to the prayer-wheel that a Thibetan missionary once taught me: "*O mane, padme hum*: 'O the jewel in the lotus!'" is a phrase that in its very reiteration shows the potency of the flower in the Asiatic mind. We have seen jades and crystals from China carved in lotus patterns. We have seen beautiful pictures of the Kamakura Buddha sitting on the big lotus flower. The lotus means all the million contradictory things which stand for Asia from the beginning. All those that mourn, all those that rejoice, in the East, turn to the lotus.

In like manner, the rose means Europe and America from the beginning. Christ says: "I am the Rose of Sharon and the Lily of the Valley." Dante found that Paradise was one great rose. A medieval romance was "The

Romance of the Rose.'' Then the ''Wars of the Roses'' were the tragedy and song of certain days in England. The most beautiful thing in the Gothic Cathedral is the rose window. Anywhere in the world the humblest Catholic home has a picture of Mary with a wreath of roses around her heart. And she is prayed to with the rosary. All those that mourn and all those that rejoice, in the West, turn to the rose.

So, long before the opening of the Panama Canal, as I walked alone in Springfield, I was thinking of those flowers and their separation from the beginning of time. My first song about them is ''The Canticle of the Rose of Tennessee,'' written after my first begging trip. See the story, ''Lady Iron Heels,'' in *A Handy Guide for Beggars*.

I kept thinking of those flowers, and their separation from the beginning of time. I thought of the rose as a vine climbing westward, Europe slowly moving away from Asia, apparently forever. Then I thought of ''The Rose and the Lotus,'' meeting across the Pacific, and destined to face one another forevermore. Grainger says: ''America, instead of being the most westerly interpretation of Europe, is the most easterly interpretation of Asia.'' Hal Bynner has returned from China, translating the Chinese classic poems. Eunice Tietjens has returned from China with her wonderful song of ''The Most Sacred Mountain,'' and her ''Profiles from China.'' Amy Lowell has translated much from the Chinese. The recent great Japanese earthquake proved every heart in the world could love and pity Japan. The whole world sent help.

On a recent Sunday I heard my sister, Mrs. Paul Wakefield, at the Euclid Avenue Christian Church, make a speech to the Sunday School children, in the capacity of a returned missionary. She championed, at least for free argument's sake, the Confucian order of society, with the scholar and the sage ranking the highest in the caste system, because they give the most to the world. And the soldier she described as ranking lowest, according to Confucius, because he only destroys. She said that which is a commonplace, anywhere but in Sunday School, that Confucius existed as a great sage and teacher many hundred years before Christ, that Confucius had a great deal to teach every Christian. I felt the chill going up and down the spines of some of the hundred per centers as she spoke. Nevertheless she continued to teach the children the Confucian proverb: ''Under Heaven, all one family.'' She taught them to say it in Chinese. She showed them how shameful race prejudice is, in the eyes of a good Confucian. She showed that the best Chinese Christians understood Christ better than the average nominal Christian of the West, because of inherited Confucian training. She said that open-minded missionaries went to China as much to learn as to teach. Representing a medical mission, she could speak thus boldly. Also, I remember her sending me a picture of the Kamakura Buddha with words of great admiration as she was passing through Japan for the first time. And these are some of the things that I meant when I drew the hieroglyphic of ''The Rose and the Lotus.'' Others may be found in ''The Jingo and the Minstrel,'' page [192].

I want the reader of this article to assume that I hope to be called to the platforms of art schools as much as any, or be backed by the art departments of the universities, the high schools and the local clubs. I hope we may offer programmes seldom discussed in the papers. We come, looking for those who desire the beautiful and holy city, and the visible arts in their most spiritual aspect. We want the art schools and the art teachers to make themselves the radiating centers of The United States Gospel of Beauty. Thus, my dear friends, will you permit me to keep close to the hieroglyphic I knew in Springfield before 1912, and close to the sea at sunrise as well, to keep all the elements of my mysterious Springfield around me, and make my "Map of the Universe" a Universal Universalist University indeed.

Mine has been a college and university circuit. There is only one art school to each hundred colleges. Yet those schools stand out to me as the most worth winning from the hieroglyphic standpoint. I hope all my friends will enter into conspiracy to win them on my behalf.

They will find in the opening pages of *The Art of the Motion Picture*, the account of an affair put on in Fullerton Hall, The Chicago Art Institute. They exhibited the film "The Wild Girl of the Sierras, as acted by Mae Marsh." I tried to point out the possible aesthetics of the future movie, as that glorious film moved along. It is my especial pride that I am the first person to have done such a thing in an Art School. These and similar questions I want to talk over with you in your town. I do not want to recite "The Congo." You can recite it yourself as well as I can. I do not want to recite "General Booth."

This essay has turned much on the date 1912. In June, 1912, I started West from Springfield, Illinois, with *Rhymes to be Traded for Bread*, and copies of the panels *The Village Improvement Parade*. People talk about my distributing my rhymes. They do not remember that I distributed these pictures with an equal zeal.

I wrote letters back to Springfield, to my father, mother and sister, and to Susan E. Wilcox and others. These letters, covering the period up to October, 1912, are all assembled in the book *Adventures While Preaching the Gospel of Beauty*. That book can be read at one sitting, and I most earnestly urge that it is a summary of all I have to say in your town for audiences, especially the proclamations at the front and back. Please read this book because it was written. This is the book I myself buy in quantity and give away as a tract. It is not even a rhymer's book. It is an art-student's book, from first to last. I consider it the final test, the central point of my work. All these pictures are implied in it. Closely related to it are: *The Village Magazine, The Art of the Moving Picture* and *The Golden Book of Springfield*. None of these are books of the jazz idea. They are all of them the books of an Art Student. My life is not an attempt to recite, but an attempt to re-apply in various ways till I find the right way, the sharpest sentences of the proclamations in *Adventures While Preaching the Gospel of Beauty*. The pouring crowds since 1912, though many of them would have none of this, have not in the least altered this fundamental purpose. I can *easily renounce the crowds forever if they seem to imperil the ultimate purpose of my crusade.*

Let us return to *The Village Improvement Parade*. Note the circle of the sun, drawn with the same compass as the circle of the moon, in the moon-plates. Note how it is really the central decorative theme of "The Village Improvement Parade." This same circle, drawn with a compass, is the central design of the "Litany of Heroes," page [435], for which, once upon a time, I did twenty-six big panels in colors with a separate symbol for each hero. I used to put all twenty-six panels around the lecture hall, and expound the twenty-six designs around which the twenty-six verses were written. I am planning now to issue the panels in a large portfolio, eighteen by twenty-four inches. The point is that there, as here, the central symbol is the circle of the sun. And that is not a jazz device, but a sound principle of picture-writing. Turn to the article on Egypt in the *Encyclopaedia Britannica*, to the hieroglyphic page of that section. There, as here, you will find the central symbol is the circle of the sun.

And what are the signs we read against the sun, written as it were by our banners on the very face of the sky:

"To begin, we must learn to smile.
Fair streets are better than silver, green parks are better than gold.
Bad public taste is mob-law, good public taste is democracy.
A crude administration is damned already.
Let the best moods of the people rule.
A bad designer is, to that extent, a bad citizen.
A hasty prosperity may be raw and absurd, a well-considered poverty may be exquisite.
Without an eager public, all teaching is vain.
Our best pictures should be good painting, our best monuments should be real sculpture, our best buildings should be real architecture.
Ugliness is a kind of misgovernment."

Among other things of which I have been accused, by friends who should know better, is that I am a millennialist, that I think the millennium will arrive to-day.

I have recently spent one week with my Gulf Park class in *Modern American Poetry*, reading, straight through, the "Revelation of St. John the Divine," King James's version. We read it as a sort of test and measure of all poetry, ancient and modern. Men will differ forever on that book, but all will agree that it is full of splendor and hope, the very heart of the Christian future. Reading with these eager young Americans, it seemed to me that they were also a living Apocalypse, close to the sea at sunrise, close to the Ultimate Divine Hieroglyphic, the Alpha and the Omega, the soul of America. Yet the magnificence of which they are a prophecy, will have no sudden achievement. I see the glow of century after century in their eyes. *For youth does not prophesy tomorrow so much as the hundred thousand years after tomorrow upon this earth.* This America will take long to ripen. It will be longer to our goal than from Adam to Mary of Bethlehem. If we are millennialists, we must be patient millennialists. Yet let us begin to-day as though the Millennium were tomorrow, and start our "Village Improvement Parade" down Main Street, and turn the corner east toward the rising sun to a land of clear pictures and young hearts. Close, indeed, to the hieroglyphic, and close to the sea at sunrise, close to the Percy Grainger "Colonial Song."

My publishers have decided on "The Map of the Universe" as the frontispiece of this book. So I here insert, in the latest revision of this copy, poems relating to this map. Many of them are from my very oldest, privately printed pamphlets, "War Bulletins," and the like, others reprinted from the middle of this book to show the relation.

But first please re-read "Lucifer" and "The Tree of Laughing Bells," with the map before you.

Sunrise on Sun-Mountain

GOING-TO-THE-STARS from
Going-to-the-Stars

One starry night my wife and I left our home in Spokane, the city of locust trees, for a journey toward the stars. This is an account of it we write together:

"We left our home in the Davenport Hotel wearing the uniform of the road. This included pack boards such as the Indians use, and Sierra sleeping bags. By way of the Great Northern, we arrived next morning at the eastern entrance of Glacier National Park, Glacier Park Hotel. There we danced and swam after the manner of conventional tourists at any conventional hotel.

"Going-to-the-Sun Mountain, our first goal, we reached next day at noon by official park motor through the perils of the Blackfeet Indian Reservation. We say perils because on his only journey afoot through this reservation, Vachel Lindsay was repeatedly shot at by some aborigine who did not recognize a brother.

"As we approached Going-to-the-Sun, we came out of American into United States jurisdiction. We left the reservation and entered the National Park. We crossed St. Mary's Lake, which we have renamed 'Going-to-the-Stars.' Our pilgrimage begins and ends with this starry lake, the whispering lodge of our songs. In it are reflected nine mountain peaks: Reynolds, Singleshot, Fusilade, Citadel, Goat, Whitefish, Little Chief, Red Eagle, and Going-to-the-Sun. In it are reflected also that day-star, the sun; that queer and irregular planet, the moon; and all the little stars. One of the daisies that bloom profusely on the edge we have renamed Going-to-the-Stars.

"Sun Mountain Chalet is a peaceful and kindly place where, unmolested and untroubled, one may gather these flowers as he chooses, and look up at mystifying slopes of the mountain. There is something about the way this mountain is drawn that makes one an astronomer. And he who has once drunk deep of the water of this lake is forever climbing toward the stars, then making his return journey to the mountain and the lake for renewal.

"There are all sorts of ways of climbing toward the stars. Some star climbers are disguised as mere hikers, hiking hither, thither, and yon. So on the following night we climbed, and slept for the first time under the open sky at the head of Swift-current Pass.

"From August 8 to September 15, 1925, we two were for the most part alone in the open. Official chalets and camps, deserted log cabins, and, many times, our own camp fires gave us protection by night. It was a pair traveling, not a group. Our companions were, first, the government contour map; second, Roeder's *Grammar of Egyptian Hieroglyphics* and the first volume of Warren's *Chinese Primer*; third, and certainly the most companionable, Edgar Lee Masters' *Spoon River Anthology* and his *New Spoon River*.

"Starting at Many Glacier Hotel, we walked to Granite Park; thence along Mineral Creek to Flattop Mountain, and down the Little Kootenai to Waterton Lake. From the lake we tramped over Indian Pass to Crosley Lake, and back; and we also walked one rainy Sunday into Canada. Later, leaving Waterton by way of Brown's Pass, we went over the Divide and down to Bowman Lake on the west side. There we found the automobile highway, and in the last lap of our journey took the romantic mail coach to Belton. From Belton by railroad, automobile, and launch, we returned to the east side of the Divide and to Sun Mountain, which became thenceforth the central point for our walks.

"This is the bare outline of the excursion. What are the things we fondly remember about it? Many of the poems in this book were written concerning three previous walks in the same region. One of the walks Vachel Lindsay took with Stephen Graham; the two others he took alone. Now in 1925, we two, trying to discover the same Glacier Park, found a new one, alternating fifty-fifty with the old. Of our new park we will speak some other time. We will say only this of it now: we did our first housekeeping, anywhere, in the deserted log cabins of the deepest, loneliest, farthest forests of that park.

"Of the old Glacier Park, known and loved of all men, this book attempts to be a souvenir. We shall speak now of certain aspects of our 1925 hike which touch on these songs.

"Log cabins mean Nancy Hanks, and log cabins mean Andrew Jackson. Wherever there are national parks and national forests there are log cabins still. You may not realize how much log-cabin territory there is in the United States; get from the Departments of Agriculture and of the Interior, maps of the national forests and parks, and you will see how tremendous an area it is. Every park is in the center of an endless forest, every forest enshrines a park. Despite optical illusions to the contrary, there is a vast America in our national parks, utterly inaccessible to the automobile, to be reached only by the slenderest of trails through the brush. When man reaches these places, he is in log-cabin conditions again, where the tallow candle and the ax are the main weapons against darkness and storm. The deeps of the national parks, though assumed to be playgrounds, actually represent conditions similar to the much larger national forests. The forests even of Glacier are interminable and for the most part utterly unvisited. The log cabins we chanced upon were symbols of all this. They were five in number.

"The worst and oldest of them was better than the one that Nancy Hanks slept in for two terrible winters, a half-face camp in Indiana. A half-face camp is a one room shack with no doors, no windows, no floor, and the fourth side open to the weather, where a fire may be built. With little Abraham Lincoln held against her heart, she endured cold and exposure, sleeping on the bare ground.

"The log cabin so emphatically elected Jackson that his enemies and the enemies of his lackey, Van Buren, developed the 'Tippecanoe and Tyler, too' campaign to steal the Jackson and Van Buren thunder. These seem old tales, but after a month or two of finding refuge in deserted log cabins in the western woods, generously left open to all comers, we decided that it might be assumed that Andrew Jackson is not yet dead. Certainly the *Spoon River Anthologies*, first and second, owe some of their power to the fact that Edgar Lee Masters is a stern Jacksonian. The vast organization of skilled, highly educated outdoor men who have in hand the national parks and forests are necessarily living the log-cabin Andrew Jackson life. One beautiful cabin we slept in was still in process of making, a one-room house of magnificent design, all the logs in the round, to be lighted, of course, by the world's eternal tallow candle. We took a candle from our pack and slept there. It was in a towering grove of canoe-birch and aspen, in a circle of cliffs that crowded it so closely and soared so high, that the cabin was like a jewel in the bottom of a giant's well. The old old trail leading to it and away from it had no human footprints; trees like the pillars of Baalbek had fallen across the path every half mile and stayed to gather moss three inches deep. What were the footprints in the soft mud near the streams? Many deer, many bear cubs, a few big bears, a few wolves, a few moose. In these log cabins by candlelight, we were far from the saxophone, and nearer to Noah's Ark, for instance.

"Flattop Mountain is the loveliest of all the high valleys our eyes have looked upon. It is a great serene inland sea of bear grass overtopped by the long ridge of Mount Kipp. It was there we met the stormsoaked flowers after three days of wind and snow. There is the flowery bush called 'Going-to-the-Fountain-Springs.' There, too are the Forty Waterfalls of the Forty Kisses, the Fairy River of Desire, the Great Rock of Wonderland, and the Lake Called the City of Glass. The story of Flattop would take a new Milton to tell. But there are endless fields of the flower we call 'Going-to-the-Stars.'

"Almost as an afterthought, on our last afternoon in the mountain, at four o'clock, we started up Mount Kipp, which marks the Continental Divide. By the merest chance, we found at the very top, in a crevice of the boulders, a sort of Pass of Thermopylae, the only way over, and the only way down, in miles of summit. So down through the perilous crevice we crept, feeling like John Ridd and Lorna, sneaking down the Doone Pass. On that other side we found the Secret Place of Glacier Park, The Place That Nobody Knows. In it, across a little glacial lake far below the natural balcony on which we stood stranded in mid-air, were the strange deserted peaks we called 'Egypt's Last Stand,' and 'The Secret Door.' Here, to this hidden place, let the traveler climb with faith to find the ghosts of the flower-fed buffaloes, trooping up a distant valley toward that ancient iceberg lake; here also let him find celestial flowers and trees, for here winged seeds can take root and grow. No breaker of spells ever dares come up through the Pass of Thermopylae: that circle of many-colored rocks encloses an enchanted fortress. Almost to the very summit, are tossing inaccessible fields of the flowers we call 'Going-to-the-Stars.'

"One of the people we mentioned constantly on first entering the park was the admired Stephen Graham. We kept telling each other how he tramped and camped, until we almost learned how to tramp and camp ourselves. We sent him letters pledging devotion. With even more emphasis, we thought of him as guide, philosopher, and friend when we crossed the Canadian line on Waterton Lake. One needs a British shepherd in the British Empire. Some boundaries are guarded by soldiers or by Chinese walls. Stephen is now tramping in bristling, difficult eastern Europe, still meditating on his philosophy of boundary lines. He is the man with Wesley's motto, 'The world is my parish'; the man with a globe in his head. He is sometimes in Saskatoon, Saskatchewan, sometimes holding the hand of my Lady London. There is no boundary in the world that is more the property of Stephen Graham than the Canadian, a wide swath cut in the lonely unguarded forest where any man may walk east or west. North or south, east or west in this forest, a man will find nothing but friends.

"We, Elizabeth and Vachel Lindsay, cannot pretend to be Egyptologists, but in our idle reconnoitering days on Waterton Lake, before we planned the second half of our holiday, we went into Gunther Roeder's *Short Egyptian Grammar*. It is based on the grammar of the great Adolph Erman, so we are starting in the way we should go. Here, in this park, struggling with so much unhewn western rock, we indulged in amateur meditations upon that people who made unhewn rock over into carven stone, and cut their immortal word upon that stone. The Egyptian hieroglyphic is the only stone-cut language in the history of mankind, and has so remained from the beginning to the end. Therefore it is so magnificent, so pictorial, so all conquering. The nearest thing in civilization to the Egyptian basalt hieroglyphic tablet is the American zinc-etching block which is even more rigid and sharp-edged. It is used to reproduce the drawings in this book and all pen and ink drawings whatsoever, anywhere. By way of the zinc-etching block and other similar devices, we have returned to Egypt again. And so we philosophized hieroglyphically a great deal and studied hieroglyphics a little.

"Then we thrust all books behind us, put on our packs, made the tremendous circuit of the more moss-grown west side of the park, and finally arrived at Sun Mountain again on the east side. All the way we were going to the stars. Days are short, between overwhelming cliffs, and nights are long. At the bottom of a well you can see the stars at noon; we were so far down sometimes that the sun was a star. We were so high on the passes, at other times, that the earth beneath us was a star. Of course we do not want to boast; we never reached the stars or we would not have come back. Many times they were as close and as hard to touch as the rainbows of the glacial ice caves. So it was on our last climb around Sun Mountain when we visited Sexton Glacier and went over Siyeh Pass.

"Our home is the Davenport Hotel, Spokane, but this account ends on the slopes of Sun Mountain and in the Alpine meadow to the north of the mountain at midnight. Until that hour the clouds had rolled around us; then, in an instant, every cloud was gone and every star was in the heavens, in its rightful place. All the mountains were outlined in a great hieroglyphic circle by starlight. We had left our packs behind at the chalet. Against the dampness and the thick cloud, for six hours, we had kept a gigantic fire burning. Slowly we had moved the fire five paces to the east, and on the fire-cooked ground we now made our spruce-bough floor and bed. So our best log cabin had a spruce floor, mountains and wild fire for logs, and a star roof."

A NOTE BY THE POET AND ARTIST from
The Candle in the Cabin

The Spencerian System of Penmanship, known to our fathers, used the watch spring for a decorative unit. It built up both writing and drawing from the watch-spring curves, most mechanical. In the copy books birds made in that script flew around with stamped and sealed letters in their mouths. When it had disappeared from the public schools, the Spencerian System still prevailed in the script of the steel-engraved calling cards and wedding invitations of our elect.

Spencer was the only man in the Anglo-Saxon world who taught the public to build up handwriting into birds and flowers. If he had used the natural autograph of each man, instead of a watch-spring curve, as the basis of his system of teaching, it might have become a school of art, instead of a discarded curiosity.

The Arabesques of the Arabs are evolved from carefully made scripts: — texts from the Koran, following to the last limit of decorative evolution the natural stroke of the scribe. Every school of Chinese and Japanese painting is evolved from the brushwork of the language. Still the young Chinese and Japanese artist is the boy in writing school whose script is most individual and interesting. He is later encouraged to combine the same brush strokes into drawing and painting.

Even the Chinese and Japanese architecture is an enlargement of their right-angled, brush-written ideograms. Half the history of art goes back to handwriting. Gothic architecture is close to the illuminated manuscript of the Monk. Old Irish design is a kind of writing.

So Spencer used a sound principle when he evolved his personal script into a bird.

In all the pictures in this book I have used the letters of the alphabet, capital and small letters, upside down, in circles, on top of one another, and all sizes. In short, these pictures are written, not drawn.

INSCRIPTION FOR THE ENTRANCE TO A BOOK from
Every Soul Is a Circus

DEAR PARENTS:

This is a book for precocious children, twelve or fifty years of age. All mothers admit their youngsters are precocious. They are right. The budding human race does not stay that way because of false grammar school education. I leave this statement general, so that every educator can agree with me, however he may differ from his neighbor educator on the details.

Ten years hence I want a group of precocious first voters, twenty-one or twenty-two years of age, to be my fast friends. I want the youngest younger generation along with the oldest older generation and here stake out my claim. I want some of those first and last voters to put me in as Mayor of Loami, Illinois. The only way to get votes is to sit in the hotel lobby and hand people your card with your picture on it, and be appallingly frank about it. This book is my card.

Precocious children of any age are teachers. They teach the rest of the world all it ever learns or forgets. Here you will find a fraternal poem for young Marquis De Talleyrand, and one for twelve-year-old Horace Mann, one for some infant T.B. Macaulay, and one for Confucius, and one for the young Jennie Lind, and the young Harriet Beecher Stowe, and the young Sacajawea, and the next Carrie Nation, and the next Frances E. Willard, and the next Anthony Comstock, and the next Francois Rabelais, and the next John Brown, and the next Artemas Ward, and the next Robert E. Lee, and the next Robert G. Ingersoll, and the infant Jean Jacques Rousseau, and the next Phillips Brooks, and all the rest that are coming, including the next Methuselah.

Badly as they conduct themselves, my words behave better than I do. Dear Parents, it is easier for me to set an example for your young than my young. As I write my naughty boy and girl, whose traits are utterly inexplicable, are raising awful Ned in the next room, here in this house where I was born. I wish someone would indite them a new book with such strong, refreshing, fraternal language in it that they would sneak behind the haymow with it for half a day. Dear other parents, on the other side of the world, that I have never met, you have the same wish, and here I try to fulfill it for you.

Do you know that Tom Sawyer and Huckleberry Finn were forbidden to the infants of their day, till it was discovered that to give those two books to the young was one way of keeping them quiet? Then it was that little Rollo died. Huckleberry Finn and Tom Sawyer were the principal pallbearers.

And here is *my* wreath for the mossy, ivy-clad tomb of little Rollo.

In my more helpless infancy when I was seven years old, I had a public library card, but the dour old librarian would not let me take out anything but Jacob Abbott's Rollo books. I read them all. Also one Lucy book, which I found at home, blistered with my mother's infant tears, which she had read in her day. Now in the fiftieth year of my age comes my revolt. I come roaring forth with a book which is the opposite of little Rollo and little Lucy.

We must admit that to counterbalance Rollo our grandmothers had McGuffey, politics so hot that most any man would be arrested for talking that way now, selections from Jefferson and the revolutionary forefathers, red speeches from Edmund Burke in defense of the American rebels, long orations skinning Aaron Burr to a fare-you-well, and going into that love affair with the wife of B. on the island in the west in a way that must have provoked infant curiosity. Then there was the fiery reply of young Pitt to Walpole on being accused of being a young man. A certain amount of hot stuff was allowed. Then there was Spartacus to the Gladiators that won every oratorical contest in its day until it had to be debarred. These memories of old McGuffey read in my grandmother's attic when I was a child, under the dusty pictures of George and Martha Washington, give me courage for the United States precedent of plain speech with children.

My old art school chum, George Mather Richards, collaborates at every point in this volume. I furnish the rhymes, and this preface. I sneak in a few of my better hieroglyphics and then he illustrates the book all over the shop. He designs it, paper, print and all.

That is the way we planned to work together away back in 1905. We have been hoping to put it over ever since. I know I cannot draw. So does he. But just the same we patiently studied art together for years and years. We ran a studio on West 57th Street one winter, where he furnished the pictures and I furnished the conversation. He has two great talents. He can fill a whole studio full of masterpieces of his art and he has more varieties of conversational silence than any other man I ever met. He is a Plymouth Rock (born in Washington, D.C., with charming irrelevance). I am a Virginian born in Springfield, Illinois, with the same charming irrelevance. He has returned to Connecticut. I have returned to Springfield, Illinois, to the house where I was born, from Spokane, where I had five glorious years.

Our friendship is an anacronism, but if it stands the strain of this volume, the reconstruction period is over. The south has eaten crow, and the stars and bars are temporarily furled, at least in the studio. Anything he has not liked in this book or this preface he has marked out.

So do not consult the poet about further changes in the work. Make them yourself. If there is anything in this book, dear parent, that you in your magnificence deem too strong for little Willie or little Susie, or Methuselah, mark it out or tear it out before handing it to them.

That is the way the book censorship societies and the Hollywood movie saints treat books and movies for you. Pass on the noble gesture. Transmit it to the tender and sheltered generations. Let them also feel the touch of volunteer, amateur, uninstructed authority, and watch how they like it.

As for me, what I want is peace without victory.

This is a book for Tom-boy girls and goshawful boys, as I said, a book for precocious children. Find the top commanders in any department of the United States from college presidents to railroad presidents and you will often find those who read the fundamental works in their profession before twelve years of age. There is not a biography in the world but is full of queer books the kid read before twelve, sometimes they were just terrible books, like the Greek Classics in the original, which were plain tough in some parts, and are still translated with dots and dashes, in the ponies used in the universities.

And now for more serious discourse. As Longfellow says, and as Robert Frost so aptly quotes:

"A boy's will is the wind's will.
And the thoughts of youth are long, long thoughts."

This book of mine is aggressive, however sinful, and full of pride. If they do not like aggressive verse at twelve, they never will. Not that all of this text is controversial. Far from it. But I choose to be serious when I please. I do not believe in simpering with twelve-year-olds as though they were two-year-olds, if they are by any means readers. Of course I like to punish wicked and dull and annoying twelve-year-olds by simpering at them in conversation till it is a positive torture for them and they leave the room for keeps and all. But even bad children indulge in good jokes when they have left the room. Parents indulge in what they think are exquisite, high-minded jokes when the children have left the room. It is hard to tell who is the wittiest. Notice, if you have the self-control, when you are talking down to your progeny in a moment of excitement, and you pause for a reply they talk down to you. The joke is on you.

Yea, all parents use what they think is very strong, subtle Henrik Ibsen language of the wild duck variety when the children are asleep. All the children use very strong and subtle and devil's disciple Bernard Shaw language when the older people are off on an alleged picnic. Why not get together in this matter? All parents shamelessly, unblushingly and blatantly use very poetical and passionate language when they are sure the children are absent. All children use even better poetical and passionate language when the parents are absent. Why not get together in this matter? And now for an even more serious discourse.

If this book is for twelve-year-olds and Methuselahs of a precocious turn, some of them will be high-school freshmen in a few months, eventually if not now.

I have had a hand in a high-school freshman class in the dancing of poetry in the Lewis and Clark High School of Spokane. This was done with the help of Miss Edith Haight of the Physical Education staff, now head director of Physical Education, University of Wyoming, Laramie.

Many other Spokane groups have helped in the special Spokane development of the Poem Games. Stoddard King, the poet, and Lenore Glen, the actress and dancer, have for two seasons developed the idea for us. With their help we entertained passing artists who were going on to proclaim our gospel to the ends of the earth. We have been gratified to receive press clippings from Scotland and England discussing the games and speculating upon them. It is no doubt that this general work by Miss Glen and Mr. King has greatly helped to give wide impetus and ambition to the high-school experimenters and helped in their conquest of the town. Of all this, more will be said elsewhere, at great length.

But the class of Miss Haight is my special theme now. She has proved that anything that seems to be poetry to the listener can be danced by him while it is read to him. Her group has danced many things from Shakespeare to Coleridge, also the more rhythmic moderns like Lanier and Poe and Swinburne. Tennyson's bugle song became instantly an improvised ballet, as a group marched abreast from side to side of the room.

There is only one rule: Leave out all musical instrumentation and singing. To elucidate: leave out thumping, drumming, and musical notation and any imitations of singing, and orchestras. Elaborate reading is what is required, reading that comes to the edge of a chant without having the literary meaning clouded by the chant.

The solo dancers developed a talent for inspired improvising of poems they had never heard of before they stepped to the dancing floor. The soloist improviser stands in the middle of the floor and the reader sits on the side lines. The improviser is instructed to keep one-half a second behind the meter of the reading and dance one syllable at a time, thinking only of the music of the poem and not the meaning. It becomes writing in the air. The second time through, novel and beautiful rhythms are discovered in established but neglected poems, and the dancer often produces remarkable tableaux, rising into realistic acting.

Setting poetry to music, even the best music, is the destruction of poetry and the production of an amorphous and confused result. All poetry that has been set to music has been blasted thereby.

On the other hand, poetry carefully read and set to dancing is recreated, made social and troubadourish, raised from the dead golden treasuries into life again.

The high-school freshman dancers went through four stages this season. The first stage they were so used to thumping their feet when they danced that they liked only poems in which they could impersonate ponies and buffaloes, and their feet were but drums on the floor. In short, they stripped music of everything that had been held over from a bad past and left only the drums.

In the second stage, the drums disappeared. They had forgotten even the lightest thump on the piano keys, which they had used for dancing in former days. After all, the piano is only one kind of a drum, and poetry read like the best piano playing is choppy and nippy. The rhythm of the most seemingly regular poetry should be like a stream, and the seeming surface rhythms are only emerging stepping-stones near the river bank, which the landscape gardener has put there at regular intervals.

Sometimes the music of poetry is a subterranean stream, as in the caverns "measureless to man" in Coleridge's Xanadu. Entering upon this second stage they were listening for the subterranean river. They learned to float on their feet till not a foot-fall could be heard as they swept from end to end of our apartment, like butterflies, dancing only the ripples that lie between the beats that are scanned in poetry. The readers learned also to control and ignore the mere march-tune of the poems and read for the subterranean river under the rhyme. In this stage they did Coleridge's Kubla Khan with splendid pageants in motion. There are forty musical schemes in that poem, all different, none of them drum tunes or piano tunes, all blended like a magic carpet, on which they seemed to float to Cathay.

In this period we did Swinburne's couplet: —

"All the feet of the hours that sound as a single lyre
Dropped and deep in the flowers with strings that flicker like fire."

Third stage. As a result of the discovery of this secret rhythm, even in the most casual reading of verse, our little butterflies became too aesthetical and floated around in dissolving views, after the manner of all bare-foot dancers the world over that have not themselves in hand. They were cloudy little beauties luxuriating in their own sufficient selves and whirling scarfs around, but getting no further into the mysteries than downy chicks. You have all seen groups in movie news films doing this in parks and have said, "Very pretty," and let it go at that.

Fourth stage. Toward June they became literary people. This was the goal. Their faces had the look of writers, not of performers. They were writing in the air with great seriousness and precision. This was natural, for they were all volunteers from the English classes, not picked in any sense. They were merely the students who cared enough for poetry to try to dance it.

Individually they were what society queens would call extremely awkward. This was natural, because it was the awkward age, but it is the most fluent age also, and the body is almost a river, more of a river than a tree. In groups they became friezes and storms, and every gesture harmonized. What one lacked in one rhythm, three others supplied at that point, so four awkward children made a graceful army. A simple line of Lanier they found had a hundred rhythms in one, and an acting possibility that came out of the literary rather than the dramatic instinct.

Yes, in the fourth and last stage, toward June, these children, with the look of writers on their faces, the passion of literature in their hearts, were confidently on the edge of discovery. They rushed rapidly through all sorts of improvising of the classics of British and United States poetry, with that sharp listening expression on their faces. They abandoned themselves to a new kind of printed page on which they, themselves, were the twenty-six letters of the alphabet, the forty or more sounds of the English language, the thousand separate syllables which make up poetry.

Pick your poem game dancers for their marks in English and their disposition to write little rhymes without urging. They will write well with their own awkward little bodies in a year. They will be no more worried or ungraceful about it than boys playing baseball as hard as they can. Each dancer developed her own style of improvising, discovered the one poet she could do best. I was delighted to free the idea from my own work and to prove out that it applied to any rhythmic writing. We looked up the precedents in history, which are many, for this kind of expression all the way back to the Greek Tragic Dance.

In this fourth and last stage the students tried composing couplets as they went along. The composer would stand in the middle of the floor and the leader on the side lines would say, "Compose and dance a couplet at the same time on . . . 'The Beach Tree,' or 'April,' or 'Indians,' or on 'Graduation,' or on 'Discovering a Mountain.'" The couplet was forthcoming and the dance at the same time, with slow, unbroken stateliness, the word and the gesture at the same moment springing from the great deep. This was an action of the sub-conscious stream, well worth while, a thing clairvoyant. I recommend it to parents tired of psycho-analysis. It goes further back than the whirling dervishes of Arabia. And please study the footnote [at the end of this essay].

A couplet is, after all, only two lines long and the composition and incantation took but sixty seconds, no longer than it takes to let the old oaken bucket down into the well and bring it up brimming. The poetry was as good as the best high-school verse ever is, and that is better than most poetry published.

In this last stage the group were freed forever from the idea of scanning verse by tapping with a pencil on the desk, or writing rhymes for examination papers in English while scrooging and squirming. This composition of a couplet in midair, as one might say, takes as much nervous strength and concentration as to produce four pages of essay, and the result is far more pointed and to the point. Of course, the child's work is done for that day. It is exhausting if glorious.

In this last stage we were not trying anything new. Various phases of the poem games exist in a scattered way all over the world, remainders from ancient time. For instance, the composing of couplets and the capping of rhymes has been a Chinese social custom for ages, whereby one scholar introduced himself to another, when they were strangers in an inn, or the like. The old Chinese stories are full of this form of mutual recognition of belonging to the gentility. In some Latin-American countries the guests are entertained by an improviser who walks about the room and turns the occasion by word of mouth into presentable verse, putting everything into verse as fast as it happens, with the proper gesture. Then in a certain popular novel the story of a South American dictator, they play the old game in which scraps of poetry are improvised and tossed from one guest to another to be completed.

Stately and well-established social and conventional precedents for various phases of the games may be found in all races, but turn to the greatest international influences of today. Isadora Duncan, who being dead yet speaketh, danced poetry, without music, in the poetry hour. Not a few chapters in her brilliant autobiography mention occasions of this kind when the poetry was separated from all other forms of music and danced and read for its own sake. The Denishawn Dancers try experiments that are on the edge of this idea. But it is an idea that has existed wherever poetry has been spoken, not printed or written. Only the printing press and the consequent banishment of poetry to the libraries has made poetical games seem obsolete. Obviously many of the Elizabethan madrigals and the songs in Shakespeare are for appropriate action while being read, and in both cases the tune was but a flowering of the words and not imposed upon the words by orchestra, saxophone, megaphone, radio, talking movie, telephone, or other mechanical intruder.

It is my opinion that the standard John Barrymore manner of acting Hamlet is first of all a stately dance to a chant. Sensitive people cannot avoid dancing those words. The Hammest of Ham actors and the greatest Barrymores step that play off to the same chant and much the same gesture and foot work, and the main difference is the final item of intelligence with which it is done. The acting comes out in the final production as the ultimate edge of the dance and the poem emerging to the top.

The fourth and last stage of my little dancers in June, just before they scattered for their summer picnics, has set me thinking as nothing else for many a long day. If you want mental stimulus and a new basis for speculation, try this out in your parlor. Always after an hour of these experiments, however awkward they seemed at the time, we all had our heads in a whirl of speculation, reconstruction, and poetical music for two days.

The title poem of this book is intended in an especial way as a poem game, hence the repetitions of the refrains. It often requires the repetition three times of a refrain for the dancer to complete the appropriate action, or fill out the step and the gesture, for words are at least three times as fast as music in expressing an idea, and generally three times as fast as dancing. This also is proved by ancient precedent. All choruses, so called, are packed with repetitions, going back to the day when the words had to be repeated in order to be danced completely. So in dancing *Every Soul Is a Circus*, or any other work in this volume, repeat any line when necessary over and over again, and let the chanters on the side lines repeat it until the dancer in the middle of the floor has been able to fill it out into a complete action story.

I have expressed in many places an impatience with the best orchestras in the world, as well as the worst music and the radio howling, and the talking moving picture howling. Artists may be offended that I have bunched all these things together, but they are all a part of the mechanical weight against which poetry and the spoken word has to struggle. Not one of them but has its good moment and its moment when it touches poetry to animate rather than to destroy, but the selection of that moment is difficult, unless you are in a tremendously exhilarated condition and able to keep up your spirits for a long time of waiting. Let there be one hundred times as much good music! But let the poetry-hour be a separate, literary-dancing matter. Let the best boy-actors in the dramatic societies act and speak the poems, while the girls dance in circles, round them. Boys like to be known as actors, not literally as dancers.

I found a great moment the other day in a talking motion picture news film. It was a perfect poem game. What was the music? The murmur of a gigantic crowd in the background in a grand stand, far enough away for it to have the rhythm of a subterranean river, far enough for it to be the true basis of a chorus. It was this crowd that made the occasion, assembled for a championship tennis game. There would be no championship games if the crowd did not assemble and murmur and rustle. Much nearer to the talking moving picture machine was the championship tennis player moving silently, but to the rhythm of the subterranean river. A beautiful dance! The drum music was gone, there was no regular percussion of that sort, but there was a very musical tinkle with a curious rhythm all its own, the impact of the tennis ball against the tennis racket. Right then I was prompted for one fanatical moment to say the tennis racket is about the only musical instrument we have left, and *that* when it is in the hands of Helen Wills when she is playing a championship game. Pallas Athena herself in motion! The poem was the chanting adoration of the crowd, the dancing was magnificent and triumphant tennis by California incarnate. All the youth and hope and glory of California and all the nonsense left out! Even the little white eyeshade worn by the player was like the helmet of Pallas Athena flashing in the sun of eternal Olympia.

If you have almost given up the talking movie, watch for news reels of Helen Wills' championship games. The diminished roar of that crowd far off was like the murmur of my own little dancers who whispered to themselves as they danced Kubla Khan, a couplet that never failed to lift them into tragic power,

> "And midst this tumult Kubla heard from far,
> Ancestral voices prophesying war."

As a final footnote, in the matter of the chanting of verse, I quote from the Tulsa, Oklahoma "Tribune," August 4, 1929:

John Masefield, in England, organized the Oxford Recitations that are doing more in England than anything else to show the advantages of recited poetry over poetry that is read in quiet.

The Englishman organized what were to be called the Oxford Recitations in July, 1923. Calling in judges who were poets or writers, and announcing the verse-speaking contests in the papers of his country, Mr. Masefield was rewarded with five hundred entries in the first contest.

It has come now to where twice five hundred young men and women enter the contests held annually in Oxford. Where the judges alone were all that came formerly to hear them, we have Mr. Masefield's word for it that some hundreds of others attend the contests and follow them as keenly as the judges. "An audience has been made," says he. "People have begun to listen."

Perhaps the chief result of the contests in England, Mr. Masefield explains in his preface to "The Oxford Recitations" just issued by the Macmillan Co., has been that hundreds of people have discovered how intense a pleasure listening to poetry can be. The American people, so much on the lookout for new sources of pleasure, might think of sampling this one.

Following his introduction there have been published in this volume "Love in the Desert" by Laurence Binyon, a genuinely effective thing when read aloud (even by a reader as poor as ourselves). "A Parting" and "The Return" are by Gordon Bottomley, while "Polyxena's Speech" and the "Messenger's Speech" are translated from the Hecuba of Euripides by Mr. Masefield. These are the plays and poems performed by various speakers in the Oxford Recitations at Oxford on July 24, 25 and 26, 1928. The winning selections of this year, we anticipate, will appear in September.

TITLE INDEX

Note: "(cont.)" following a title indicates continuation

INDEX OF TITLES

Note: "(v)" following a title indicates a variant title.